Welcome to the revolution.

"The Growers Guide is chocked full of useful and time honoured growing techniques. Hamilton's writing makes it an easy and entertaining read. Highly recommend it to anyone who is thinking of starting an indoor garden."

Eric Coulombe
Garden Culture Magazine.

The Growers Guide

to indoor gardening & horticulture

Introduction

The Growers Guide has had a clear game plan right from the start, it is devoted to what the novice grower is asking for, a concise, easy to follow guide that will get you started in the world of indoor growing. This book will show you how to grow in a 1.2 x 1.2 x 2m growing tent/room in both soil and coco coir using a hand fed, run to waste watering cycle. The book takes you right through from the earliest point of the grow process, the germinating of a seed, to the very finish which is the harvest and curing of your fruits. Whilst this may currently seem extremely daunting and as if I am talking complete gibberish, I guarantee that by the time you have read the whole of this book that you will feel fully informed and able to confidently complete an entire growing cycle.

We are the only book on the market to date that brings together all the most popular and well respected brands in hydroponics in one publication. These brands include Plagron, Jiffy, Dutchpro, Growth Technology, Method Seven, Grodan and Gavita to mention a few. This gives us a platform from which to get you fully informed and up to date on what products and brands you should be looking out for when you first go into a hydroponics store, as the sheer range of products and brands available can be massively overwhelming in the beginning when you haven't grown before.

Obviously in time you will find your own preferences as to what you like to use as you experiment and gain confidence. You should however, rest easy for now as all the hard work has been done for you. All the products I have chosen and talked about throughout the book have been selected due to their high, consistent performance, meaning you can rest assured that from the start point onward you are giving yourself and your plants the best chance possible. It is also testament to the book that such high profile and respected brands have agreed to be involved with the Growers Guide and have allowed their products to be featured in it and this should only serve to give you more confidence in the book's teachings and advice. It's at this point that I would like to take the opportunity to thank all the brands who have supported The Growers Guide and helped to make it possible.

I'm not saying that this is the only way or the best way to grow indoors but what I am saying is that this book will arm you with the basic skills you need to produce wonderful results, shockingly fast. It is categorically a tool to enable you to grow all kinds of fruits successfully within an indoor environment.

Every chapter covers a different step of the growing process in full, it is written in order to be concise and easy to understand. You will find that each chapter is packed full of colour pictures, diagrams and step by step instructions. Each coming with a complete "shopping list" of items needed for each stage of your Grow. Chapter by chapter you will be walked through the entire process in simple layman's terms, telling you exactly what to expect and look out for and when to expect it. I will not only tell you what you need but also what each item does and why it does it. I will talk you through all the available options giving you my experienced opinion aalong with the pros and cons of each. I will show you how each element is best implemented into your working growing environment, including how to get the most out of it and so enabling you to produce the best end result possible.

Think of The Growers Guide as a cookbook of sorts, I have taken inspiration from all the many years of experience that I have accrued and all the differing ideas that you will find out there on the hydroponics market that growers are currently using.
Every word and sentence in this book has been debated and every single stage has been streamlined in order to create this comprehensive beginners guide. It is inevitable that not everybody in the industry is going to agree with what I say in this book or how I think things should be done and they are entitled to their opinions, as am I and this is how I do things and what works for me, it's a starting point for you to add to and build on with your own experiences.

The processes or "recipes" if you like, in this book have been tried and tested to ensure that this book serves as a reliable companion for you, and hopefully to the people to whom you recommend it to after seeing the results of using it yourself. It's by far the most balanced and clear guide to starting off in hydroponics that is out there on the market to date. So I ask you to trust in all the effort that has gone into this book and know that as long as you follow what I have written and have the essential equipment that is vital for success, you'll be enjoying bountiful yields of your own making in no time.

As well as being an excellent introduction and starting point into the world of indoor gardening for the beginner grower, this book is also a valuable source of knowledge for those that perhaps are more experienced in their growing. Maybe you want to find out more about why we do what we do? Or better understand the theory behind the practice of indoor gardening? Perhaps you feel that your plants are not reaching their full potential and you want to take your growing routine back to basics and try a new approach in order to increase the quality and size of your yields? Maybe you are just bored and fancy a look at what other people are doing? Well if this is the case then this book is for you too. No matter how long you have been growing or how much you already know there is always more that you can learn to make you a better grower. Remember that knowledge is key after all and that more knowledge can only lead to greater success.

Ultimately The Growers Guide is a philosophy "you get out what you put in" or if you prefer "what you give is what you get" and I think if you give it a go you'll really get into it. Yes, the first couple of times that you grow you may stumble, make a few errors or find that it takes a little longer to get the bountiful yields that you desire but do not be put off by this. Remember that this is just human nature and an inevitable part of the learning curve. Once you fully embrace the process, learn to read your plants and get fully into the spirit of the shortcuts and tips that I have given you, you will definitely start to reap the rewards of your efforts. So take the philosophy on board and run with it as I guarantee that if you put in the maximum amount of effort, you will get the maximum output from your crop time after time.

Armed with a basic knowledge, you will inevitably find your own individual style of growing, what works for you and what doesn't. It's not just about me as an experienced grower being able to do it. These ideas have been tested by growers at all levels and ages and their response has mirrored the results that I have had and if they can do it, so can you.

Rich Hamilton.

www.TheGrowersGuide.co.uk

www.machiavellianmedia.co.uk

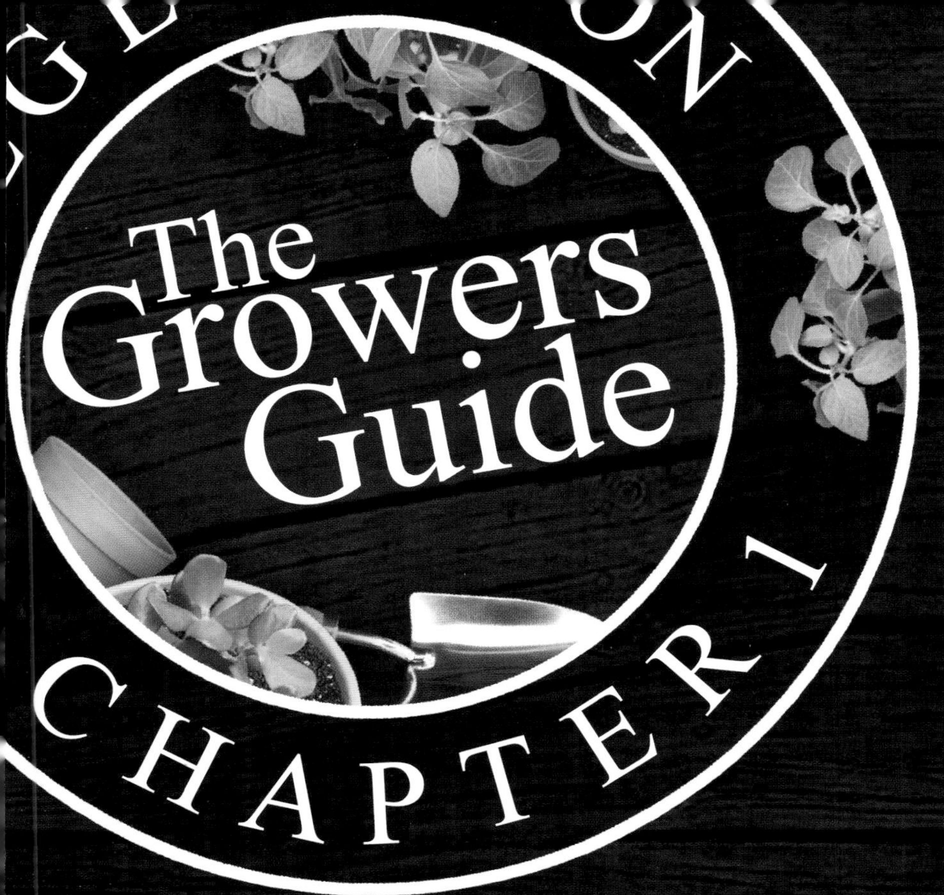

Know your plant

In this first chapter we will be looking at a basic overview of the plant. In order to make this more digestible I have broken it down into 6 easy to follow sections, each covering a different part of the plant's structure. Additionally I will walk you through an example of the plant's lifecycle, looking at the 4 different stages that the plant goes through during its lifetime and what you need to take into consideration for each. A good understanding of all the separate elements which make up the plant and what each does is essential for you to get the most out of your crop and to give you the potential to be a successful grower.

Know your plant

The Basics

First things first we are going to go over the basics. There are many different types of plants.

The types of plants which we will be looking at in this book are typically "dioecious" flowering herb plants. This means that each individual plant is either a male or a female. The photoperiod which the plants are subject to affects/controls the stages of the plant's lifecycle.

These plants are normally annual plants, however by controlling the light photoperiod, the environment and by using the techniques demonstrated in this book you can go through the whole of the plant's lifecycle from Seed to Harvest in 3–4 months.

To make it easier and more digestible I'm going to break this chapter down into 6 simple sections.

1. **Plant Overview**
2. **Roots**
3. **Stems**
4. **Leaves**
5. **Buds**
6. **Fruit**

You may be tempted to overlook this section or bypass it to get to the more juicy bits but don't, as even if you're an experienced grower it's good to recap and you never know you might learn something new. Knowledge is power after all!

1.Plant Overview

So the basics of the plant are laid out for you here. They may seem pretty simple on the outside but the closer you look the more complicated they are. A well-learned friend of mine told me a long time ago that it's all about balance. The general law is that, what is above is essentially below. What you put in you will get out. Yin and yang, if you will.

A plant's lifecycle

A plant's life is basically separated into 4 stages:

1. Seed – no light
2. Propagation – 24hr light
3. Vegetation – 18hrs lights on, 6 hours lights off
4. Flower stage – 12hrs light on, 12hrs lights off

We will go through each of these stages later in the book one by one. The light cycles above are the most commonly used, however other light cycles can be just as effective.

Plant Overview

Flowers.

Stem.

Fruit.

Leaves.

Roots.

2.Roots

We will start at the bottom with the roots and work our way up.

One of the most important parts of the plant to grow is the root.

The roots are the beginning of the vascular system, which is the main pipeline that feeds the plant's leaves, stems and fruit with water and nutrients in exchange for sugar. Any sugars left over after they have been used for the growth and well-being of the plant are turned into starch and are stored in the root ball, one of the plant's fuel tanks! The roots also anchor the plant to the ground providing it with stability for strong upward growth.

The bigger the root system is on the plant, the more nutrients the plant can take up and thus the bigger the plant will be. What is below is above.

Roots do not like the light! Exposing a plant's roots to the light for a prolonged amount of time will stress the plant and can essentially kill it. Therefore when transplanting your plant from pot to pot it's best not to mess around. Minimising the exposure of the roots to the light will minimise stress to the plant.

There are plant pots out there that "air prune" the roots. These plant pots are basically designed to encourage the roots of the plant to grow out of the sides of the perforated pot. In doing this the roots are exposed to the light, which then die off and allegedly send the energy and root growth back into the plant pot creating more roots............ does it work? Is it a gimmick? Well they are popular in the hydroponics world but the very idea of exposing the roots to the light seems unnecessary to me. I wouldn't recommend stressing the plant at all if possible.

I have tried these plant pots/air pruning pots before and I have found that over the 3 month period in which I would be growing the plant, the feed and nutrients which I have given to the plant would make the roots grow so aggressively, that they would grow out of the holes and before they could "air prune" (stress the plant out) they would look for feed/nutrients and grow back into the pot!!! This would leave a section of root exposed to the light, thus giving the plant long term root stress, or cause it to die off leaving the other end of the root to rot in the pot. Not a good thing at all.

Commonly overlooked mistakes with root systems (probably because they are mostly underground/covered up) include being exposed to the wrong temperature and assuming that roots don't need oxygen. They do, in fact it's essential that the roots are as well oxygenated as possible and this can be achieved and optimized in a number of ways depending on which system/technique you are using to grow. Getting the right temperature will also increase the roots uptake.

There are four main sections of the root system.

- **Root ball**
- **Tap root/primary root (vertical roots)**
- **Secondary root (horizontal roots)**
- **Root hairs**

Root ball

The root ball is the main mass/heart of the root system. Located at the base of the plant it connects the plant's stem to the root system. This is where the plant turns the sugars sent from the leaves into starch and stores it. It also, in turn, feeds the main plant with the vital waters and nutrients taken up via the roots.

Tap roots

The tap roots/primary roots are the main roots that grow directly downward, elongating the root mass and forming anchors for secondary roots to branch out laterally. Tap roots develop from the seeds radicale root (the first root you see when germinating a seed).

Tap root

Secondary roots

The secondary roots tend to grow horizontally out from the main tap roots; increasing the diameter of the root mass. However, when restricted by a pot they can grow up and down vertically.

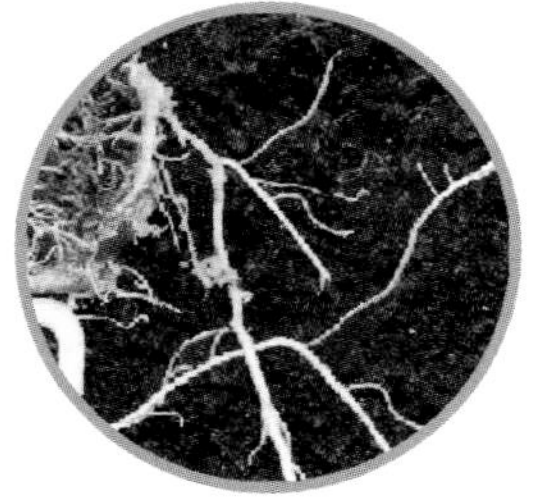

Root hairs

The root hairs grow out of the secondary roots and are predominantly found in zones of lateral maturation. Their primary function is to collect/absorb feed and nutrients that are present in the medium in which the plants are growing. They also secrete an acid (H+ from malic acid) which helps solubilize the feed and nutrients in order to make it easier for the roots to take it up.

The root hairs themselves are very fine and delicate. As you can see in the close up picture below, to the naked eye they look more like fuzz surrounding the root than they do hairs. This however is the start of the plant's vascular system.

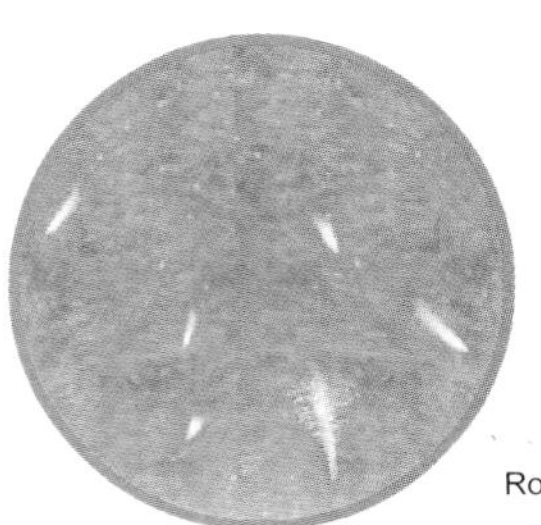

Root hairs.

Stems

The stem is the second main part of the plant's vascular system (the roots being the first). The stem has a number of functions other than being the nutrient highway of the plant. The stem increases the height of the plant to ensure it reaches as close to the light source as possible. It can also store nutrients for later use. The stem is divided up into sections by nodes and internodes.

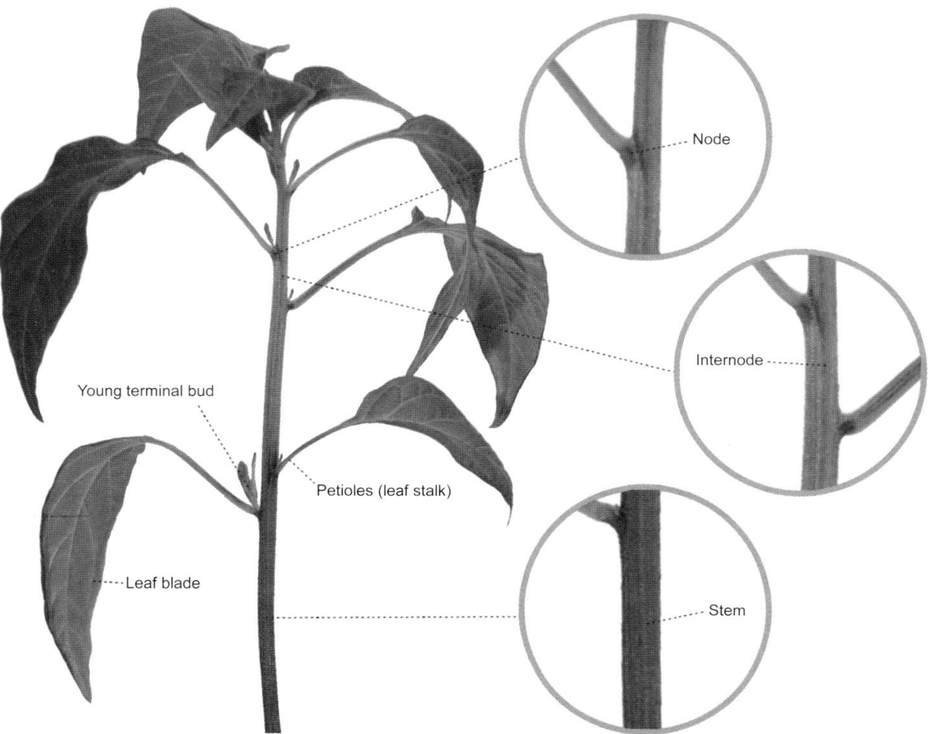

As the stem develops it creates nodes. Nodes (which are sometimes referred to as knuckles) are the points of the stem from which the leaves, buds and branches grow.

A normal node should look like the image above. As a rule it will have two axillary buds, which may turn into terminal buds. Below the axillary buds there should be petioles (leaf stalks) with leaf blades on the ends. At the base of the petioles there are normally stipules.

If it is a male plant then in the crease there are small sacks called staminate primordial. As the male plant grows the sacks will reproduce, creating small sac formations which look like a small bunch of grapes.

Leaves

A complete leaf structure is made up from a petiole (leaf stalk), a lamina (leaf blade) and stipules (small whisker looking hairs) on either side of the leaf stalk.

Leaves come in all shapes and sizes. They are typically very thin and flat in order to maximise the surface area exposed to the sun/light in order to get the most photosynthetic production.

The leaves are mainly used to produce sugars via the process of photosynthesis. This is a very complicated process, so I will try and break it down to its easiest explanation.

Photosynthesis is the chemical change that happens in the leaves of green plants. During this chemical exchange carbon dioxide and water are converted into oxygen and glucose sugar. In order for this to happen there has to be a light source/energy which is absorbed by green cells in the leaf of the plant containing chlorophyll. The basic formula is;

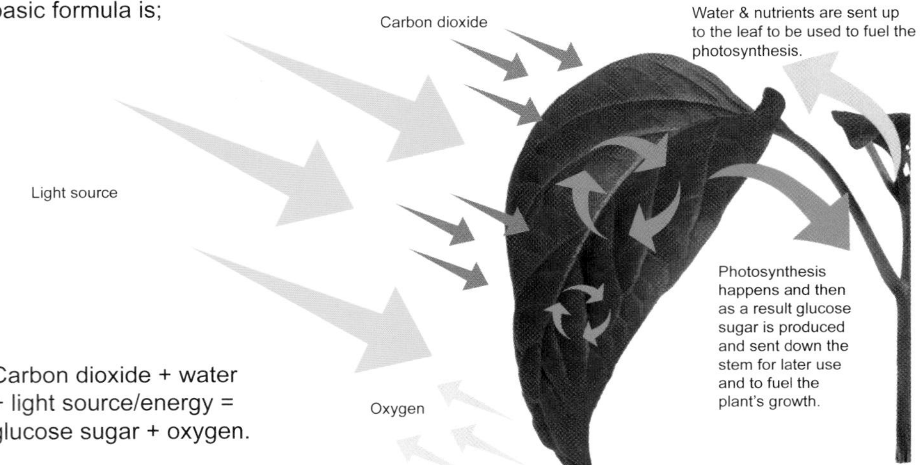

Carbon dioxide
Water & nutrients are sent up to the leaf to be used to fuel the photosynthesis.
Light source
Photosynthesis happens and then as a result glucose sugar is produced and sent down the stem for later use and to fuel the plant's growth.
Oxygen

Carbon dioxide + water + light source/energy = glucose sugar + oxygen.

It is important to note that this is a basic formula. The amounts of each of the factors as shown in the diagrams can increase and decrease the production/efficiency of the photosynthetic process.

With this in mind, more light is not (as some people think) always better. A plant's leaves can only produce a certain amount of glucose sugar depending on the ratio of light, to water, to carbon dioxide available. The trick is to get them working at the right levels in order to make the leaves the most productive they can be.

In order to explain this I have drawn out some graphs to help.

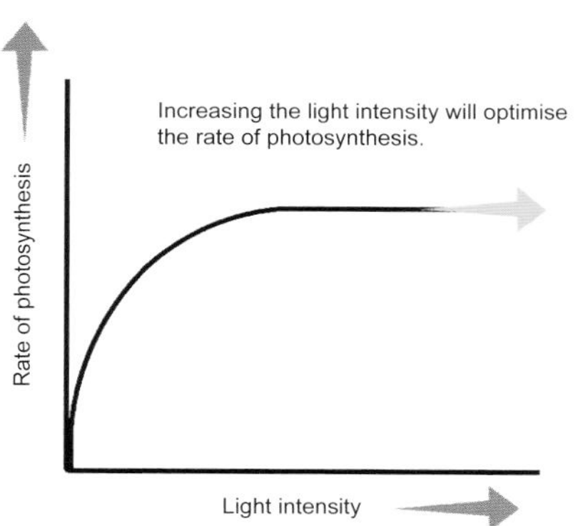

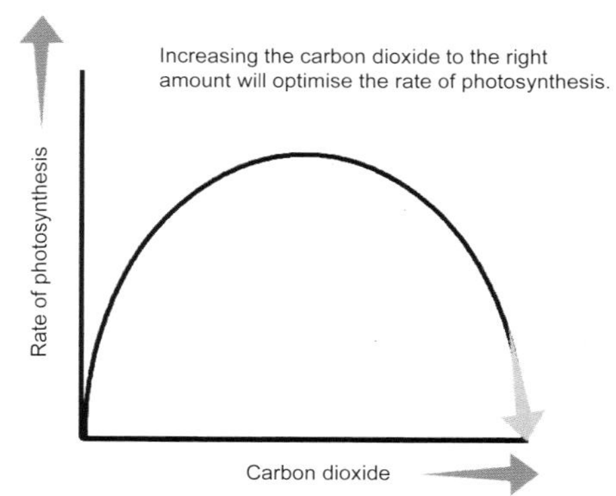

Too much carbon dioxide will however decrease the rate of photosynthesis.

If there is not enough light, the rate of photosynthesis will decrease massively very quickly but remember also that the more light you need, the more carbon dioxide you will need. If there is not enough carbon dioxide then the rate of photosynthesis will still decrease.

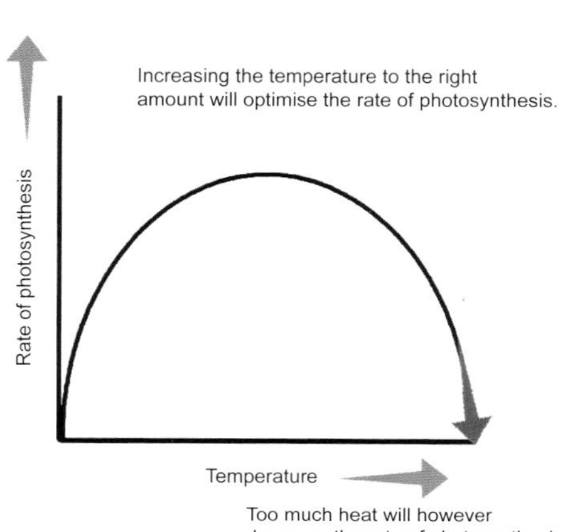

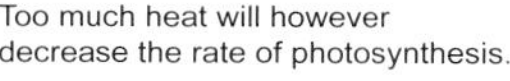

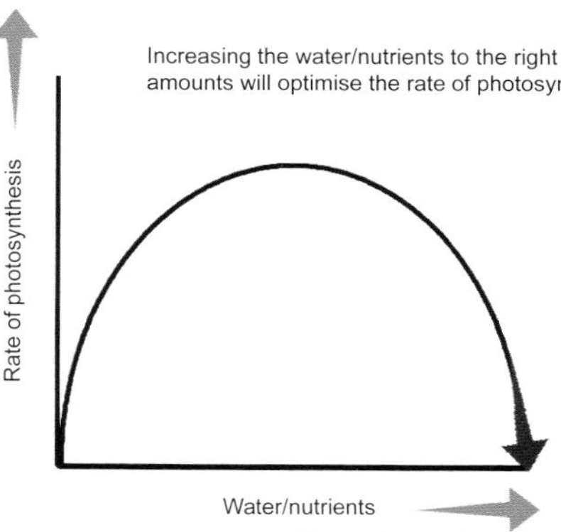

Too much water/nutrients will however decrease the rate of photosynthesis.

If its too hot or too cold, the rate of photosynthesis will decrease massively regardless if you have the correct light to carbon dioxide ratio.

Any one of the factors as explained and shown in all the graphs could limit the rate of photosynthesis.

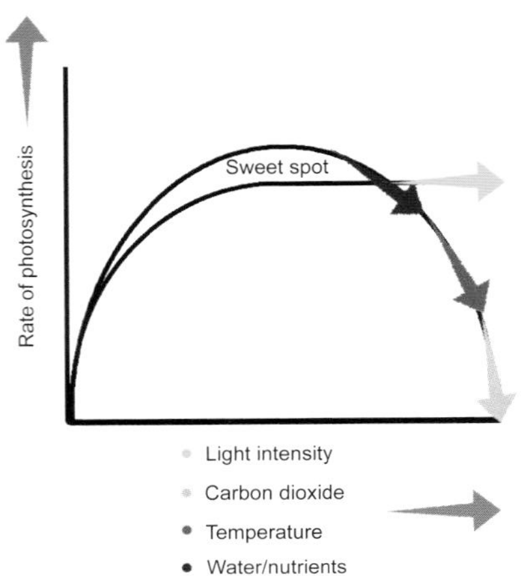

As you can see when we put all of these graphs together there is a common "sweet spot".

So in layman's terms its all about balance, it's pointless having a lot of light source if there isn't enough carbon dioxide. You will also be wasting your time if you have the maximum amount of light and the right ratio of carbon dioxide and then the plants are too hot or too cold. The amount of water the plant receives is also important; unless you are watering the plant properly there will be a decrease in the plant's photosynthesis process.

I have also put together a cross section of a typical leaf in order to show you what is going on inside the leaf, where the photosynthesis process happens, how the carbon dioxide enters the leaf and where the oxygen leaves it.

On the leaves there are openings called stomatas, this is where the plant allows the exchange of gases; carbon dioxide in and oxygen out. The leaves are covered in stomatas, however, there are normally more on the underside of the leaf blade than there are on the top in order to reduce the amount of water lost through vapour escaping from the leaf.

Cross section of a leaf.

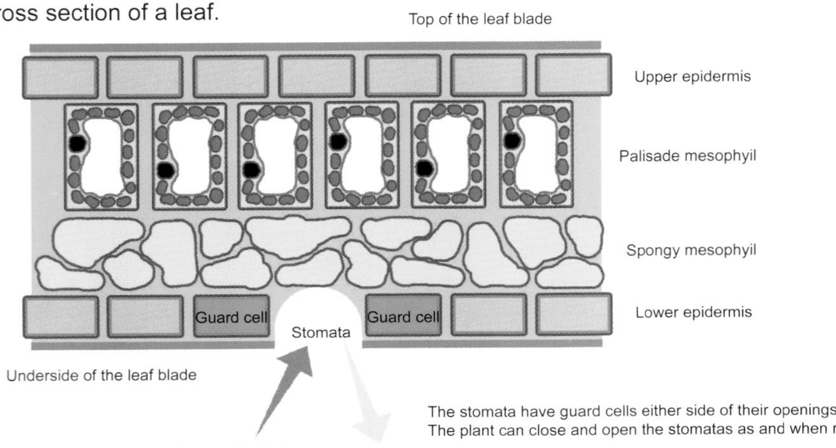

The glucose sugar which is produced by photosynthesis is used to fuel the plant's growth. Any surplus glucose sugar is turned into starch/carbohydrates and is then stored for later use.

The bottom line is that the more productive you can make the photosynthesis process, the faster and larger your plant will naturally grow.

Buds

Don't get too excited about the word bud! In botany a bud is an undeveloped shoot which is normally located at the main elongating, vertical growing points of the plant which are in the axil (just above a node) of the leaf stalk or at the tip of the stem.

Axillary buds

Terminal bud

The terminal bud shown in the circle was an axillary bud but has now developed into a terminal. As this is now a terminal bud it will grow towards the light creating nodes and internodes as it reaches higher. From the nodes it will produce more axillary buds which may then turn into terminal buds.

As you can see there are two main buds, the terminal buds and the axillary buds. Terminal buds are located at the end of the stem or a shoot. Axillary buds are located in the axil of a leaf stalk. Axillary buds can start to grow into a new shoot/branch, making the original axillary bud a terminal bud. On this new shoot the plant will naturally develop nodes and internodes. As it does this it will create new axillary buds, which again in turn may or may not turn into terminal buds and so on as the plant grows.

As a rule of thumb all this growth happens within the Vegetative stage and at the beginning of the Flower stage of the plant's life. When the plant is put into Flower the transfer period from Vegetative to Flower (or as it's called "the stretch") normally takes around 2 weeks. In these 2 weeks the plant can double in size before it sets into the true Flower stage of it's life. When the plant is in the Flower stage, all the energy is taken from the stem and shoot/branch growth and is put into the growth of the fruit.

If you wanted to stop or slow down the vertical growth of the plant there is a method which people use called "topping" or "pinching out". This is the process of removing the terminal bud in order to stop vertical growth in the Vegetative stage and encourage lateral growth and thus more terminal bud sites.

When "topping" it is advisable to use surgically clean scissors or a surgical knife. These can be bought at any Garden or Hydroponic store.

When cutting a plant in any way, shape, or form you are going to stress it out; so it's best to try and make the cut in one slice/movement. By doing this you will give the best chance of the plant recovering quickly. It should take no longer than a week to heal, during this time the open cut will be very susceptible to infection so no touching and keep an eye on it.

Below is a very young plant which we will "top" to show you how this will affect the plant as it grows.

The main terminal bud/head of the plant removed.

Single headed non topped plant.

Single-headed, non-topped plant.

Double-headed, topped plant.

Above is a a set of pictures of the same plant. On the left is the plant before we have "topped" it. As you can see it has one clear centre point. This is commonly called the main head or master terminal bud. This plant clearly is growing from the centre out. The plant on the right is the same plant but after it has been "topped" and left to grow and as a result there are now two main heads. The plant will now grow outward of the two main heads, increasing the overall mass of the plant to the source of light. This process can be done again and again, the end result being that you can train your plant to have 50 or even 100 main heads.

Double headed topped plant.

If you are doing this multiple times then the plant will need to be supported as the top will be much heavier than the bottom.

The double headed topped plant on the left clearly shows the two (now) main heads growing from where the original head was. This process will also reduce the height of the plant. If this plant wasn't "topped" by the time this photograph was taken it would be twice as tall.

The fruit of the plant is really what we are here for. Everything we do is to increase the size of the fruit and the plant's yield, the bigger and heavier the better.

To most people the word "fruit" means a fleshy seed filled structure, for example apples, oranges, grapes etc, which are derived from a flowering plant. In botany the word "fruit" not only includes the above but also refers to other structures such as bean pods, wheat grains and so on.

Some plants are grown for their fruit's medicinal proposes, such as Codeine (a commonly used painkiller) which is derived from the poppy plant.

Plants can grow fruits without seeds, this is done in a number of ways. One is by genetically modifying the plant and the other, which is much easier and what we will be looking to achieve, is by not pollinating the female plant. In order to do this the males and the females must be kept separate. Normally a female plant needs pollen in order to start the fruiting process, but this is not always the case. We will be concentrating on the types of plants that are put into the flowering process by the change of the photoperiod.

Photoperiod - meaning the changing of the light cycle.

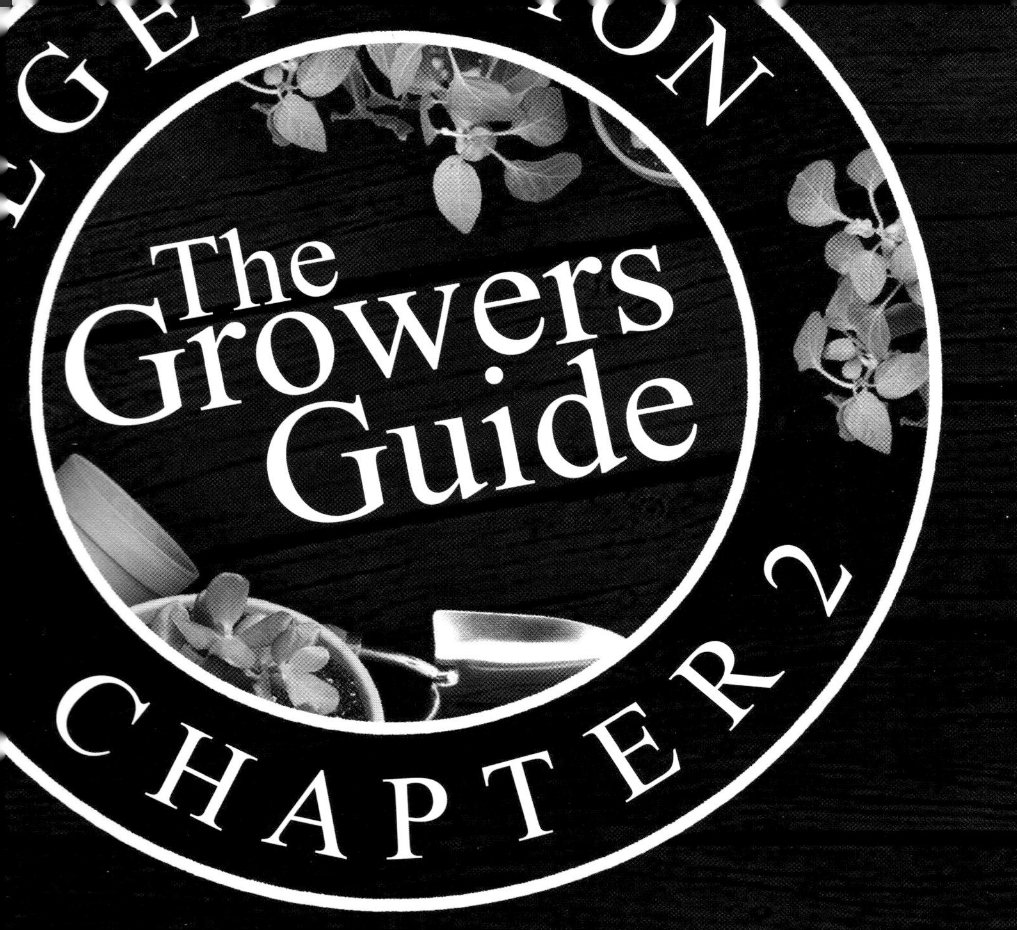

Understanding water and nutrients

Now that we have a good basic understanding of the plant the next things to look at are the water and nutrients that are used to feed the plant. Understanding water, types of water, pH and E.C are all fundamental and crucial elements of the growing process.

In this chapter we will go through the basics, giving you a good all-round knowledge on the subject. I will go through what water pH is, how it affects plants and how to adjust it. We will look at E.C, what it stands for and how to control it, as well as what feeds to use and when and how to mix them correctly in order to get the best out of your plants.Understanding this chapter will give you a great foundation on how and when to give your plants the correct chemical elements, ensuring that you achieve monster bumper yields.

The feeding schedules which are featured in this chapter have been proven and tested over years of refinement. Trust me! They work and they work well.

Water - Nutrients and understanding pH and EC

It is fundamental to know what type of water you have and the pH and E.C of your water before you start adding nutrients/chemicals to it. It is also important to know what chemical nutrients to put into the feed solution and when.

To achieve this you will need the following;

Equipment

- **pH chemical test kit**
- **E.C reader (E.C stands for electrical conductivity)**
- **Mixing tub**
- **Measuring jug 1 litre**
- **Measuring syringes 10ml and 20ml**

pH chemical test kit – this is used to measure the level of acid or alkaline level of the water. It is a very simple and cheap kit that you can buy from any Hydroponic or Gardening shop. They are pretty much idiot proof, will give you a fairly precise reading every time and can be bought for under a fiver. So all in all it's a no brainer!

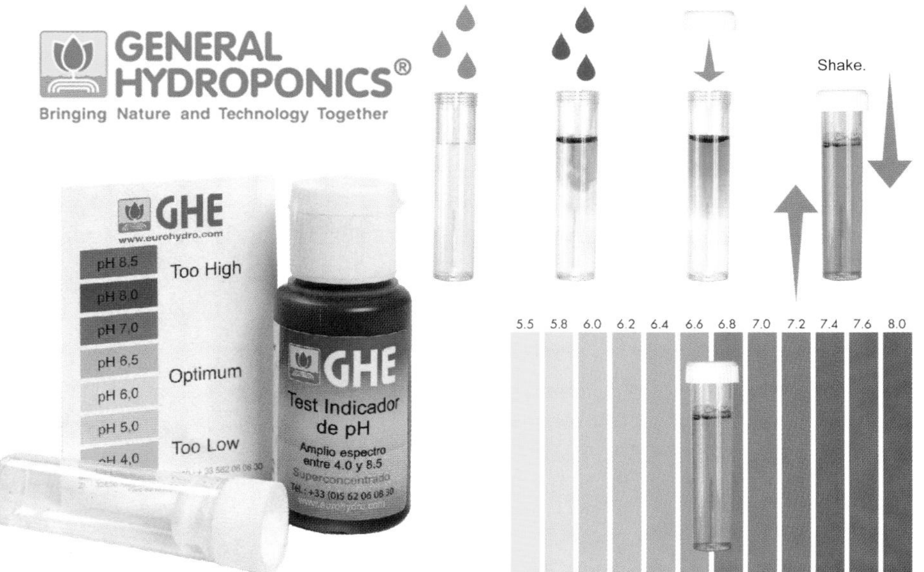

There are digital pH test readers on the market which will give you the exact pH reading. These are perfect for giving you the ultimate control over your pH, however, they are expensive and if not maintained correctly can give a false reading which could be detrimental to your plants. My recommendation for the beginner therefore, would be to stick to a pH chemical test kit.

E.C reader – E.C stands for "Electrical Conductivity". What the E.C reader does is to measure the electrical conductivity of a solution and thus gives you a reading of how strong or weak the level of added chemicals are in the water. As tap water and distilled water already have a level of chemicals in them you will have to take what is called a base reading of the water first before you add any nutrients.

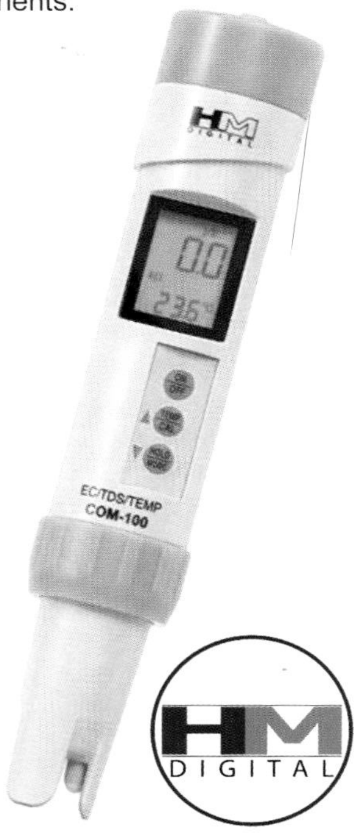

Think of it as like making a cordial drink diluted with water. Everybody likes it a little bit stronger or weaker. With cordial its easy to judge your preferred strength by tasting it but with plant feed solutions you will need an E.C reader to tell you how strong or weak the solution is. Every plant will prefer different E.C levels at different times. Some like higher/stronger levels and some like lower/weaker levels. By using an E.C reader it will make sure that the E.C is at the optimum level for the plant to absorb the most amount of nutrients available.

If the E.C is too high it means that there are too many chemicals in the water for the plant to efficiently take up nutrient. Another issue is that if the E.C is too high it will give the plant what's known as "nute lock". Nute lock is when the feed is far too strong for the plant. In these cases the plant will completely shut down any nutrient uptake in order to try and save it from poisoning itself.

If the E.C is too low the plant will slow down in growth, lighten and show signs of nutrient deficiency across the board.

Mixing tub – In order to mix your feed solutions you will need a large clean tub. For the purposes of this book we will be mixing in batches of 10ltr's so instead of buying a 100ltr water butt we will be using a 10ltr bucket! Something basic, clean and cheap will do the job.

Top tip for making up your feed is to pre-pour the water you will be using the day before and allow it to stand for 24hrs. Doing this will allow some of the chemicals which the water board have put into the tap water to evaporate; making the water more suitable for plants.

If you want to super charge your feed it can be made oxygen-rich by adding a small air stone (attached to an air pump) to the water while it is left to stand. This will help the process of evaporation and make the water turbocharged with oxygen.

Measuring jug 1ltr – this will help you measure out the 10ltr's into your Mixing tub and it is also a good size to use when hand feeding your plants.

Measuring syringes 10ml and 20ml – You will need these to measure out the correct amount of chemicals when making your nutrient solution. A 10ml and 20ml syringe are perfect for smaller measurements. The 1ltr measuring jug can be used for anything that needs to be measured out in larger doses.

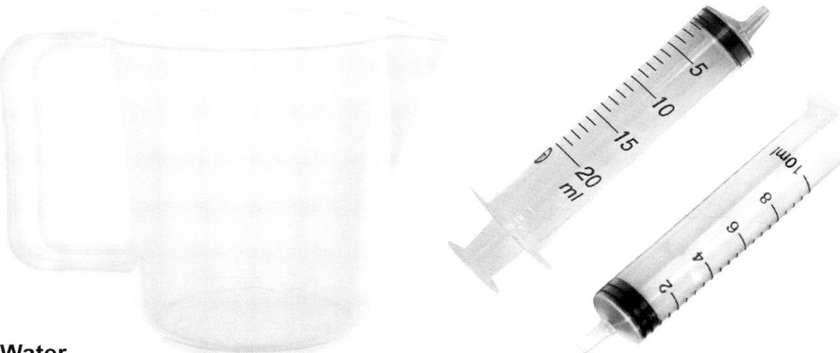

Water

There are two main different types of water which come out of UK household taps; soft water and hard water. Both are vastly different and would ideally need a nutrient base that would take into consideration the chemical differences.

Below is a rough map of the UK and the soft and hard water areas.

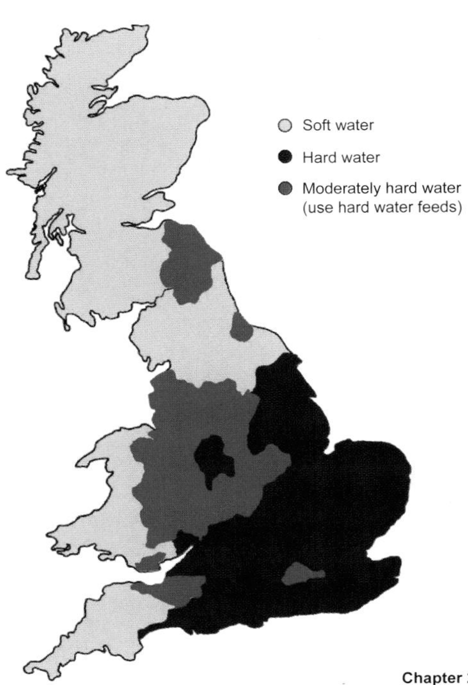

What makes soft water different to hard water?

Hard water is water that has a high mineral content, mainly deposits of calcium and magnesium rich minerals such as limestone and chalk.

Soft water is water in which the above listed chemicals levels are much lower; if not non-existent.

Both are fine for human consumption, however, hard water does cause more adverse issues with equipment such as kettles, dishwashers etc.

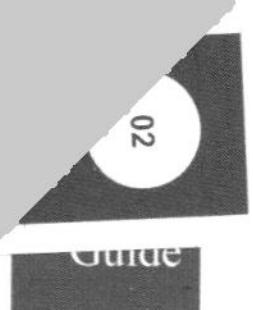

If you want to make sure whether you have soft or hard water there is a very complicated test which can be done.

Look in your kettle!

If there's no limescale then it's a soft water area. If there is limescale then it's a hard water area. Simples. Failing that, if you ring your local water provider they will tell you.

In an ideal world plants would prefer pure fresh water, not tap water which has been recycled and/or had an array of jaw dropping chemicals added to it in order to make it "allegedly" fit for human consumption by your local water board.

There are water purifiers/distillers out there on the market which are affordable and easy to fit but are not essential, however, if you intend to grow long-term I would suggest looking into the purchasing of one of these units.

The next thing we need to look at is the pH of the water. pH stands for "power of hydrogen" and is the measurement of the level of how acidic or alkaline the solution is. As a rough guide I have given below a measure of every day household items and their pH/level of acidity or alkalinity (base).

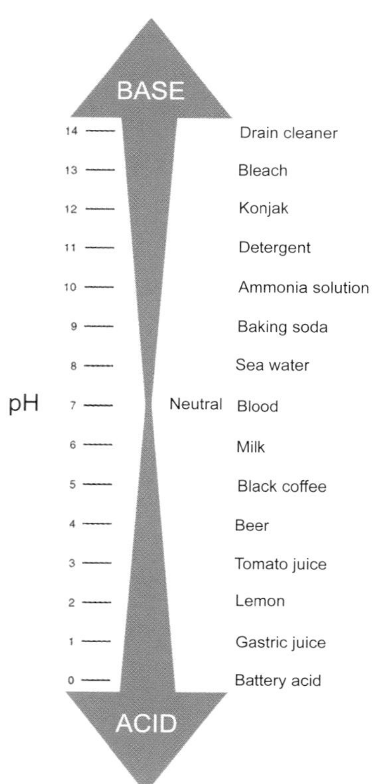

It is important here to point out that a high level of alkaline can be just as harmful if not more so than a high level of acid. Acid is known to burn but as you can see in the guide one of the most common strong alkaline solutions on the market today is bleach and as we all know bleach is a very corrosive and dangerous solution.

Whether you grow in a soft water or hard water area the pH will nearly always be different.

It is good practice to take the pH measurement of the water that you are using every time. This will give you a better understanding of the base solution (water).

If the pH of the water is not where it needs to be it can be adjusted using pH-Up or pH-Down. It is important to note at this stage that when adding your nutrients to the water it WILL change the pH. So it's best to leave the adjusting of the pH until the nutrients have been mixed into the water.

I must point out at this stage that when adjusting the pH after the nutrients have been added to the water that it must ONLY be

adjusted one way. What I mean by this is that if the pH is too high it can be brought down by adding pH-Down until it's at the right level. If you add too much pH-Down and it goes below the required level you can NOT then add pH-Up into the mix to bring it back up (and vice versa if its too low). If this is the case then this nutrient mix is no good and you will need to start again.

pH-Up and Down is strong stuff so I would always recommend to read the bottle first and be sure to always wear gloves and eye protection when handling corrosive chemicals.

There are nutrients on the market now that claim to be "pH perfect". What this means is that when the nutrients are added to the water solution the chemical mix will automatically alter the pH to the right level. If I was you however, I would still always check the pH after making a feed mix and before feeding any plants.
The graph below shows you that the correct pH levels will give you the most even amount of nutrient element uptake for your plant.

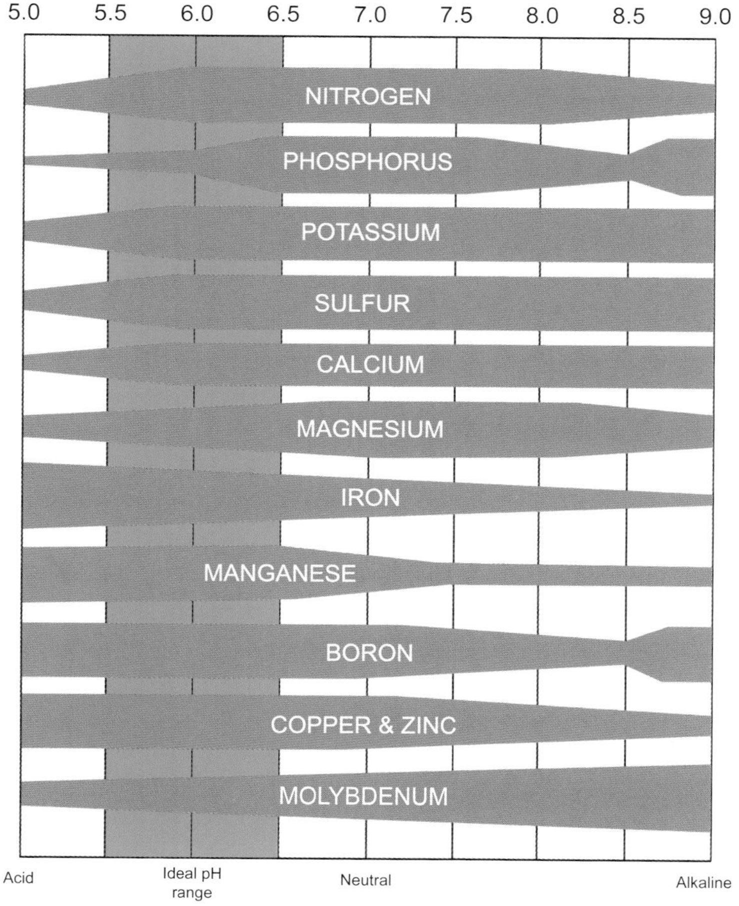

5.0 5.5 6.0 6.5 7.0 7.5 8.0 8.5 9.0

NITROGEN
PHOSPHORUS
POTASSIUM
SULFUR
CALCIUM
MAGNESIUM
IRON
MANGANESE
BORON
COPPER & ZINC
MOLYBDENUM

Acid
Ideal pH range
Neutral
Alkaline

Nutrients – are fundamental to the plant's life and without them the plant will not survive. In the plants natural habitat the plant would get all of its required nutrients from the earth in which it is grown. Growing indoors means that you can make the most of what the plant needs, when it needs it and doing this will super charge your plants giving you super sized bumper yields.

In the hydroponic world the "nutrients" as they are commonly called for the entirety of the plants feeds are normally split into two different groups. Group 1 is "Nutrients" which refers to the base feeds. Group 2 is the "additives" which can refer to the enzyme, root tonic, PK 13/14, foliar spray, bloom and combined bloom boosters. Both the nutrients and the additives are used together in order to give the plants exactly what they need when they need it to produce the maximum yield.

Nutrients and additives

In order to get the most out of a high energy plant it is imperative that you use a full range of feeds which cover all bases.

The basic feed range you will need is;

- **A Base Feed**
- **Enzyme**
- **Root tonic**
- **PK 13/14** } **Combined Bloom Booster**
- **Bloom**
- **Foliar Spray**
- **Flush**

A Base Feed– This normally comes in three different types;

1. **A one part**
2. **A two part**
3. **A three part**

1.A one part base feed is as simple as it gets; all the chemical elements required for the base come in one bottle. There is one for the "Veg" stage (sometimes referred to as the "Grow" stage) and one for the "Flower" stage. Normally one part base feeds tend to be at the cheaper end of the spectrum and are only available for soil and coco.

If you are growing in soil the one part that I would recommend to use would be Plant Magic's Oldtimer.

2. A two part base feed is the most common of all the base feeds. It comes in a Grow A and B for Vegetation and also an A and B for Flower. Some nutrient companies have the same A and B mix which is used through the whole of the plant's life. These come in an "A" bottle and a "B" bottle. When adding the chemical nutrients to the main water solution they should be added in the order A first then B. Two part feeds are sold in two bottles because the nutrient brands that sell them state that the chemicals that are in both A and B bottles should only be mixed when in water so that they are diluted.

So how come you can buy one part feeds?

This is a good question that is debated a lot, for my mind it's better to have a two part feed. In one part feeds more chemicals are added, in order to stop the chemicals that are normally separated in the two part feeds from reacting with each other.

When growing in coco like we will be doing for the purposes of this book I would go with Plagron's A and B as your first choice.

A quick point to make here is that when mixing up your nutrient feed, the base feed should always be added to the water first. When using a two part base feed it should be added in the order A then B. It's always good practice to wait a few minutes between each nutrient application to ensure that the nutrients you are adding have had time to dilute properly into the water.

3. A three part base feed is normally only reserved for hydroponic feed schedules and comes in a Grow, Flower and a Micro solution. How they work is pretty simple; every nutrient mix made up will contain a certain amount of all three solutions but, depending on where you are in the growing process will depend on how much of each bottle goes in. In the Veg stage more "Grow" would be used and in Flower obviously more "Flower" feed would be used.

In my opinion GHE (General Hydroponics Europe) do the best three part.

GENERAL HYDROPONICS®
Bringing Nature and Technology Together

The Grow (green) and the Bloom (red) parts come as standard but the Micro (brown) comes in both a soft water and a hard water option.

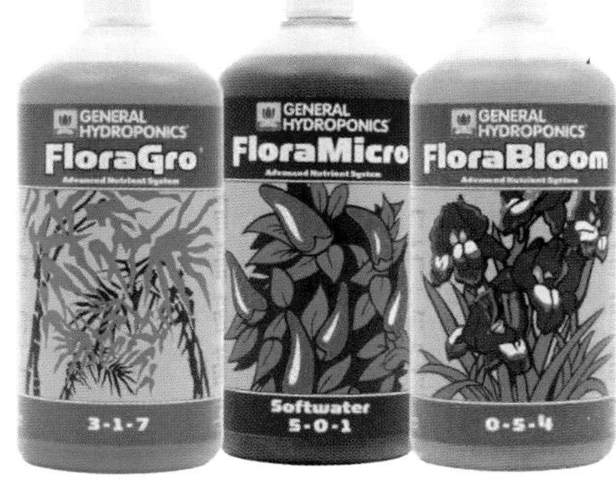

Enzyme – is an often overlooked part of the plant's feed range. Some people don't use them at all, but for me they are essential. Enzyme will help with the breakdown of older roots and help/speed up the regeneration of fresh new roots. Enzyme should be used throughout the whole of the plant's lifecycle. Some are used every other week, where others are used every week at every feed. My recommendation would be either Plagron's Pure Enzym pictured here on the right or Dutch pro's Multi Total (not shown).

Root Tonic – is basically a root steroid which will super charge the growth of your roots in the Veg stage of the plant's life. Root tonics can be used for the whole of the plant's cycle but as I will explain later I only use them in the Vegetative and the start of the Flowering stage.

For my money Dutch pro's Take Root is the best on the market. It also has a good concentration rate so you will find that a small bottle will go a long way for the price you are paying. Dutch pro's Take Root is a growth stimulant capable of radically improving the inner and outer qualities of your young plants! The active components are of natural origin, including several plant hormones and micronutrients. These combine to boost cellular division, cell elongation and nutrient transport – all of which help with overall root development during early vegetative growth. In addition to this, Take Root is classed as an organic product and also slows down the ageing process for prolonged good plant health.

Dosage: 1 ml per 1 litre water.

PK13/14 – is a chemical concentrate mix of **P** potassium and **K** phosphorus that should be used in weeks 4 to 5 in the Flower period of the plant's lifecycle to chemically stimulate and accelerate the growth and flowering process. It is normally used in connection with a standard bloom booster as opposed to a combined booster. However, saying that, if you are using a combined booster I would still recommend using it in week 4 and 5 of Flower at a reduced dilution rate.

Dosage: 0.5ml per 1 litre of water.

Bloom Booster - A good bloom booster shouldn't be cheap. With bloom booster feeds you get what you pay for, it's as simple as that. Some of the companies selling bloom nutrients do push it to be honest, I mean £180.00 for a litre is a lot to spend. On the flip side of that coin there are 1ltr blooms on the market for less than a tenner which will not be great and certainly will not have all the true chemical elements in them to get the most out of your plants. Bloom booster feeds should only be used in the Flowering stages of the plant's life.

Combined Booster - This is basically a combination PK (potassium and phosphorus) and bloom booster in the same bottle, an all in one booster if you will.

There are lots of these about nowadays but for me, I would recommend Explode from Dutch pro. It is a brilliant bloom booster stimulator/top shooter and PK in one that delivers precious nutrients and minerals to your plants throughout the Flowering stage. It consists of micronutrients, vitamins and acids, it does exactly as the name suggests – explosively drives flowering growth and bigger yields in addition to increasing your plants resistance against diseases.

Price wise you should be paying a little more for a combined booster than a standard bloom booster as it is essentially two products in one bottle. The other thing to look at is the dilution rate. Some of these products might seem expensive but they have a higher dilution rate than others, meaning that although they seem expensive the fact of the matter is that they will last 2-3 if not 4 times longer than some of the cheaper brands.

Dosage: 1ml per 1 litre of water

Flush - What does a flush do? At the end of your plant's flowering cycle the plants will need to be flushed of all the extra nutrients which you have been using. Most nutrient brands have a flush on the market but only Plant Magic have a flush for hard water and flush for soft water. All of this and for less than £15 it's a no brainer. Plant Magic's flush will remove metallic tastes; enhancing both flavour and aroma from your fruiting crops. It gives a boost of plant hormones, allowing the plant to use up any residues of excess nutrient as well as aiding the plant to mature. The correct balance of salts is also used to aid with the removal of salt residue and nutrient build up in the root zone and the plant sap. This in turn will promote sugar production, increasing the flavours and aromas of your crop to their full potential.

Foliar Spray - To get the most out of the Vegetative stage of the plant's life I would highly recommend the use of a foliar spray. Plant Magic's Evolution will significantly speed up Vegetative stages and prepares the plant to begin forming bountiful fruits and flowers, this is due predominantly to the sheer amount of new growth that forms and the number of healthy new shoots.

So now that all the separate feeds have been explained one by one, lets have a look at how it all works together. I've broken the next section down into 2 very easy "back to basics" run throughs;

- One for coco coir
- One for soil

Both chapters will run through the very basics of mixing the feeds needed from start to finish for the Vegetative and the Flower cycles.

They may seem repetitive but I have gone through each this way in order to avoid any confusion.

Coco coir - Vegetative stage

We will be mixing up feed in 10 litre batches and hand feeding. As we are hand feeding each plant and the run off ("run off" meaning - the feed which may come out of the bottom of the pot if you over feed them) will not be reused, this technique is known as "run to waste".

The nutrients you will need for this stage are;

- Plagron A and B (1 litre, that's 1 litre of each) for the base feed
- Plagron Pure Enzym (1 litre) for the enzyme
- Dutch pro Take Root (1 litre bottle) for your root tonic
- Plant Magic Evolution (1 litre) for your foliar spray

Here is the feed schedule which we will be following.

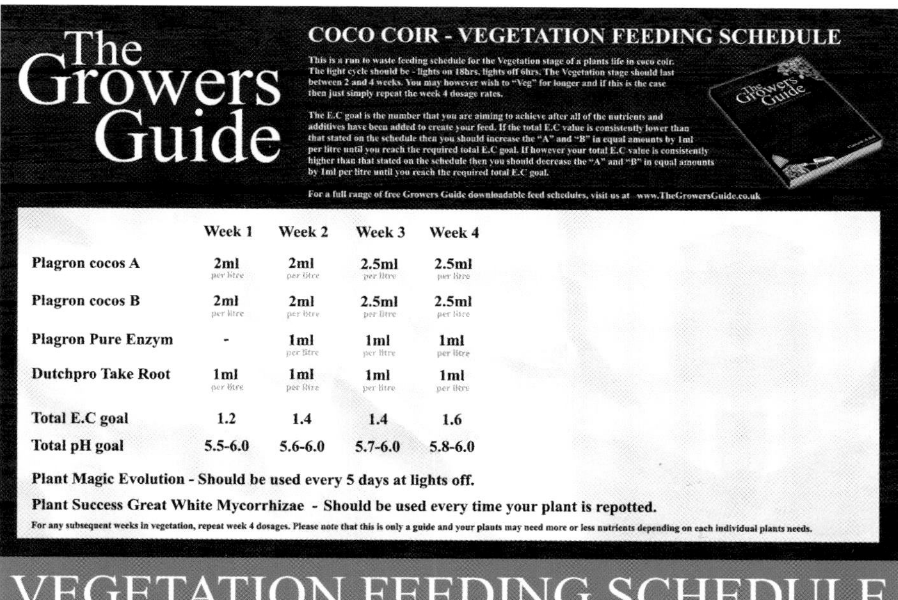

The Growers Guide

COCO COIR - VEGETATION FEEDING SCHEDULE

This is a run to waste feeding schedule for the Vegetation stage of a plants life in coco coir. The light cycle should be - lights on 18hrs, lights off 6hrs. The Vegetation stage should last between 2 and 4 weeks. You may however wish to "Veg" for longer and if this is the case then just simply repeat the week 4 dosage rates.

The E.C goal is the number that you are aiming to achieve after all of the nutrients and additives have been added to create your feed. If the total E.C value is consistently lower than that stated on the schedule then you should increase the "A" and "B" in equal amounts by 1ml per litre until you reach the required total E.C goal. If however your total E.C value is consistently higher than that stated on the schedule then you should decrease the "A" and "B" in equal amounts by 1ml per litre until you reach the required total E.C goal.

For a full range of free Growers Guide downloadable feed schedules, visit us at www.TheGrowersGuide.co.uk

	Week 1	Week 2	Week 3	Week 4
Plagron cocos A	2ml per litre	2ml per litre	2.5ml per litre	2.5ml per litre
Plagron cocos B	2ml per litre	2ml per litre	2.5ml per litre	2.5ml per litre
Plagron Pure Enzym	-	1ml per litre	1ml per litre	1ml per litre
Dutchpro Take Root	1ml per litre	1ml per litre	1ml per litre	1ml per litre
Total E.C goal	1.2	1.4	1.4	1.6
Total pH goal	5.5-6.0	5.6-6.0	5.7-6.0	5.8-6.0

Plant Magic Evolution - Should be used every 5 days at lights off.

Plant Success Great White Mycorrhizae - Should be used every time your plant is repotted.

For any subsequent weeks in vegetation, repeat week 4 dosages. Please note that this is only a guide and your plants may need more or less nutrients depending on each individual plants needs.

VEGETATION FEEDING SCHEDULE

welcome to the revolution.

So first things first, you will need 10 litres of water. Pour it into the bucket and leave it for 24 hours, this will allow the majority of the unwanted chemicals which tap water contains to evaporate.
If you want to super charge the water, this can be done by putting an air stone in the water which is hooked up to an air pump.

Next thing is to check the pH and then the E.C.

Here my water's pH is 6.7 (which is too high, so we will adjust later) and the E.C is 0.2 (which is about normal)

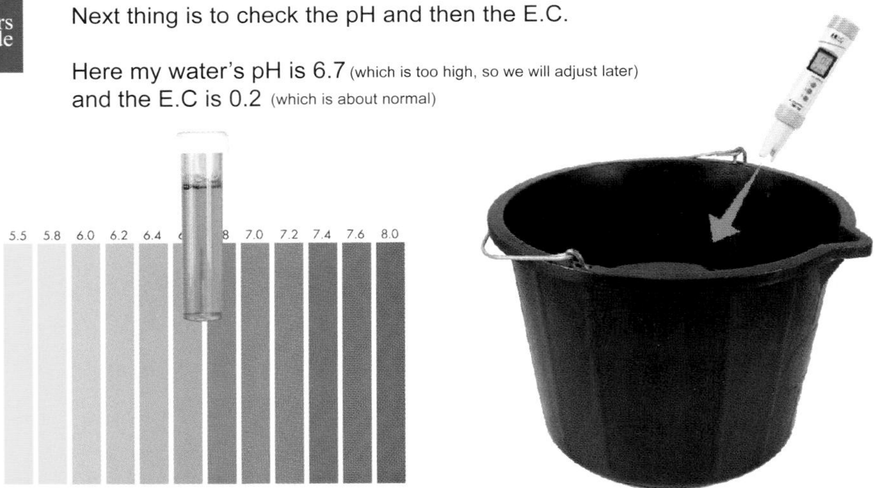

Make sure you note these numbers as they are your base line. Now you need to add your nutrients in order as follows.

First to be added is the base feed, at the correct dilution rate. We are using Plagron's two part Cocos A and B feed. The first to be added is the "A" and for this you can use the 20ml syringe.

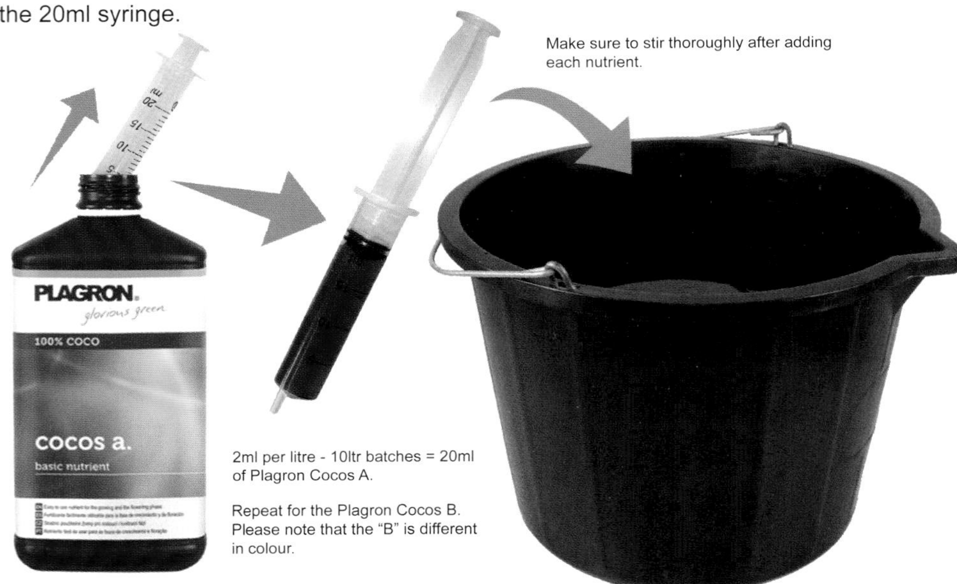

Make sure to stir thoroughly after adding each nutrient.

2ml per litre - 10ltr batches = 20ml of Plagron Cocos A.

Repeat for the Plagron Cocos B. Please note that the "B" is different in colour.

Now repeat the same process for the "B" part of the feed. Then mix/stir, making sure to check the E.C.

Second into the mix is the enzyme. We are using Plagron Pure Enzym (1 litre). Make sure the 10ml syringe is clean before use and add the enzyme, as soon as this is added it will need a good mixing/stirring.

Make sure when adding each nutrient to stir thoroughly.

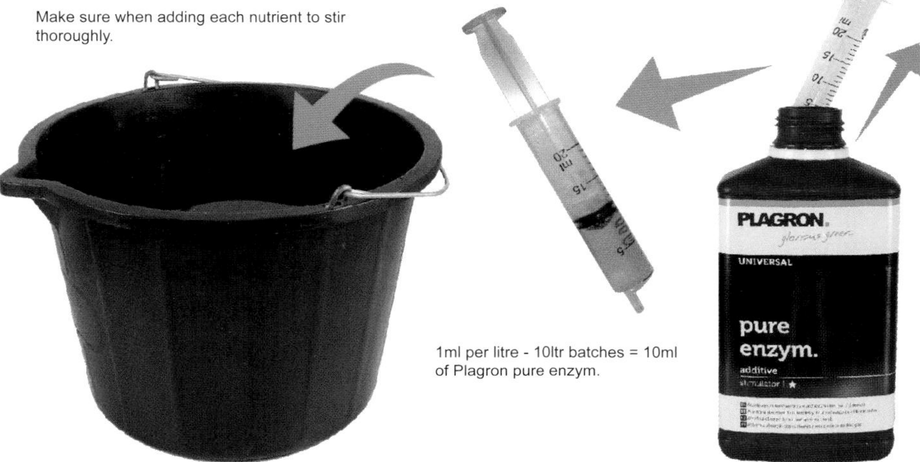

1ml per litre - 10ltr batches = 10ml of Plagron pure enzym.

Third to be added is the root tonic. We are using Dutch pro's Take Root which is highly concentrated so be careful to stick to the dilution rate on the schedule. Once again ensure that the syringe is clean before using it and make sure you shake the bottle first.

Make sure when adding each nutrient to stir thoroughly.

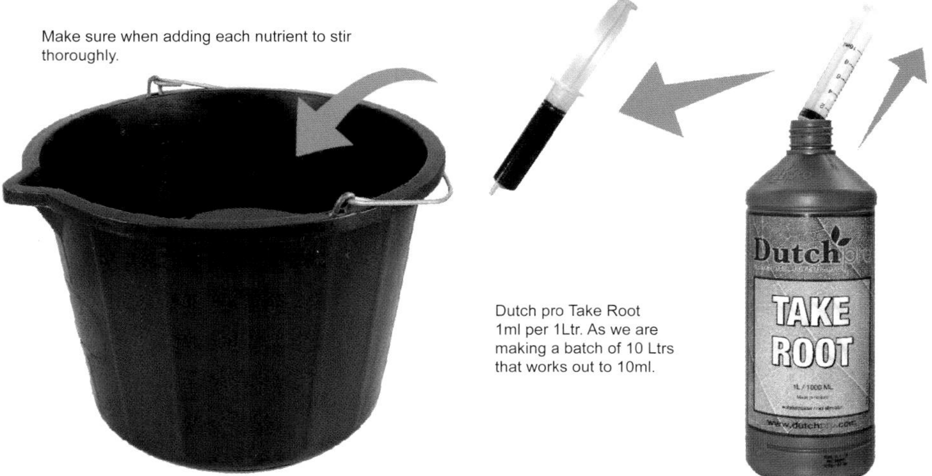

Dutch pro Take Root 1ml per 1Ltr. As we are making a batch of 10 Ltrs that works out to 10ml.

Now check the E.C. of the mixture and if all has gone well the E.C should be at 1.6 if it is over 1.6 you will need to add water in increments of 1Ltr at a time in order to reduce it. If the E.C is under, you should add more of the base feed (Plagrons two part Cocos A and B) in equal quantities until it reaches the desired level of 1.6.

You will now have to check the pH, it is vital that the pH of the feed is correct. If it is not correct then the plant will not be able to take up the nutrients in the right amounts, at the right times. This could and often does lead to toxicity problems (toxicity–meaning that the plant is taking in dangerous amounts of one element which is poisoning it) and deficiency issues (deficiency–meaning that as a result of the pH being wrong the plant is not taking in/up a vital element and thus starving itself as a result).

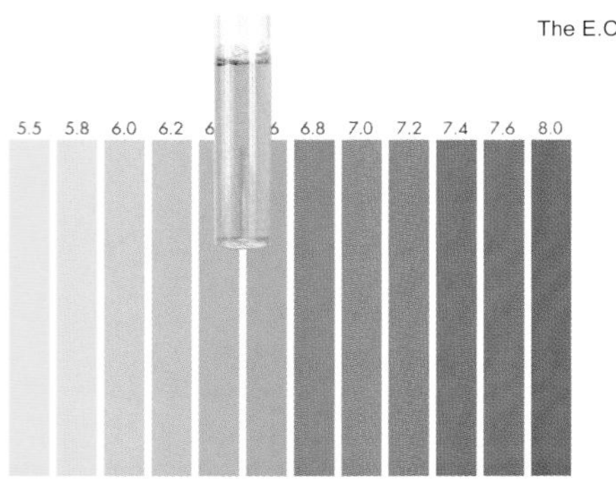

As you can see after we have added all of the nutrients our pH is coming out at about 6.4 which is too high. Ideally we want the at pH of 5.5

The E.C has come out at a value of 1.6 which is perfect.

If the pH is too high you will need to add pH Down in order to reduce it and vice versa if the pH is too low you can use pH Up to increase it. Please be aware that both pH Down and pH Up are strong and hazardous, so make sure to follow the instructions on the bottle to the letter. Whenever I use it I always use gloves and eye protection. Add the pH Down/Up in small very quantities until you reach the desired pH level that you are looking for.

Its super important to point out here that if by adding pH Down you go below the desired pH level, you cannot then add pH Up in order to rectify the situation. In this instance this batch of feed is no good and you will have to start again from scratch. The same goes the other way round, if your pH is too low and you increase it by using pH Up, you cannot then lower the level by using pH Down.

As you can see here I have added some pH Down in very small quantities until I have got the final mixture down to the desired pH.

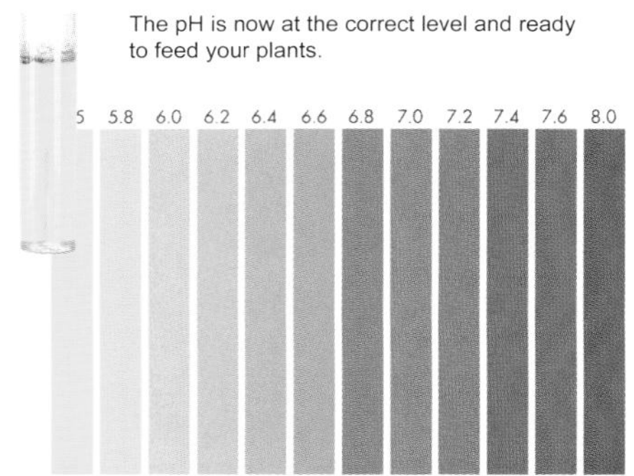

The pH is now at the correct level and ready to feed your plants.

The foliar spray (Plant Magics Evolution) should be used every 5 days at lights off, in the Veg stage only. The closer you can apply the foliar spray to the lights going off the better. All the leaves will need to be sprayed until they are wet.

DO NOT use foliar spray when the lights are on, if you do you will burn the plants.

So there you have your coco coir, "run to waste" plant feed mixed and ready to use. If however you are now wondering when exactly to water your plants and how often? Do not worry as I will go through this in the Vegetation chapter of the book.

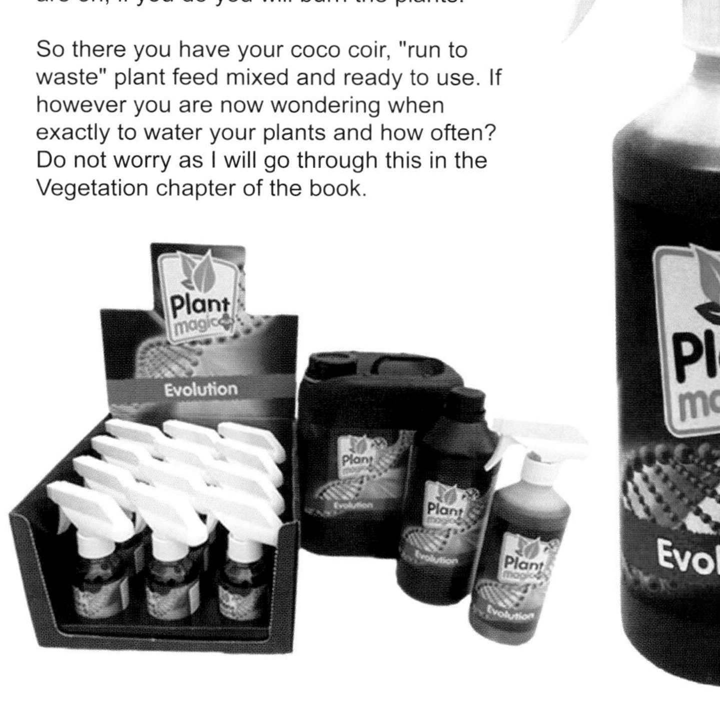

Plant Magic Evolution Foliar Spray.

Coco - Flower stage

For the Flower stage we will be mixing up the same amount of feed as we did for the Vegetative stage (10 litre batches) and hand feeding using the run to waste technique.

The nutrients you will need for this stage are;

- Plagron Cocos A and B (1 Litre, that's 1 litre of each. Plagron A and B is the same for Flower as it is in the Vegetation stage) for the base feed
- Plagron Enzym (1 litre) for the enzyme
- Bio Green PK 13/14 (1 litre)
- Dutch pro Explode (1 litre)
- Plant Magic flush (1 litre)

Here is the Flowering feed schedule which we will be following.

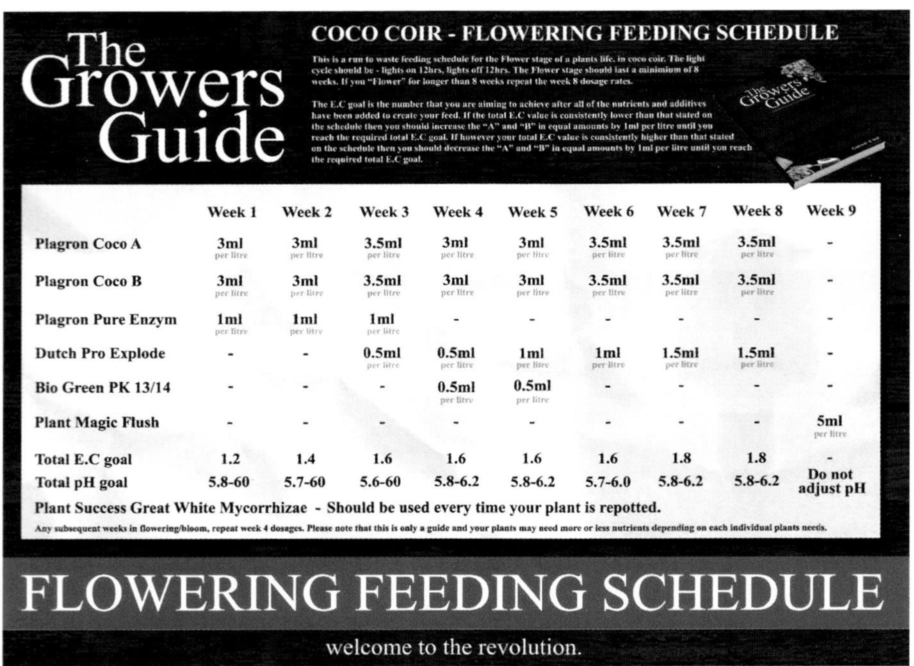

The Growers Guide

COCO COIR - FLOWERING FEEDING SCHEDULE

This is a run to waste feeding schedule for the Flower stage of a plants life, in coco coir. The light cycle should be - lights on 12hrs, lights off 12hrs. The Flower stage should last a minimium of 8 weeks. If you "Flower" for longer than 8 weeks repeat the week 8 dosage rates.

The E.C goal is the number that you are aiming to achieve after all of the nutrients and additives have been added to create your feed. If the total E.C value is consistently lower than that stated on the schedule then you should increase the "A" and "B" in equal amounts by 1ml per litre until you reach the required total E.C goal. If however your total E.C value is consistently higher than that stated on the schedule then you should decrease the "A" and "B" in equal amounts by 1ml per litre until you reach the required total E.C goal.

	Week 1	Week 2	Week 3	Week 4	Week 5	Week 6	Week 7	Week 8	Week 9
Plagron Coco A	3ml per litre	3ml per litre	3.5ml per litre	3ml per litre	3ml per litre	3.5ml per litre	3.5ml per litre	3.5ml per litre	-
Plagron Coco B	3ml per litre	3ml per litre	3.5ml per litre	3ml per litre	3ml per litre	3.5ml per litre	3.5ml per litre	3.5ml per litre	-
Plagron Pure Enzym	1ml per litre	1ml per litre	1ml per litre	-	-	-	-	-	-
Dutch Pro Explode	-	-	0.5ml per litre	0.5ml per litre	1ml per litre	1ml per litre	1.5ml per litre	1.5ml per litre	-
Bio Green PK 13/14	-	-	-	0.5ml per litre	0.5ml per litre	-	-	-	-
Plant Magic Flush	-	-	-	-	-	-	-	-	5ml per litre
Total E.C goal	1.2	1.4	1.6	1.6	1.6	1.6	1.8	1.8	-
Total pH goal	5.8-60	5.7-60	5.6-60	5.8-6.2	5.8-6.2	5.7-6.0	5.8-6.2	5.8-6.2	Do not adjust pH

Plant Success Great White Mycorrhizae - Should be used every time your plant is repotted.

Any subsequent weeks in flowering/bloom, repeat week 4 dosages. Please note that this is only a guide and your plants may need more or less nutrients depending on each individual plants needs.

FLOWERING FEEDING SCHEDULE

welcome to the revolution.

Following the same principles as the Vegetation stage, you will need 10 litres of water. Pour this into a bucket and leave it for 24 hours. Remember to check the pH and note it down before adding your nutrients.

Following the same technique as you have used in the Veg stage, add all of the nutrients at the right doses as stated on the feeding schedule.

Check the pH and E.C as before and adjust accordingly.

It is important to follow the feeding schedule as closely as possible, but saying that, every plant is different and will sometimes need more (or less) particular nutrient elements at different stages of its life.

The key is to read your plant. This is only learnt through experience, time and hard work. Your plant will show you tell tale signs of what it needs and when, you just need to look out for them.

Soil - Vegetative Stage

Again just like the coco coir Vegetative stage we will be mixing up feed in 10 litre batches and hand feeding using a run to waste technique. I will run through it in the same amount of detail as I have for the coco coir stages.

The nutrients you will need for this stage are;

- Plant Magic Oldtimer Grow (1 Litre) for the base feed
- Plagron Pure Enzym (1 litre) for the enzyme
- Dutch pro Take Root (1 litre bottle) for your root tonic
- Plant Magic Evolution (1 litre) for your foliar spray

Here is the feed schedule which we will be following.

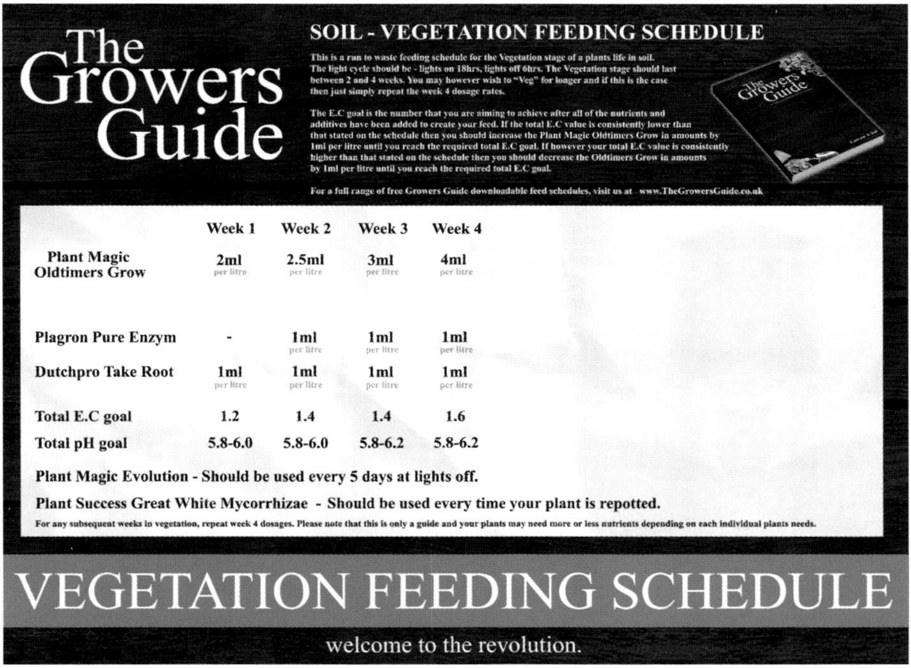

The Growers Guide

SOIL - VEGETATION FEEDING SCHEDULE

This is a run to waste feeding schedule for the Vegetation stage of a plants life in soil. The light cycle should be - lights on 18hrs, lights off 6hrs. The Vegetation stage should last between 2 and 4 weeks. You may however wish to "Veg" for longer and if this is the case then just simply repeat the week 4 dosage rates.

The E.C goal is the number that you are aiming to achieve after all of the nutrients and additives have been added to create your feed. If the total E.C value is consistently lower than that stated on the schedule then you should increase the Plant Magic Oldtimers Grow in amounts by 1ml per litre until you reach the required total E.C goal. If however your total E.C value is consistently higher than that stated on the schedule then you should decrease the Oldtimers Grow in amounts by 1ml per litre until you reach the required total E.C goal.

For a full range of free Growers Guide downloadable feed schedules, visit us at www.TheGrowersGuide.co.uk

	Week 1	Week 2	Week 3	Week 4
Plant Magic Oldtimers Grow	2ml per litre	2.5ml per litre	3ml per litre	4ml per litre
Plagron Pure Enzym	-	1ml per litre	1ml per litre	1ml per litre
Dutchpro Take Root	1ml per litre	1ml per litre	1ml per litre	1ml per litre
Total E.C goal	1.2	1.4	1.4	1.6
Total pH goal	5.8-6.0	5.8-6.0	5.8-6.2	5.8-6.2

Plant Magic Evolution - Should be used every 5 days at lights off.

Plant Success Great White Mycorrhizae - Should be used every time your plant is repotted.

For any subsequent weeks in vegetation, repeat week 4 dosages. Please note that this is only a guide and your plants may need more or less nutrients depending on each individual plants needs.

VEGETATION FEEDING SCHEDULE

welcome to the revolution.

So first things first you will need 10 litres of water. Pour it into a bucket and leave it for 24 hours, to allow the majority of the unwanted chemicals which tap water contains to dissolve.

Next is to check the pH and the E.C of your water

Here my water's pH is 6.5 (which is too high, so we will adjust later)
and the E.C is 0.3 (which is about normal)

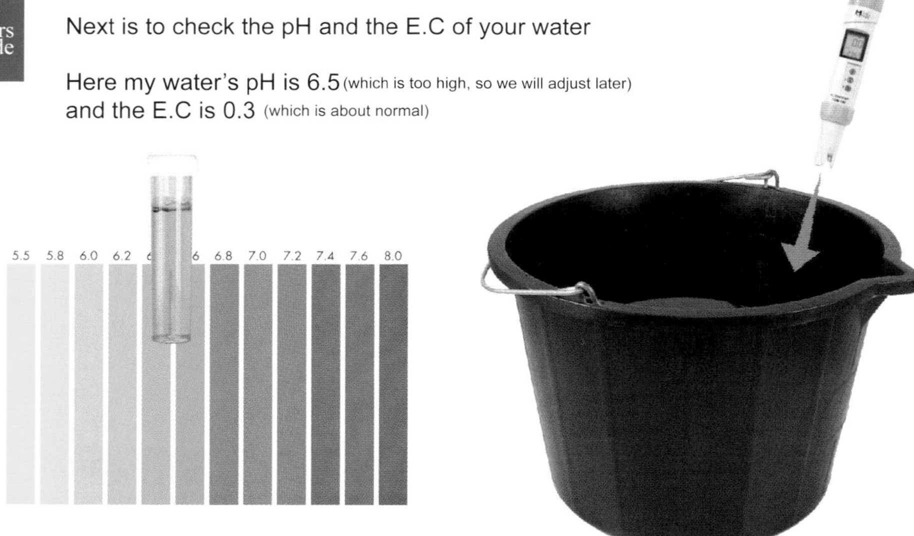

Make a note of these numbers as they are you base line. Next you will need to add your nutrients.

First is the base feed which requires adding at the correct dilution rate. We are using Plant Magic Oldtimer Grow Feed and for this you can use the 20ml syringe.

Make sure when adding each nutrient that you stir thoroughly.

2ml per litre - 10ltr batches
= 20ml of Oldtimer Grow.

Second to go into the mix is the Enzyme. We are using Plagron Pure Enzym (1 litre). Make sure the 10ml syringe is clean before use.

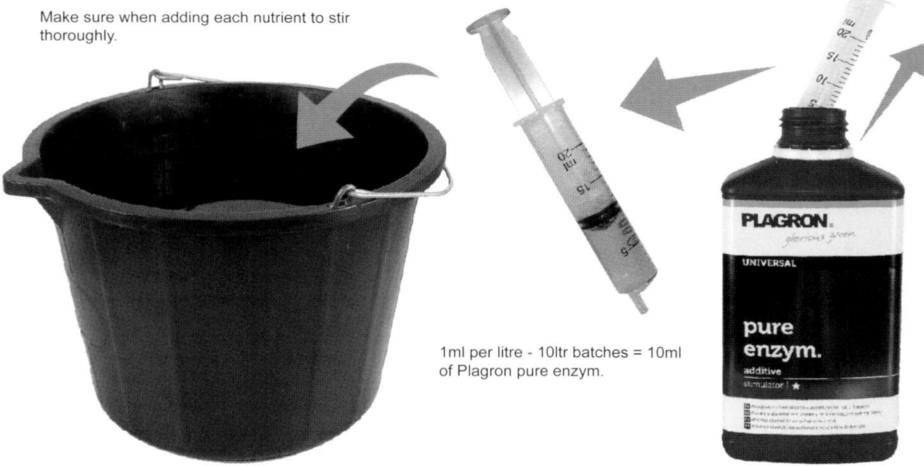

Third to be added is the Root Tonic. We are using Dutch pro's Take Root which is highly concentrated so be careful to stick to the dilution rate on the schedule. Once again ensure that the syringe is clean before using it and make sure you shake the bottle first.

Make sure when adding each nutrient to stir thoroughly.
Dutch pro Take Root 1ml per 1Ltr. As we are making a batch of 10 Ltrs that works out to 10ml.
TAKE ROOT

Now check the E.C. and if all has gone well then it should be at 1.6, if it is higher than this then you will need to add water in order to reduce it.

If it is under the desired level then you should re-add the base feed (Plant Magic Oldtimer Grow) until the E.C reaches the desired level.

You will now need to check the pH, it is vital that the pH of the feed is correct. If it is not then the plant will not be able to take up the nutrients in the right amounts at the right times. This could and often does lead to toxicity problems (toxicity–meaning that the plant is taking in dangerous amounts of one element which is poisoning it) and deficiency issues (deficiency–meaning that as a result of the pH being wrong the plant is not taking in/up a vital element and as a result is starving itself).

If the pH is too high you will need to add pH Down in order to reduce it and vice versa if the pH is too low you can use pH Up to increase it. Please be aware that both pH Down and pH Up are strong and hazardous, so make sure to follow the instructions on the bottle to the letter. Whenever I use it I always use gloves and eye protection. Add the pH Down/Up in small quantities until you reach the desired pH level that you are looking for.

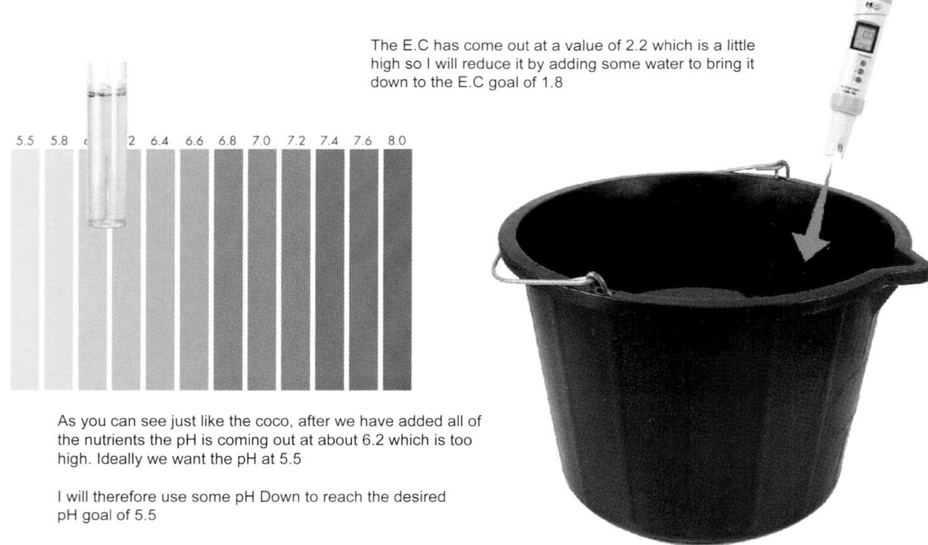

The E.C has come out at a value of 2.2 which is a little high so I will reduce it by adding some water to bring it down to the E.C goal of 1.8

As you can see just like the coco, after we have added all of the nutrients the pH is coming out at about 6.2 which is too high. Ideally we want the pH at 5.5

I will therefore use some pH Down to reach the desired pH goal of 5.5

It's super important to point out here that if by adding pH Down you go below the desired pH level that you cannot then add pH Up in order to rectify the situation. In this instance this batch of feed is no good and you will have to start again from scratch. The same goes the other way round, if your pH is too low and you increase it by using pH Up, you cannot then lower the level by using pH Down.

The other items I have on the Vegetation feeding schedule are foliar spray and mycorrhizae, these should only be used as stated on the feed schedule.

The foliar spray (Plant Magic Evolution) should be used every 5 days at lights off, in the Veg stage only. DO NOT use foliar spray when the lights are on, if you do you will burn the plants.

Soil - Flower stage

We will be mixing up the same amount of feed for the Flower stage, 10 litre batches and hand feeding them using the run to waste technique.

The nutrients you will need for this stage are;

- Plagron Cocos A and B for the base feed (1 Litre), that's 1 litre of each.
- Plagron Enzym (1 litre) for the enzyme.
- Bio Green PK 13/14 (1 litre)
- Dutch pro Explode (1 litre)
- Plant Magic Flush (1 litre)

Here is the Flowering feed schedule which we will be following.

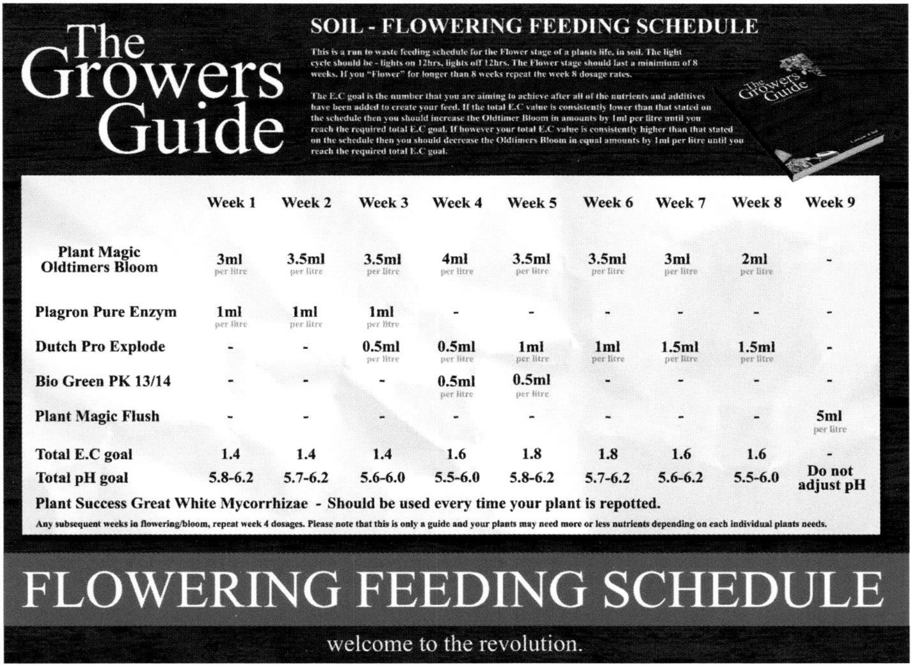

The Growers Guide

SOIL - FLOWERING FEEDING SCHEDULE

This is a run to waste feeding schedule for the Flower stage of a plants life, in soil. The light cycle should be - lights on 12hrs, lights off 12hrs. The Flower stage should last a minimium of 8 weeks. If you "Flower" for longer than 8 weeks repeat the week 8 dosage rates.

The E.C goal is the number that you are aiming to achieve after all of the nutrients and additives have been added to create your feed. If the total E.C value is consistently lower than that stated on the schedule then you should increase the Oldtimer Bloom in amounts by 1ml per litre until you reach the required total E.C goal. If however your total E.C value is consistently higher than that stated on the schedule then you should decrease the Oldtimers Bloom in equal amounts by 1ml per litre until you reach the required total E.C goal.

	Week 1	Week 2	Week 3	Week 4	Week 5	Week 6	Week 7	Week 8	Week 9
Plant Magic Oldtimers Bloom	3ml per litre	3.5ml per litre	3.5ml per litre	4ml per litre	3.5ml per litre	3.5ml per litre	3ml per litre	2ml per litre	-
Plagron Pure Enzym	1ml per litre	1ml per litre	1ml per litre	-	-	-	-	-	-
Dutch Pro Explode	-	-	0.5ml per litre	0.5ml per litre	1ml per litre	1ml per litre	1.5ml per litre	1.5ml per litre	-
Bio Green PK 13/14	-	-	-	0.5ml per litre	0.5ml per litre	-	-	-	-
Plant Magic Flush	-	-	-	-	-	-	-	-	5ml per litre
Total E.C goal	1.4	1.4	1.4	1.6	1.8	1.8	1.6	1.6	-
Total pH goal	5.8-6.2	5.7-6.2	5.6-6.0	5.5-6.0	5.8-6.2	5.7-6.2	5.6-6.2	5.5-6.0	Do not adjust pH

Plant Success Great White Mycorrhizae - Should be used every time your plant is repotted.

Any subsequent weeks in flowering/bloom, repeat week 4 dosages. Please note that this is only a guide and your plants may need more or less nutrients depending on each individual plants needs.

FLOWERING FEEDING SCHEDULE

welcome to the revolution.

As with the Vegetation stage you will need 10 litres of water. Pour it into a bucket and leave it for 24 hours. Remember to check the pH and note it down before adding the nutrients. Following the same technique as you have used in the Vegetative stage, add all of the nutrients in the right doses as stated on the feeding schedule.

Check the pH and E.C as before and adjust accordingly.

When using soil as a medium, less is always more. Don't forget that soil is already enriched with nutrients.

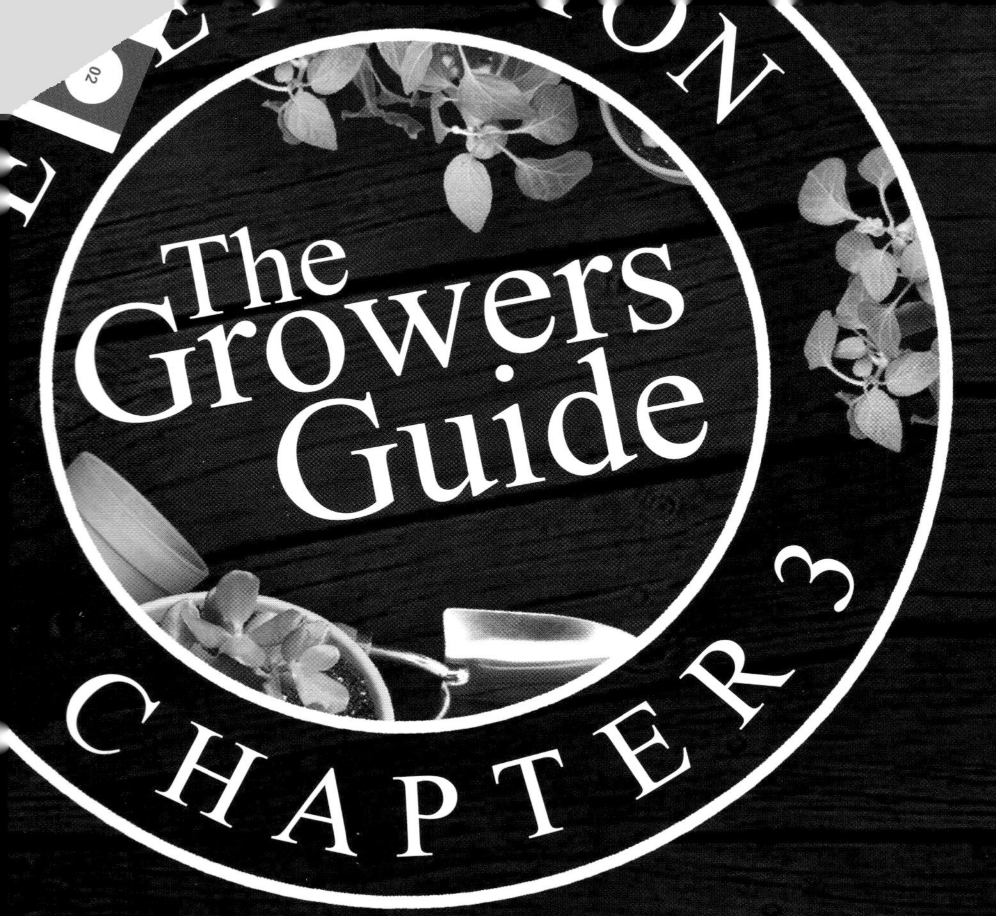

Seeds

In this chapter we will be looking at seeds; the differing types and whats inside them. Understanding what's inside a seed and how it develops will help to give you an overall knowledge of the plant at both the very first stages and hibernation stages of its life. We will also be looking at entropy, what this is and how using this system can give you the greatest possible chance of growing the very best plant from a number of seeds.

This chapter also shows you the most efficient way to dry seeds for stasis/hibernation, how to store them and for how long.

Seeds and types of seeds.

There are an uncountable amount of seeds and strains of seeds out there in the world.

My advice would be to get your seeds from a reputable retailer or breeder. You get what you pay for! At first it may seem a lot of money to spend on something so small but believe me when I tell you that it is worth every penny. A good batch of seeds, handled correctly, should get you approximately a 90% successful germination rate, which is spot on where you need to be.

Growing from seed will always give you a better yield if it's done correctly from the start. Buying from a reputable seed breeder will also ensure that your seeds have come from a disease-free mother plant and environment.

In this day and age a lot of people try to keep it as simple as they can by buying pre-rooted cuttings/clones, which I will go through in the "cuttings/clones" section of this book.

An important thing to remember here is that cuttings can be expensive and can have their problems, some of which can be devastating not only to your plants and crop but also to your equipment and grow room.

The bottom line is that starting a seed from scratch and getting it through Propagation to Veg is a fundamental part of the growing process and thus should be carried out and learnt by all growers. This will make you a better grower and increase your yield, trust me.

The days of secret and regional specific strains of seeds are all but gone. All good worthwhile strains can now be readily brought very easily from retailers, seed distributors or online seed suppliers.

Seeds can be brought in feminized packs, mixed packs and autoflowering packs (commonly know as "autos"). To keep things simple and to make things easy on yourself I would say to use feminized seeds.

Feminized seeds – are seeds which have been treated/modified to increase their chances of becoming a female plant. There is no 100% guarantee that they will be female, but there's a good 99% chance.
Some people (me included), believe that treating/modifying the seeds in this way can affect the overall stability of the plant and yield, they can however produce phenomenal results. This is why I would recommend the use of feminized seeds brought from a reputable seed breeder.

Mixed seeds – are natural untreated seeds. The female seeds in "mixed packs" are nearly always more stable and yield more then feminized treated/modified seeds. The drawbacks with these seeds however is that it can be hard to "sex" the males from the females without knowing exactly what you are looking for. I have gone through the basics of spotting the tell tale signs of sexing a plant in the section "Know your plant". Chapter 1. Just one male or even hermaphrodite plant can ruin a whole crop. Normally in a mixed pack there is around a 50/50 split of male and female seeds. This should be accounted for when you are buying and germinating your seeds.

Autoflowering seeds – are genetically modified/bred to flower automatically after the plant reaches a certain maturity regardless of the photoperiod.

Photoperiod - meaning the light cycle of the plant.

Normally to put a plant of this nature into Flower you would have to change the light cycle from Veg (normally - 18hrs light on - 6hrs light off) to Flower (normally - 12hrs lights on - 12hrs lights off). Autoflowering plants normally go into Flower after 3 weeks regardless of wether you have changed the light cycle or not.

The good points about autos are that they grow quickly and are hardy. The bad points are that they are small and thus yield less.

It is impossible to be 100% sure whether a seed is male, female or a hermaphrodite until it grows and shows the tell tale signs. It is important to note that plants can change their sex from male to female, female to male and from either male or female to both sexes, a hermaphrodite at any time. They can be tricky little buggers!

With seeds you will always have genetically stronger and weaker ones from the same source. I like to think of it like children from the same parents, although they are from the same source they will inevitably have different attributes of their predecessors; taller, shorter, stronger, weaker, dominant, passive, ginger and yes there is always a runt! I've found that seeds, cuttings and plants are very similar. Their offspring, clones and cuttings all can have different attributes, even exact genetic copies of a plant can and do develop different characteristics depending on their environment and feed.

In order to even out, what I call the "runt rate" (technical term is "Entropy") what I do is the following.

Let's say I want 10 plants. Those 10 plants I will grow from seed all the way through to yield. To do this I wouldn't go out and buy 10 feminized seeds, I would look at buying 20. Out of the 20, 18 germinate (90% germination rate is pretty good). Now I'm left with 18 little plantlings (yes "plantlings" is a new word I've invented meaning young plants from Germination up to Veg) at this stage they're too young for you to see their attributes, ie; which ones are strong and which are weak. For this reason I would take all 18 through Propagation and into the end of the first week of Veg. This is the point when I would check for males and hermaphrodites, any found should be taken out and destroyed. I would then select the strongest, best looking 10 young plants to take through the rest of Veg and Flowering up to yield and I would destroy the others.

This may seem a little extreme and some would say a waste of money but I've been using this tried and tested method over all the years I've been growing and can safely say that it has never let me down.

When I ran a Hydroponic shop, I lost count of the amount of times people came in and moaned that they had 1 or 2 plants in the corner of their grow room which were half the size of the rest, or that didn't yield as much as the rest, etc. Sometimes, some plants are just genetically weaker than others, you can do everything right but it doesn't help. In some of these cases people can spend all their time losing focus of the crop as a whole whilst trying to remedy the runts, which can end up being to the detriment of the other plants.

Using the above method levels out the amount of runts but you will have to accept that you will always have the odd few that get through and my advice would be to either treat them like the rest, with maybe a little more TLC or get rid of them as soon as they become an issue.

In order to help you understand seeds and what they are made up of, here is a cross section of what's inside a seed before germination.

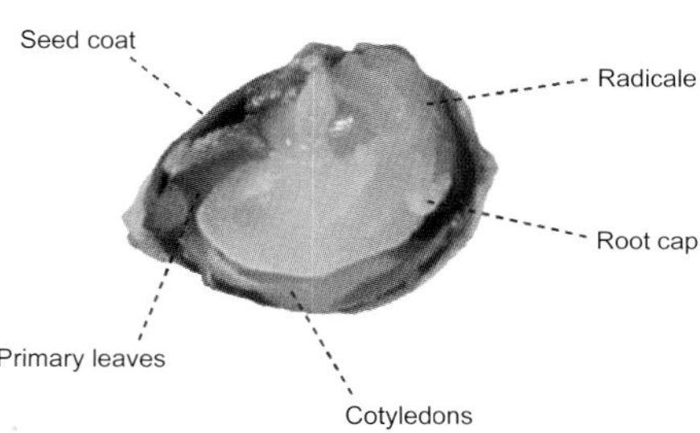

Drying seeds/preparing them for storage

If you have seeded a plant and want to store the seeds for a later date the first thing you will need to do is to remove the fruit containing the seeds from the plant. The next process of drying the seeds can be done in a number of ways.

The first is to dry the fruit with the seeds still attached/inside the fruit. This can be tricky if not done properly and if the fruit is dried in the wrong conditions. One of the most common problems encountered here is botrytis. Most people know botrytis as bud rot or grey mould. This is common in the drying of fruit if the air where the fruit is being dried is not ventilated properly or the humidity levels are too high. I will go through in full detail how to dry fruit in the "Harvest and curing" section of the book. As a quick rule of thumb however you want it to be as dry as possible, as dark as possible, with good ventilation and the temperature to be at a constant 30°c with a humidity of 8% or less. The fruit can take a while to completely dry out and will need rolling/turning every day to make sure that it is drying evenly as this will reduce the chance of botrytis taking a hold. As every fruit is different in size and moisture content it is impossible to put a set time on drying all the fruit out completely, but saying that, if you have the right conditions it should take no longer than two weeks.

When the fruit is completely dried it's just a simple case of removing the dry seeds and storing them.

The second method of drying, is to remove all of the seeds as soon as the fruit is taken off the plant (when ripe). It's best to lay them out on two layers of good quality kitchen towel somewhere dry and dark with good ventilation and again at a constant 30°c and with a humidity of 8% or less. The average time seeds will take to dry out like this is 7 days. As I mentioned above it is best to roll/turn them every day.

When dried properly the seeds should be rock hard. If they are soft or bendy, then they are not fully dried out.

Storing seeds

The best place to store seeds is in bags of 5 or 10 in a light-tight, waterproof, air tight container in a consistently cool or cold environment (don't forget to label and date them).

How long can they be stored for? Technically they can be stored forever but I think "fresher the better". I personally would set a use by date on them once dry of 12-24 months.

FORMULA-XL

Propagation plant feed & pre-soak

FORMULA-XL is a scientifically designed, bespoke premium product which is specifically tailored for the propagation stage of a plant's life, full of all of the micro and macro elements that are crucial for a plant's early development. Each bottle is batch coded and comes complete with a guaranteed chemical analysis and can be traced via a batch numbering system to ensure that the highest of standards are always maintained.

The exact NPK is;

2.10 – 0.85 – 3.36

Most nutrient brands do not label products with the exact NPK ratios, they normally round the figure up or down to allow for slight differences in the products elements when manufactured, which as a result can negatively affect the feeds efficiency. By showing the exact NPK on each bottle and always manufacturing it to these ratios, **FORMULA-XL** is leaving no room for error and as a result it gives a consistently high performance that you can rely on every time.

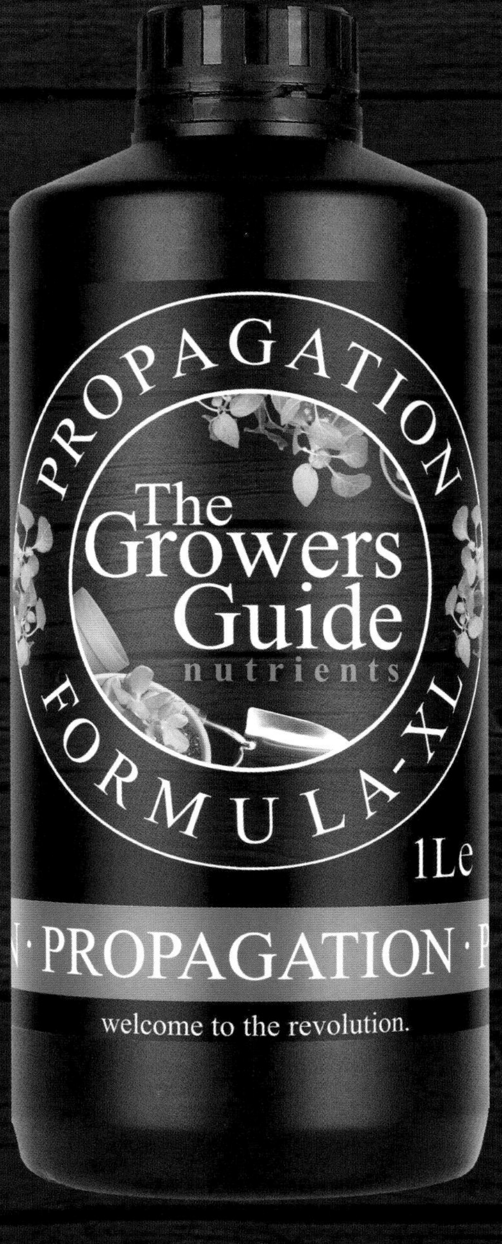

Give your plants the best start possible

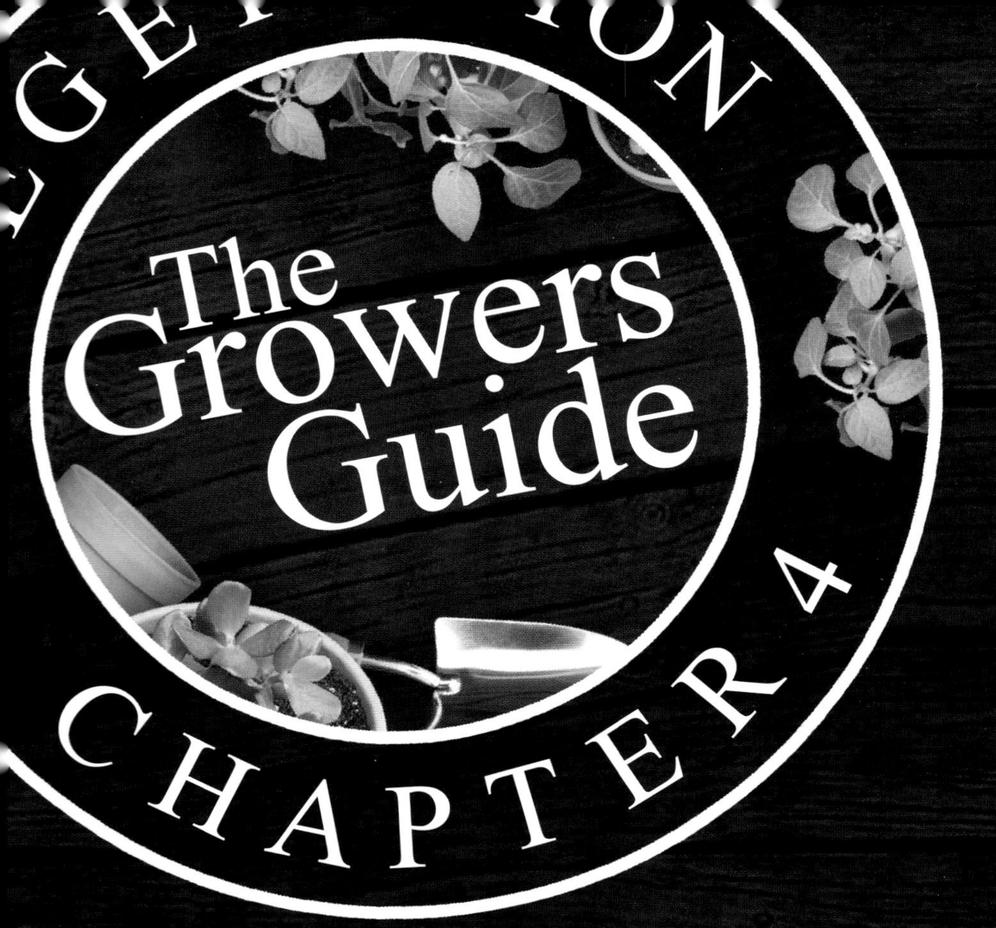

Germination

To germinate simply means ‘to bring to life’.

In this chapter we will go through several different methods of germinating a seed and the vital elements needed to do so. When carried out successfully and in the correct way, this process can and will give your plants the best start possible. It will reduce any plant mutation and ensure that you are on the right path to achieving phenomenal results from your plants.

An often overlooked part of the growing process, the germination of a seed is the very start of bringing life back from the plant’s hibernation state. Every grower will benefit greatly from following this chapter, learning to germinate seeds efficiently and can expect to see a higher rate of success as a result.

Germination.

In this chapter we will be looking at the germination of a seed, right up until it is ready to go into the propagator.

So what does "germinate" mean?......................

Germination is the first part of a plant's life, the growth or shooting of a seed into a seedling and then hopefully a plant. There are 3 things which are vital for this to happen:

- **Water**
- **Oxygen**
- **The correct temperature**

Water - is needed to fundamentally start the process as the seed is dry and needs to absorb a lot of water in order to start the cellular metabolism of the plant, in order to expand the shell and soften it to allow for the plant to grow easier. The uptake of water into a seed is called imbibition.
Within the seed/embryo there is a storing of starch, oils and proteins and so when the imbibition process starts hydrolytic enzymes are activated which release/produce the stored proteins, oils and starches giving the plant just enough of the right chemicals in order to get it started.

Oxygen - When being germinated, seeds, like most living things need to breathe. The oxygen that the seed receives is used for aerobic respiration in order to help with the metabolism and without this oxygen the seed may drown or suffocate.

The correct temperature - Getting the temperature correct when germinating is often overlooked, I think it is an essential part of the germination process if you want strong healthy plants. Each type of seed will have a different germination temperature range, above or below this range and the seed will not germinate.

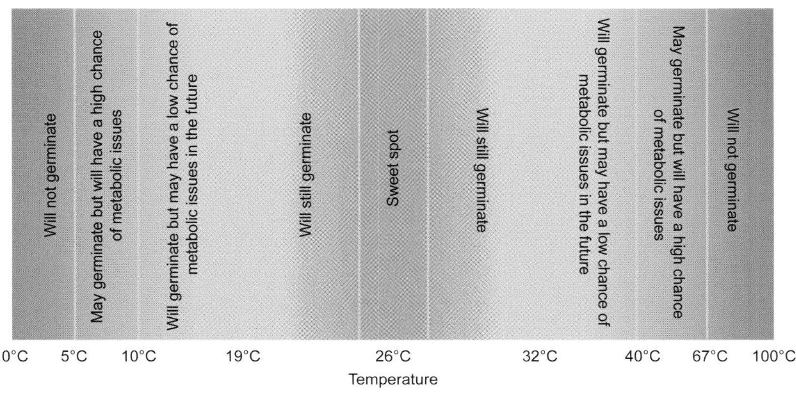

Ideally you want to get your seed/seeds to germinate at the perfect temperature for that particular seed, I call this the "sweet spot" (inbetween 21°C and 24°C). If you germinate a seed at the hotter or the colder end of its germination temperature spectrum then it will germinate, but it may have unseen effects on the metabolic rate, which may affect the plant's growth and health in the future.

Most seasonal vegetables will germinate between 10°C and 32°C

Aubergine - 24-32°C
Beetroot and Chard - 10-30°C
Broccoli, Cabbage, Cauliflower, Kale & Brussels - 7-30°C
Broad beans - 8-15°C
Carrots - 7-30°C
Cucumber - 16-35°C
French and Runner beans - 16-30°C
Lettuce - 4-27°C
Onion - 10-35°C
Parsley - 10-30°C
Peas - 4-24°C
Sweet peppers and Chillies - 18-35°C
Sweetcorn - 16-32°C
Tomatoes - 16-30°C

There are lots of different types of seed germination, the two main ones being epigeal – above ground and hoypogeal – below ground. We will be focusing on just the one, The epigeal germination. Epigeal germination implies that the cotyledons (seed leaves) are pushed upward. The seeds themselves hold starch, oils and proteins, normally just enough to get the leaves to open in order to start the photosynthesis process. Generally plants that produce epigeal germinating seeds produce lots of seeds in order to increase their chances of survival.

How to germinate...................

There are a few ways that my friends and I prefer to germinate seeds, one way is to leave them in a glass of mineral water in a dark room until the radicale/tip of the root shows (about 24 hrs later). This can, however, take longer depending on seed type; any longer than 3 days and the chances are that you either have a dud seed or that it is genetically weak. To germinate a seed you only need water, any nutrients or fertilizers at this stage will it before it has a chance to grow.

You will find this to be one of the faster ways to germinate a seed as you will get the maximum amount of water absorption, however seeds also need oxygen and so there is a possibility that using this technique coud cause the seed to die due to a lack of oxygen.

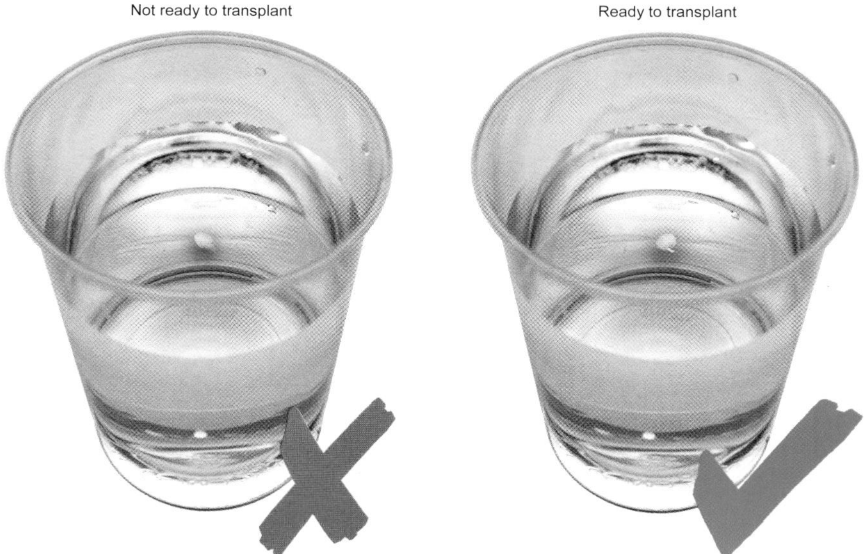

Once the radicale/root tip is showing the seed is then ready to transplant to the medium you plan to use throughout its life, ie soil, coco coir, pebbles etc.

At this transference stage it is important to treat the seedling as delicately as possible and therefore as a rule of thumb I only try to touch the seed once (from its bag/ breeders pack, to where I plan to germinate it). At any other time I will use clean plastic tweezers or surgical gloves when I need to move or touch it.

How I normally germinate a seed is a little unconventional but it has worked for me for years and years and I have never encountered any problems with it.

I take a sheet of premium kitchen towel and fold it in half, I then place the seed/seeds to the left of the centre of the kitchen towel, if you are germinating more than one seed, you can use the same piece of kitchen towel but try not to let the seeds touch. Once you have done this, fold the kitchen towel in half again so that all of the seeds are covered up and then saturate with water, tap water is fine as long as it has been left for 24hrs beforehand. You would need to give the tap water a chance to settle for 24 hrs in order to help dissolve certain chemicals in the water which may be harmful to the seedling. This is because the water that comes out of your tap at home has been treated by the water company providers for human consumption, thus they add all sorts of chemicals and compounds some of which at disturbing levels.

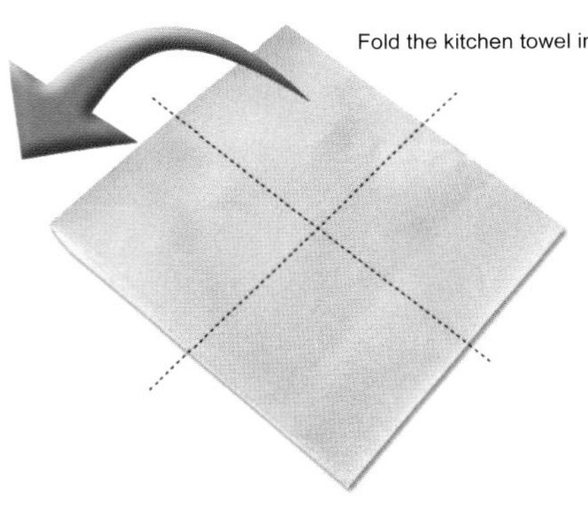
Fold the kitchen towel in half

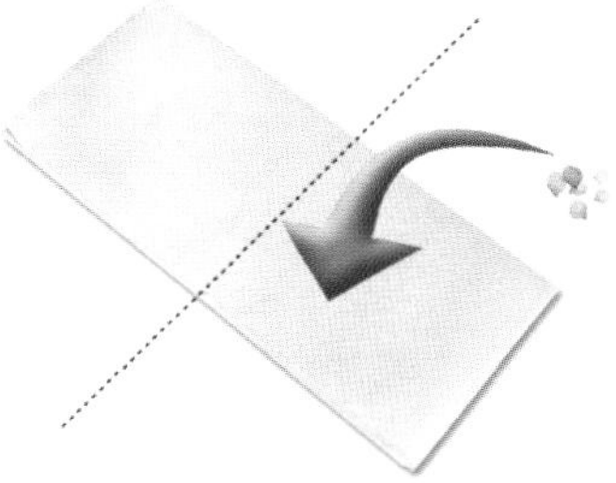
Evenly space the seeds out on the kitchen towel

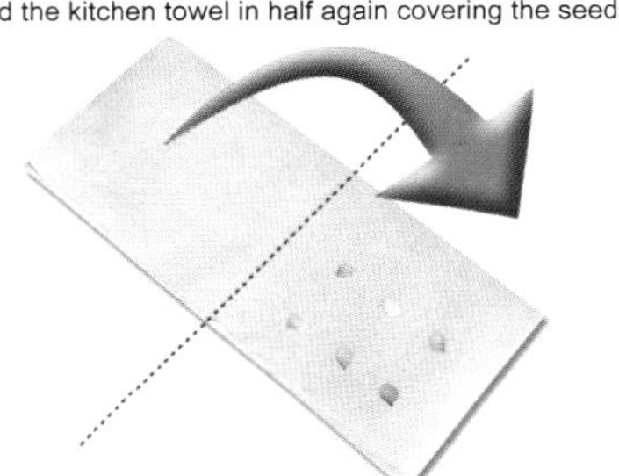
Fold the kitchen towel in half again covering the seeds

Add clean water

Due to the presence of these chemicals I would, therefore, pre-pour the water a day, If not two days before I intended to use it, unless of course I was using ionized or pure filtered water. Some people use bottled water and some swear that carbonated bottled water is the best thing to use and whilst I agree that this does work, it is best to remember that this type of water is originally intended for human consumption and not for feeding plants.

In an ideal world purified water would be ideal to use, however water purification units are normally very expensive and can be complicated to use. I use the method as just explained and it's done me fine for years its cheap, easy and not much fuss. For the next step I would then place the kitchen towel containing the seeds on a plate and leave in a dark place, infact, the darker the better. As a rule rule of thumb roots do not like the light! Humidity levels are of equal importance and keeping the seeds in the kitchen roll keeps the humidity levels up where they should be and this is why it is very important that you do not let the kitchen towel dry out. This method takes a little longer than the "glass of water technique", about 2 to 4 days in total (check every 24hrs until you can see the tip of the root, the radicale) but without fail I have always found the plants to be stronger when germinating like this.

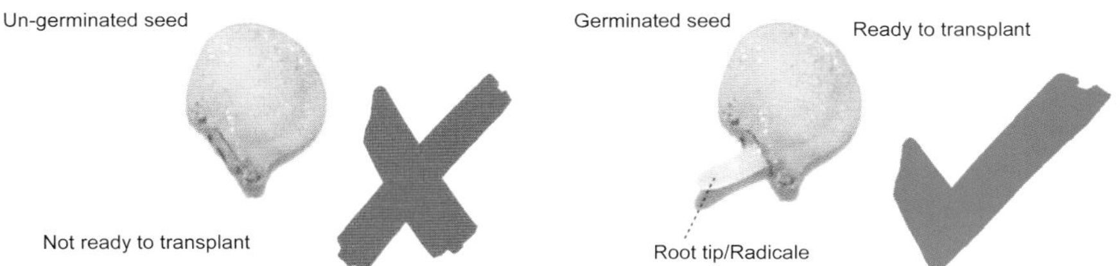

It is important to transplant each seed as and when it's ready, some seeds may take longer than others and as I said in the chapter before, as rule of thumb I only try to touch the seed once, from the bag/breeders pack, to where I plan to germinate it. When I do touch the seeds I make sure to antibac my hands first and at any other time I will use clean plastic tweezers or surgical gloves.

If the seeds don't break/germinate after say 6 days, you could leave them for a while longer or try a different method, if I'm honest though I wouldn't, I would throw them away and start again with a fresh set of different seeds from either a different breeder or a different supplier. I'm a strong believer in "you get what you pay for" so when buying seeds make sure that you go for a reputable breeder and strain and this way you should average out at around the 90% germination rate.

Usually I would say if you plan to grow in coco then the first transplant should be into coco and If you plan to grow in soil, then plant into soil and so on.

The problem I have here, however, is that sometimes I don't know which medium I will be growing the plant in and so in this case a growing sponge is perfect as it can be used in any substrate of method of growing you may choose later on. It is also a good option when selling the plantlings, because if they have been grown in a neutral sponge it means that they can easily adapt to their next stage/transplantation and to any growing medium and method.

One of the most popular mediums used at this stage by hydroponic and indoor growers is called rockwool. I find that it works just fine, but I'm not a massive fan

to be honest, don't get me wrong I have used rock wool over the years and it does the job ok, but I find a rooting sponge to be tougher which is great for making a stronger plant and root system. It may take longer for the roots to break through a rooting sponge but when they do they are nearly always stronger. The other thing which I'm sold on with the rooting/growing sponges is the structure of the rooting plug itself, because as you can see by the following diagram it is designed to help promote root growth in the right direction.

A lot of people ask me the basic question of, is there a right way up the seeds need to be put into the soil after germination?

The answer to this is obviously yes!

The radicale/root goes at the bottom and you must remember to be gentle with the seed whilst planting it.

Seed goes in root first/downwards.
As you can see the rooting sponge has a "T" Shaped cavity, this helps to hold the seed up and allows for easier lateral growth of the root downwards.

Rooting sponge

Cross section of a rooting sponge

As soon as they are ready and have been transplanted they need to go into the propagator.

The other way to germinate a seed is to germinate it directly within the medium/rooting sponge/rockwool. This is obviously a more natural way to germinate a seed however it can be hard to control as you will have to wait until the plantling first shows itself out of the medium to see if it has been successful. As the seed is embedded within its medium you cannot check on the seed during the process to see if it has begun the germination process, as if you do there is a high chance that you will either break the primary root or stress the seedling to the point where it may cause adverse effects in its later life. It is no surprise, therefore, that this process can take much longer than the alternative methods already discussed. It is also not the most reliable way of germinating, as whilst being more natural it must be remembered that a plant in its natural environment would drop many, many seeds into the surrounding medium and still then only a few will germinate successfully. It is always a gamble therefore, to try and germinate a seed this way as the odds are stacked against you.

If you do decide to use this method however, if you decide to use this method the first thing you will need to do is to make sure that the medium in which you want to germinate in is wet to moist. The seed will then need to be carefully inserted into the medium which you have chosen to use, in this case for an example I will be using a rooting sponge. The seed needs to be completely surrounded by the medium, including over the top. As you can see by looking at the cross section of the rooting sponge the seed can only go so far down and if left this way will be exposed to the light. To combat this, I would remove a small section from the side of the rooting sponge and place it in the hole on top of the seed. This will ensure that the seed is not being exposed to any light and is completely surrounded, giving it the best chance possible to absorb any water held in the rooting sponge which is needed to start the germination process.

Put your seed in the root sponge.

Wet rooting sponge

Take a section from the side to cover the seed.

Cross section of rooting sponge

The end result should look like this.

Cross section of rooting sponge with the seed covered.

As the seed grows it will push the section of rooting sponge used to cover it out of the way.

Cross section of rooting sponge as seed develops.

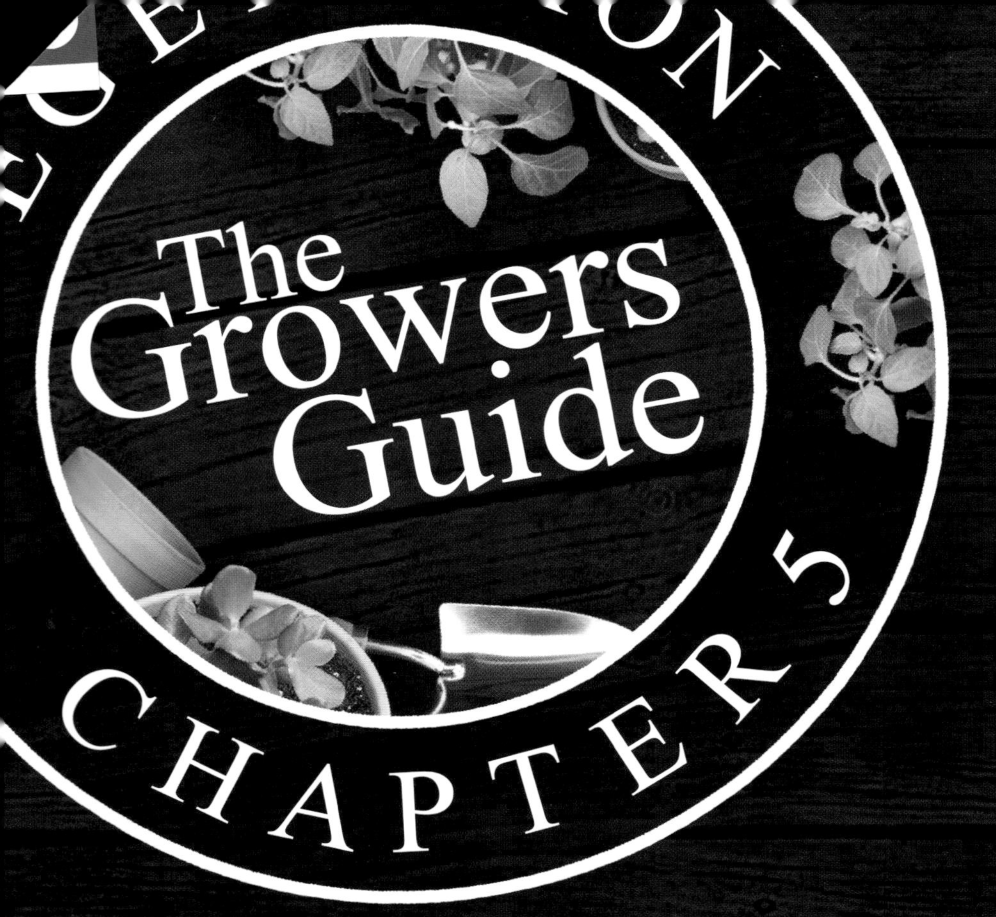

Cuttings and clones

Taking cuttings is a fundamental part of growing. All growers worth their salt should be able to competently take cuttings. When done in the right way you can ensure that you get the very best from every strain of plant that you are growing, not to mention the money which can be saved by utilizing generations of the same strain instead of buying new seeds each time, as this can be both unpredictable and expensive.

In this chapter we will go through everything you need to know to take successful cuttings, from the equipment needed to what it does and why we use it. We will then go through the technique of taking cuttings, the differing types of cuttings, where to take them from, how many to take from each mother plant and what to expect after you have taken them.

Taking Cuttings and Clones

Equipment

The basics you will need for this stage are

1. **Scalpel**
2. **Cloning/Rooting gel**
3. **A clean cup to put the rooting gel in**
4. **Medium preparation (Something to transfer the clones into)**
5. **A plant to take cuttings/clones from**

All of the above can be readily purchased from your local Gardening or Hydroponic shop.

Please note that you will hear the terms 'cutting' and 'clone' used to describe the same thing. For the purposes of this chapter I will refer to it simply as 'clone'

1. A Scalpel – it is important to use a clean scalpel. A stanley blade or craft knife will simply not do as they are soaked and coated in a thin layer of oil to prevent rust and corrosion and so as you cut the plant for the clone, before you even dip the stem into the rooting gel it will already have a thin layer of oil/grease on it. The chances of this rooting are pretty much nil. In this day and age it is easy to purchase disposable surgical scalpels. These are cheap, disposable and will give you the best results possible. When I say that they are disposable I mean after being used for a whole session, a fresh scalpel is not needed for each clone! Think about it...... if a scalpel is clean and sharp enough for surgical use then it should be clean and sharp enough for taking clones!

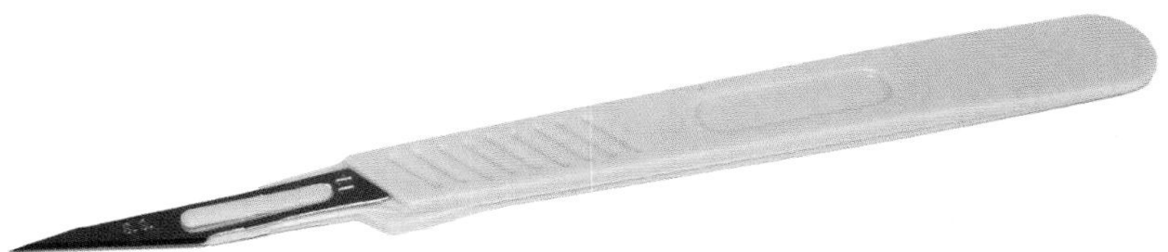

2. Cloning/Rooting gel – There are two main different types of cloning gel – organic and non-organic, so it really just comes down to personal preference. There are lots of brands out there on the market but the one I use is “Clonex” (non-organic) made and distributed by Growth Technologies. I have used it from day dot and it really does not get much better in my opinion, it comes in various sized bottles to suit your needs and at a good price too. The one thing I will say is. ... make sure that it’s in date when you buy it!

I had a friend that just could not get his clones to root, this went on for about 6 months and cost him thousands and this guy is a big commercial grower with years of experience. He would regularly ring me up and tell me all about his problems to try and identify what the issue was. We went through the method he was using

stage by stage, time and time again, until he eventually talked me into going round and having a look, to watch him go through the process to see if I could spot something he was doing wrong. Within 2 minutes of being there (cup of tea in hand) I found the problem, out of date cloning gel! As simple as that! He had bought new rooting gel each time from the same shop who, unbeknown to him had sold him out of date cloning gel and not only that but it was from the same batch each time, he just never thought to look.

3. Something to put the rooting gel in – I use plastic party cups/disposable cups. They are clean, cheap, can go in the household rubbish after use and they get the job done. For me there's no point in taking the risk of using a partially cleaned cup which has been used before....... because if it's not 100% clean it will taint the rooting gel and thus may have an adverse affect on your clones. A quick point to make here is that if you are dipping the clones straight into the rooting gel without decanting it first, then when you have finished you will need to throw the remainder away as it will be tainted.

4. Medium preparation - something to transfer the clones into. Now there are a lot of things available for the transfer, the rule of thumb however, is for stage one transfer to be into the medium in which you intend to grow the plant throughout its life. With soil therefore you would put your clone into soil, coco you would plant your clone into coco and so on. The most common and readily available of these mediums I will list and explain below, all have their pros and cons.

Coco plugs - contain dehydrated/dried coco coir pellets that you need to soak till fully expanded (about 5-10 minutes). An overlooked problem with soaking the dehydrated pellets is oversaturation, my advice would be to wait until they are fully saturated and then take them out one by and give them a slight squeeze and shake off any visible excess water. This is not the most scientific method, but it works all the same. Pretty much every company which deals in coco coir have their own version but if you want my advice and if you can get your hands on them, Jiffy does the best. This is due to the fact that Jiffy yara buff all of their coco coir which makes it ideal for clones and smaller plants as it is enriched with calcium trace elements which the younger plants thrive on. Coco plugs are also suitable for seeds.

Coco plug which has been soaked.
Dry coco plug.

Soil plugs/Peat plugs – contain dehydrated/dried soil pellets which you need to soak till fully expanded (about 5-10 minutes). As above with the coco pellets an overlooked problem with soaking the dehydrated pellets is to oversaturate them. My advice would be the same, wait till they are fully saturated, take them out one by one, give them a slight squeeze and shake off any water. Soil pellets are harder to find but still readily available in most Hydroponic shops.

The issue I have with soil pellets is the same issue I have with soil itself and that is... yes it's natural etc but for me it's about control, I know what the plants want on a chemical level and I know what they need to thrive. Each batch of soil medium has different amounts of different chemicals and trace elements in it which cannot be measured, thus the soil plug may be giving the clone the wrong (or should I say "not the most productive") chemicals and trace elements. As each batch of plugs/pellets will contain differing amounts of these chemicals and trace elements it make things very hard if you do not know 100% what you are doing.

I must however say that I do find the fruits of plants grown in soil (from the very start) to have the most natural flavour. Soil plugs are also suitable for seeds.

Soil/peat plug which has been soaked.
Dry soil/peat plug.

Plant Magic peat plug.

Peat plugs - are ready to use plugs which are dedicated to the propagation of young plants raised from clones and seeds.

A special mix of compost is used to produce peat plugs. The compost is handled with great care and as gently as possible, leaving the growing media with an airy structure. During manufacturing the moisture content is monitored and adjusted to ensure all peat plugs reach a uniformly high standard.

The plugs are wrapped in an environmentally friendly, reinforced paper which is suitable for plants which do not require a long rooting time.

Once the roots appear the new plants can be handled with ease without disrupting the plants surrounding them.

For ease of use and no messing about this really is an amazing product. Used with FORMULA-XL you have pretty much the best start money can buy for your plantlings.

Plant Magic's Peat Plugs give you;

- Uniform and consistency.
- A secure hold for the root ball.
- Minimal root disturbance when moving.
- A more rapid establishment.
- Ready to use.
- Great value for money.
- The best start possible for your plants.

Coco coir - If you do want to put your clones directly into a coco coir medium I would recommend using Nutrifield®'s Coco Premium. It is pre-washed and buffered, making it perfect for young plants.

Nutrifield®'s Coco Premium Organic Plant Medium possesses the highly coveted RHP certification for unsurpassed consistent quality which ensures you get a product that gives optimum performance each and every time you use it. Nutrifield®'s Coco Premium Organic Plant Medium comes to you thoroughly rinsed, pre-buffered with Calcium, pH stabilised and has the lowest salt index in the industry providing you with the optimum growing environment. The essential water to air ratio that Nutrifield®'s Coco Premium Organic Plant Medium gives plants an incredibly stable environment to prosper in and it is guaranteed free of pests and pathogens so you can use it with confidence. Serious gardeners use Nutrifield®'s Coco Premium Organic Plant Medium.

It is available in most Hydroponic stores.

Soil - Dutch pro's PRO SOIL/AARDE LIGHT MIX is composed of the finest, carefully selected ingredients to provide a modern and ecologically proven response to all of your growing media requirements; offering a rich blend to achieve optimum growth and yield capabilities.

- high air-porosity & elevated drainage
- high substrate stability
- high rewetting ability
- additions: NPK 15-10-20/Lime
- Perlite 2 -6 mm
- 50 % Black Peat/40 % White Peat/10 % Perlite
- Structure 0-20 mm
- pH-value (CaCl2) 5.3 – 6.0

Product free of pathogens & organisms harmful to plants, animals and humans. All Dutch pro medium carries the RHP stamp of quality.

Root sponge – Made from inert nutrient enriched sponge which normally comes moist but can be dry (if so they will need soaking till wet through). I find root sponges perfect for mass clones, especially when you don't know which medium they will be spending the rest of their lives in. I like them mainly because the root sponge itself is inert, a blank canvas if you will. I also find the sponge denser than most of the other products mentioned here. This means that the roots do take longer to come through/show but when they do they are always tougher and more resilient, thus more likely to grow into a strong healthy plant. Root sponges also hold the right amount of liquid for the clone, making it hard to oversaturate which as I've mentioned when discussing them is easily done with the coco and soil dehydrated plugs. Root sponges are also suitable for seeds.

Root sponges.

Rockwool – is made from actual rock! It is a natural product originally discovered in the mid 19th Century in Hawaii. It is formed from the process of hot steam being pushed through basalt (solidified lava) at high pressures.
Nowadays the process is reproduced on a mass commercial level in production furnaces. There are various different brands of "rockwool" on the market, but if I was you and I had a choice I would buy "Grodan" rockwool. The company has been trading for 45 years and the consistent quality is second to none. For the first clone I would recommend a 1 inch block. The 1 inch blocks are normally sold in trays as opposed to individually. They will need to be soaked in pre-pared water for a few minutes until they are wet throughout. Rockwool can get waterlogged so I would recommend after soaking to give them a little squeeze and shake off any excess water.

Sometimes when growing in rockwool a green film of alge will grow on the outside of the blocks. This is normal and nothing to worry about.

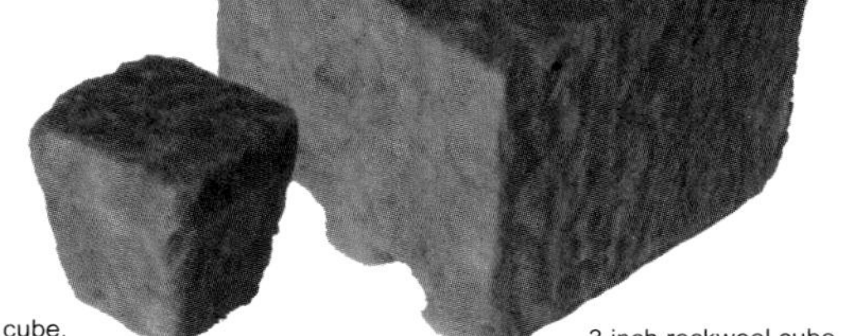
1 inch rockwool cube. 3 inch rockwool cube.

Clay Pebbles in a net pot – What it says on the tin, a small amount of hydroponic clay pebbles in a net pot (it's important to wash hydroponic clay pebbles before use). I would not advise this method unless you really know what you are doing but if you can get it right it is one of the faster ways to root a clone. You will also need a purpose built propagator and system. Clay pebbles in a net pot are not suitable for seeds.

Net pot with clay pebbles.

Net pot with neoprene collar.

Net pot – No medium just a net pot with a neoprene collar to hold the clone in place. For this you will also need a purpose built propagator and system. This in my book is the fastest way to root a clone. Net pots are not suitable for seeds.

5. A plant - Commonly called “Mothers”, “Stock Plants” or “Donors”. Obviously you will need a plant to take the clones from. I would always recommend taking a clone when the plant is in the Vegetative stage, it makes things much easier, although it is a common misconception that you can only take clones from a plant when it is in the Vegetative stage of its life. The truth of the matter is that you can take a clone from a plant at any time of its life. The difference is just that the clone has a much higher chance of rooting when taken at the Vegetative stage of the donor/mother plant's lifecycle.

Firstly everything needs to be laid out ready. It's not essential but I always use disposable surgical rubber gloves. Washing your hands thoroughly or with an anti bacterial is all very well but it is not 100%. Surgical gloves are cheap and they give me peace of mind. The other no,no is smoking. Dry/smoking tobacco can and often does carry a dangerous virus to plants known as the “tobacco mosaic virus”. If you smoke when handling fresh clones, it can be transferred onto your hands and then onto the clones. This can result in weak, slow growing and in worst case scenario, dead clones.

When taking clones from a mother plant it is good practice to not take/cut off more than 40% of the overall mass of the plant. This will give the plant the maximum chance of strong re-growth (3-4 weeks is the rough time scale for a healthy mother to recover and grow back to the stage where it is ready to give more clones). Any more than 40% and the plant will struggle to recover from the stress.

Let's say this is the plant you want to take clones from. There are two main types of clones, the first is a terminal bud clone and the second is a mid/axillary bud clone.

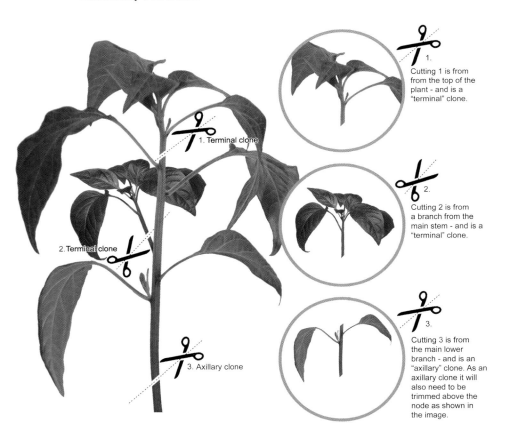

1. Terminal clone

2. Terminal clone

3. Axillary clone

1\.
Cutting 1 is from from the top of the plant - and is a "terminal" clone.

2\.
Cutting 2 is from a branch from the main stem - and is a "terminal" clone.

3\.
Cutting 3 is from the main lower branch - and is an "axillary" clone. As an axillary clone it will also need to be trimmed above the node as shown in the image.

Some people will cut a whole shoot/branch off the plant to begin with. They then put it into fresh water and take the clones from that. This way it reduces the stress to the plant as it is technically only being cut once.

I, however, like to cut my clones directly from the mother plant. The reason I do it this way is that I like to take the best clone possible while maintaining the overall shape and health of the mother plant. The other reason is as a personal preference I like to only take terminal bud cuttings. I find they grow more consistently and are easier to manage. There is nothing wrong with axillary bud cuttings but I do find that over the many years that I have been doing this that they do tend to be more inconsistent ie: double headers, triple headers, off balance when maturing, growing at different speeds and they have a much more diverse characteristics range than the terminal bud clones.

When cutting a clone from the mother plant it should be at a 45 degree angle and be done in one movement. A clean cut.

Cut at a 45 degree angle with a clean scalpel.
Not having a clean cut will reduce the chances of the clone rooting.

If you hack at the shoot, or do not get a clean cut, this will reduce the chances of the clone rooting.

As soon as the clone has been taken it needs to go into the rooting gel before the stem's cut has any chance to form an embolism. In this scenario an embolism is a small bubble of air that the stem of the clone sucks up, preventing the clone from taking up water and nutrients in the future. Speed is the key here and the faster you can get it into the rooting gel the better. When the clone goes into the rooting gel you need to make sure that the entire cut is submerged in the gel. The fresh clone needs to be in the rooting gel for a minimum of 3 minutes. After the 3 minutes is up it needs to go straight into the medium you have selected and have laid out ready.

Make sure when filling the cup up with rooting gel that there is enough to cover the entirety of the cut you have just made. As shown here, by using a transparent cup you can ensure that the whole of the cut is submerged in the rooting gel. A top tip at this point is - when you have the clone in the rooting gel, give it a little stir, this will remove any unwanted air bubbles on the cut.

A top tip here is to put a few drops of the rooting gel into the hole of the medium that you will be transferring the clones into. This is because I have found that sometimes when pushing the fresh clone into the medium that it has a tendency to wipe the rooting gel off as it is pushed in. The clones need to be pushed in enough to completely cover the fresh cut and then a little more. I would normally push a freshly taken clone about 1cm into the medium, leaving the other 4cm exposed.

Too shallow Too deep Correct depth

Every clone that you cut off the mother plant should be around the same overall mass and be as close to 5cm tall as you can get. Being nature, getting the mass and the height of the clones all the same can be impossible due to larger palm leaves. If you do have a few clones with larger than average palm leaves, simply cut the palm leaves horizontally in half as shown in the image below. This will help for two reasons, firstly it will keep the clones more uniform and thus hopefully they will grow consistently at the same rate. Secondly the leaves do need to be in the right proportion to the clone as it is all about balance. If the leaves are too big for the new stem it will stress the new clone, thus sending all of its energy to maintain the larger leaf and its growth as opposed to using the energy for the production of roots.

Before cut

After cut

The leaves should be cut as straight as possible.

All the clones should be the same mass.

It is always good practice to label your clones and note which mother they have come from.

After you have finished taking all of your clones, they should be misted with fresh water using a spray bottle and transferred evenly into a propagator ready for the Propagation stage.

Over the next 2 weeks in the propagator the clones should show little change above ground, however below they should start to root to the point that they will be showing out of a 1 inch block. Sometimes however even when everything is done right the clones will not root. Imagine that you have taken your clones, they have been in the propagator for 2 weeks but alas no roots…all is not lost however, as there is a last chance technique that you can try. This technique is commonly known as "shaving".

Everything needs to be laid out as if you were taking fresh clones. Once you have done this take the un-rooted clone out of the chosen medium and using a clean scalpel shave the side wall of the stem as shown in the image.

When shaving the stem of the clone you should keep to one clean movement. Try to avoid hacking at the stem. As soon as the side of the stem has been removed it needs to go in the rooting gel for 3 minutes before going into a fresh medium block, ready for the propagator.

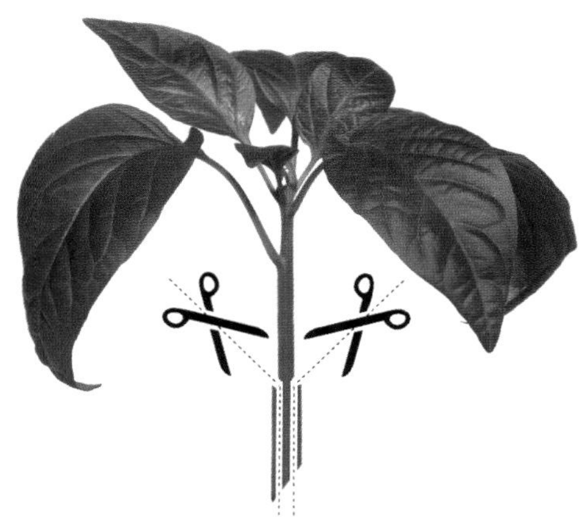

This is a last chance saloon technique so if it does not work don't be surprised. It has, however, worked for me on numerous occasions.

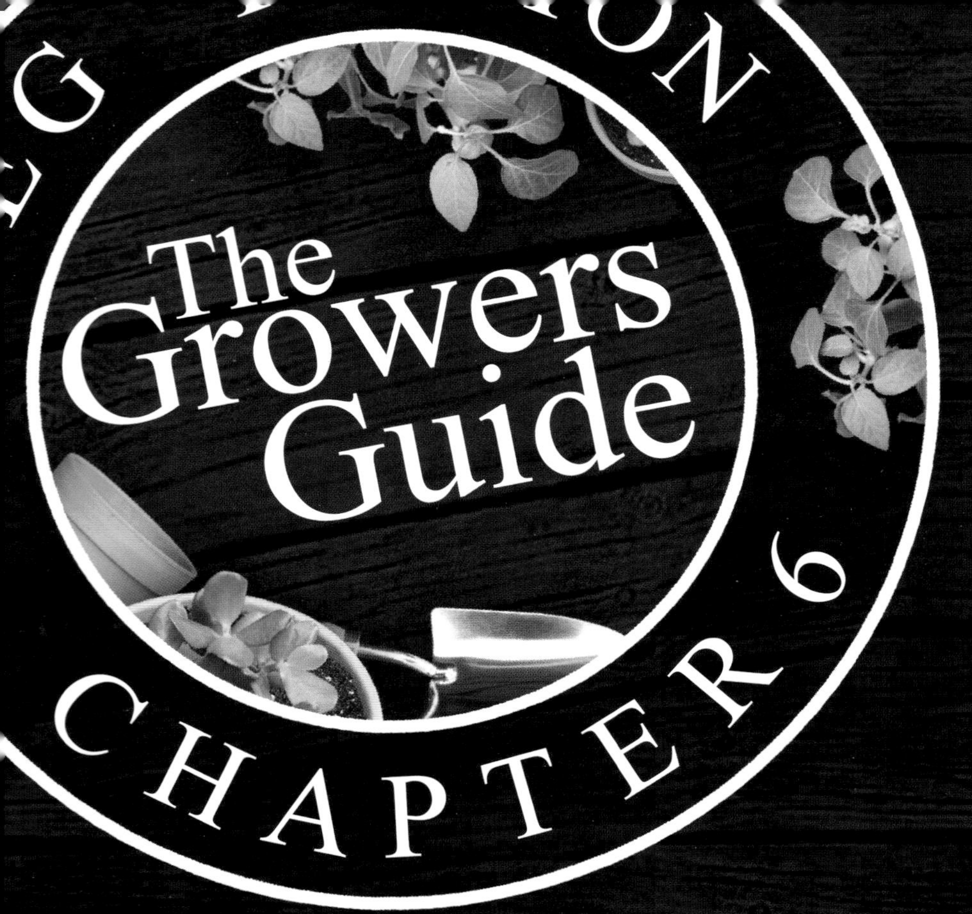

Propagation

In this chapter we will be covering everything you need to know about the Propagation stage of the plant's life. We will first look at all of the basic equipment you will need and what each item does. We will then go on to look at how it all works together including rooting your plantlings correctly. Finally, we will look at how to harden off your plants and re-pot them ready for the next stage.

It is vital that propagation is carried out properly under the right conditions and using the right feed. If executed correctly it will give your plants the best start possible to go on and produce monster yields. With a step by step guide, this chapter will go through the Propagation stage for both plantlings grown from seeds and plantlings grown from cuttings/clones.

Propagation – Light cycle – lights on 24hrs – time period 1-2 weeks or 3 internodes/stages, whichever comes first.

Equipment

The basic equipment you will need for this stage is

- **Propagator**
- **A light**
- **A spray bottle**
- **Temperature gauge**
- **Hygrometer**
- **Feed**
- **Timer**
- **Pots**
- **Medium**
- **Mycorrhizae**

All of which can be purchased in any Gardening or Hydroponic store.

Propagator – A Propagator is basically a miniature indoor greenhouse which has a clear plastic lid (a cloche) that lets the light in but retains heat and moisture. It has an adjustable ventilation port or ports (a ventilator) which allows you to cool the internal temperature of the propagator and control the level of humidity. The ventilator also allows fresh air to circulate, preventing fungal disease from spreading.

Propagators come in all shapes and sizes, ranging from 99p up to around £100. There are also heated propagators available on the market now, which I would personally recommend.

You can buy heated mats that you put in/under a standard propagator, but if I was you I would kill two birds with one stone and get an all in one heated propagator. You will find that they are readily available from most Gardening and Hydroponic stores. £35-£40 should get you a pretty decent one. I would however purchase my propagator specifically from a local Hydroponic store, as the propagators sold in Hydroponic stores tend to have larger/taller plastic covers (cloches) and are more sturdy which is ideal for tropical plants, giving them an extra 2 inches or so of space (perfect for leggy tropical plantlings and larger cuttings/clones).

The taller the cloche (lid) the better. This will give the leggy (taller) plants more room to develop.

Light - The next thing you will need is a light, you don't have to do this but again I would buy this from a Hydroponics store. The two main light units used for the Propagation stage are a strip light and a CFL.

Strip lights - are what I use, they are cheap as chips, give off hardly any heat, are pretty robust, compact and come in a range of lengths depending on how much or little you are doing. They only come in a singular spectrum of light (perfect for propagation) and so are impossible to get confused with.

A standard strip light that you would find in an office or under the cupboards of a posh kitchen will do just the same job (and normally at half of the price). You can buy them as complete kits or as separate items i.e bulbs and light shades. Shades do help but are not necessary, hence why I don't use them. I find leaving the bulb open and at the right height helps with heat transfer at the right rate and creates the correct amount of condensation/humidity within the propagator.

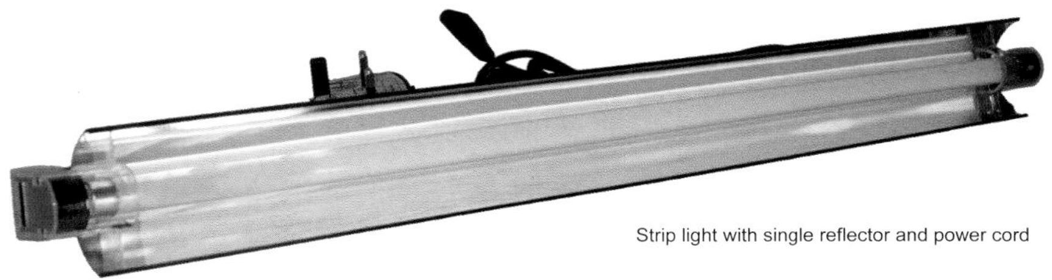

Strip light with single reflector and power cord

CFL Bulbs/Lights.- The second light unit is the CFL (Compact Fluorescent Light). The CFL bulbs comes in 3 different light spectrums;

White (some people call this "super cool") and is the one you want for Propagation.

Blue (some people call this "cool") and this is used predominantly for Veg and/or for mother plants.

Red (which some people call "warm") and this is used for Flowering.

All three bulbs normally come in either 125w or 250w. They do not need a ballast and should plug straight in to the mains via the shade or an IEC (International Electrotechnical Commission) connector.

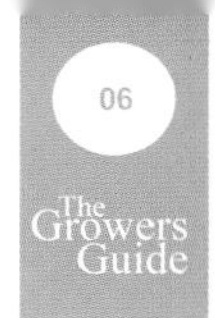

If this is your first time and you wish to go down the CFL route, I would recommend the 250w super cool white for Propagation. Please take note that it is quite a large delicate bulb which can get fiddly quick.

When buying a bulb, check it first for any cracks or damages before you leave the store and never touch the glass part of the bulb with your bare hands. If you have to touch the bulb, make sure that you wear gloves or use a lint free cloth.

So that I can sleep soundly at night I must state the obvious, which is never to touch a bulb that's warm, hot or plugged in.

To go with the bulb you will have to buy a CFL shade or what's commonly known in the hydroponics market as an IEC connection. An IEC is as basic as it gets, all it is, is a bulb connector on a cable with a plug on the end of it! There is no shade in the literal sense of the word, it is just a device which connects the bulb to the electricity supply. IEC connectors do come in different sizes and wattages so make sure that the bulb you buy marries up to the right IEC connector.

One of the most popular shades for the CFL bulbs is the dutch barn hammertone, the parabolic, and the closed box shade.

The CFL dutch barn hammertone is the cheapest of all the CFL shades. They are cheap, mass produced, affordable and able to do the job with the minimum fuss.

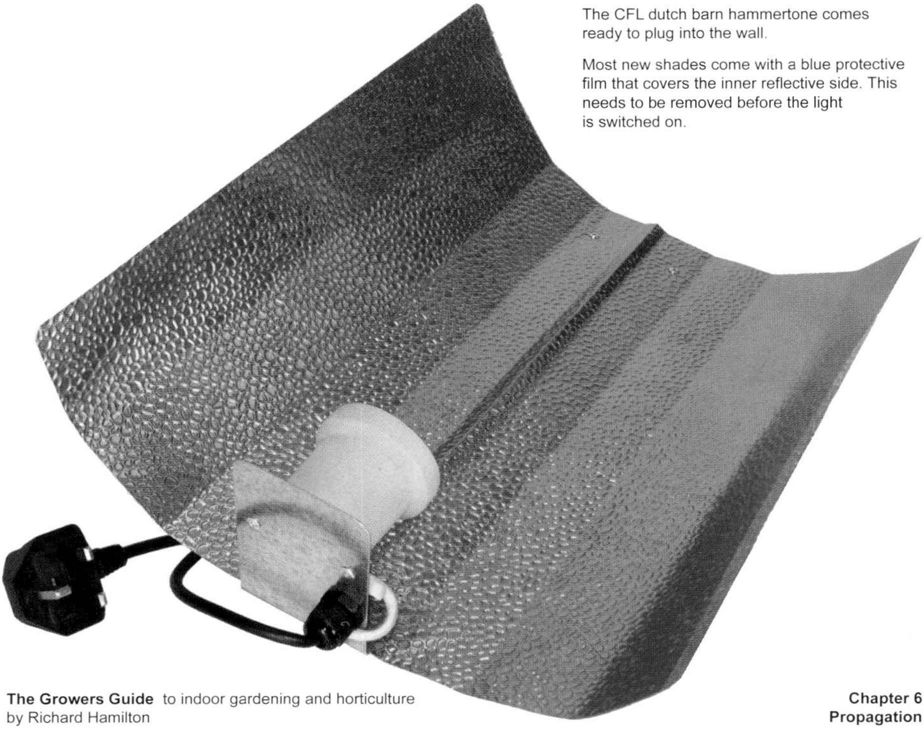

The CFL dutch barn hammertone comes ready to plug into the wall.

Most new shades come with a blue protective film that covers the inner reflective side. This needs to be removed before the light is switched on.

The parabolic in contrast is a very big shade designed to cover a lot of space and which can be very expensive. The bulb on parabolic shades hangs vertically, opposed to the other shades which normally hang horizontally.

The bulb/lamp hangs vertically on most parabolic shades. The shade which is shown here is a white parabolic. It also comes in silver. They both come flat packed which makes them great for transporting from shop to grow room.

The box shade to its own merits is a classic design that has been around for a long time. Originally used for industrial factory lighting, the design has been tweaked over time for the CFL bulbs.

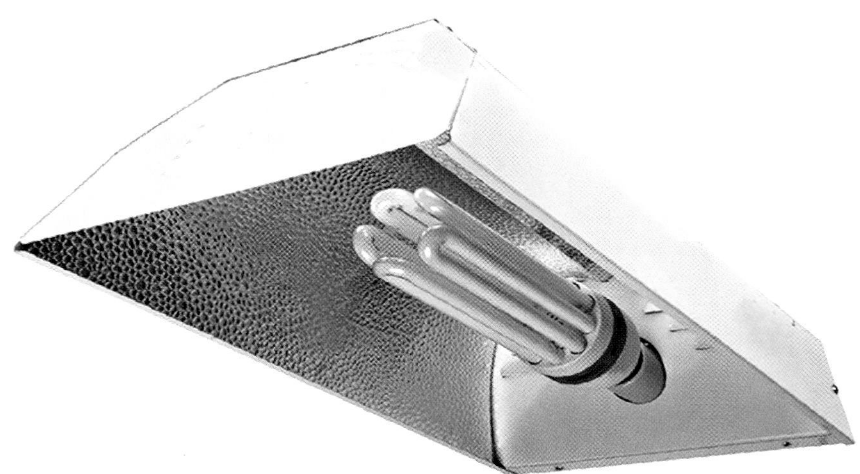

They will all get the job done but personally my choice would be the dutch barn hammertone, for the reasons I stated before. They are cheap, easy to use and get the job done.

Temperature Gauge & Hygrometer
In order to know that you are hitting the right temperatures and levels of humidity, it is essential that you buy a hygrometer and a temperature gauge to monitor the level of humidity and temperature within your propagator.

Humidity hygrometer

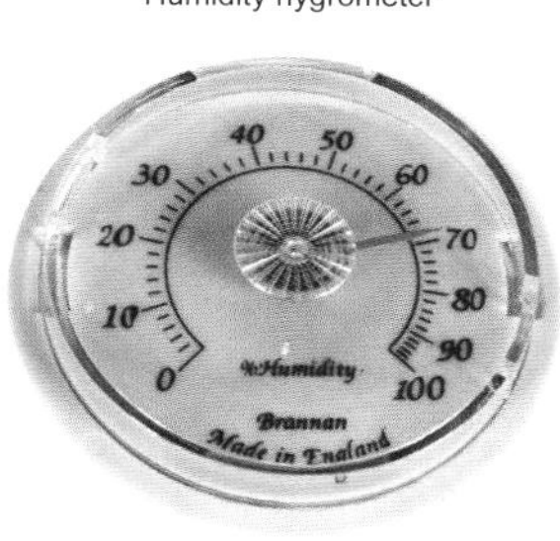

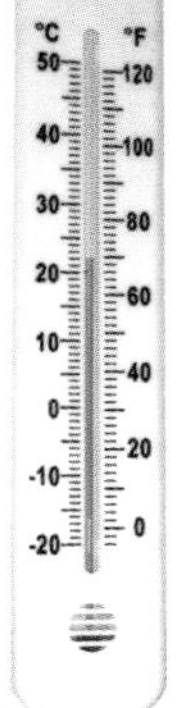

Temperature gauge

They are both pretty cheap and can be brought from most garden and hydroponic stores (please note they both should be kept at the canopy of the plants).

I use a stick on temperature gauge that is normally used for fish tanks. They are less than a fiver and sold in all aquatic stores and will last you for years. The temperature gauge needs to be kept on the inside of the propagator to give you a true reading.

Spray bottle – just a basic clean spray bottle will do. Please don't cut corners and clean out an old one! They're cheap! So buy new where you can as an old cleaned out one may still contain traces of detergent or whatever was in them before, which could be detrimental to the plant.

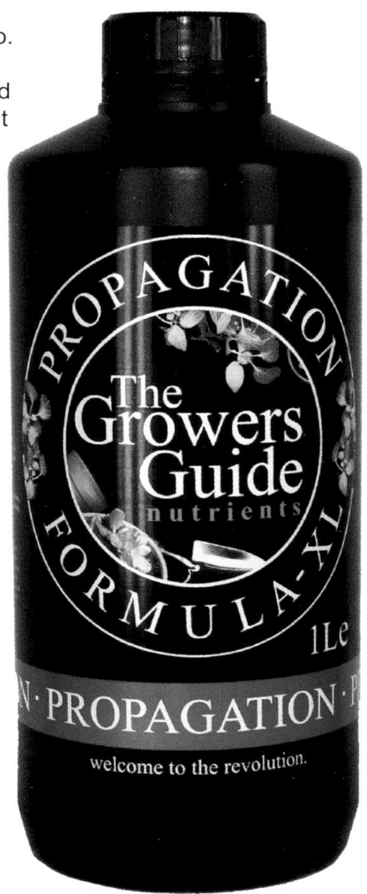

Feed – for the Propagation stage I would recommend FORMULA-XL which is available in all the best hydroponics stores. It is a one-part, premium plant feed specially designed and engineered for the entirety of the Propagation stage of the plants life. The NPK (N-nitrogen P-potassium K-phosphorous) has been dialled into the exact ratios to give your plants the vital mineral nutrients at a crucial stage of their lives. This really is a must, I cant stress enough how important it is to start as you mean to go on. The dilution rates are good, so depending how many plants you are feeding in Propagation a 1 litre bottle should last you a while.

FORMULA-XL can also be used as a foliar feed spray in the Propagation stage of the plant's life. Just half the dilution rate as stated and put into a spray bottle and your plants can be sprayed every five days as an extra feed boost through the Propagation stage.

Medium - In this book we are just looking at coco coir and soil. coco coir or as its more commonly called coco is made from coconut husks. It offers a completely blank nutrient free medium in order to grow in. A blank canvas if you will. I would advise for you use Nutrifield®'s Coco Premium for the coco coir as it has superior physical attributes. Nutrifield®'s Coco Premium Organic Plant Medium is free of pests and pathogens and has naturally occurring beneficial trichoderma so there is no need for Neem oil or other pest control. Nutrifield®'s Coco Premium Organic Plant Medium can absorb large quantities of water and nutrients while maintaining the essential 30% air porosity, creating ideal conditions in the rhizosphere to grow strong & healthy plants.

For soil I would recommend Dutch pro's PRO SOIL/AARDE LIGHT MIX it is composed of the finest, carefully selected ingredients to provide a modern and ecologically proven response to all of your growing media requirements; offering a rich blend to achieve optimum growth and yield capabilities.

For the end of the Propagation stage you will only need one pot size. 5.5ltr. This will be to transfer the 3 inch rooted rock wool cubes into before they are to go in to the Vegetative stage of the plant's life. Pots come in all shapes and sizes. If you can get your hands on them I would recommend using square to rounds for this first transfer. They are called square to rounds as they are square at the top and round at the bottom.

As a close second from using a plastic pot I would recommend using a fabric Smart Pot.

The Smart Pot is a soft-sided, fabric container that has the rigidity to hold its shape and can even support large trees.

Mycorrhizae - Great White® is the most complete mycorrhizal product on the market. The cutting edge formula contains 16 different species of mycorrhizal fungi, 14 different species of beneficial bacteria and 2 species of trichoderma all in one product. Research shows that this powerful formula will ignite plant and root growth giving plants the tools they need to maximize yields. Great White's concentrated formula ensures optimum colonization of root systems by the fungi for less money. The water soluble powder makes application a snap and delivers the spores directly to the roots for immediate germination. Users should look for explosive root growth, increased yields, increased fruiting and flowering, increased nutrient and water absorption and improved transplant success. The key to healthy and vital plants starts with a vigorous root system.

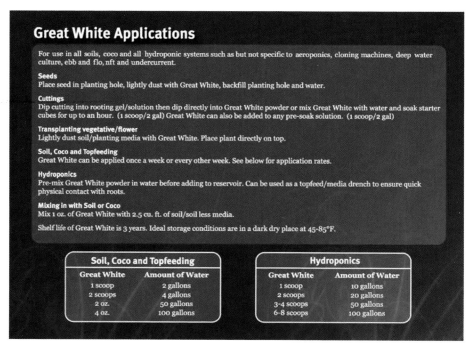

Great White Applications

For use in all soils, coco and all hydroponic systems such as but not specific to aeroponics, cloning machines, deep water culture, ebb and flo, nft and undercurrent.

Seeds
Place seed in planting hole, lightly dust with Great White, backfill planting hole and water.

Cuttings
Dip cutting into rooting gel/solution then dip directly into Great White powder or mix Great White with water and soak starter cubes for up to an hour. (1 scoop/2 gal) Great White can also be added to any pre-soak solution. (1 scoop/2 gal)

Transplanting vegetative/flower
Lightly dust soil/planting media with Great White. Place plant directly on top.

Soil, Coco and Topfeeding
Great White can be applied once a week or every other week. See below for application rates.

Hydroponics
Pre-mix Great White powder in water before adding to reservoir. Can be used as a topfeed/media drench to ensure quick physical contact with roots.

Mixing in with Soil or Coco
Mix 1 oz. of Great White with 2.5 cu. ft. of soil/soil less media.

Shelf life of Great White is 3 years. Ideal storage conditions are in a dark dry place at 45-85°F.

Soil, Coco and Topfeeding

Great White	Amount of Water
1 scoop	2 gallons
2 scoops	4 gallons
2 oz.	50 gallons
4 oz.	100 gallons

Hydroponics

Great White	Amount of Water
1 scoop	10 gallons
2 scoops	20 gallons
3-4 scoops	50 gallons
6-8 scoops	100 gallons

I will now show you how to put all these individual elements together to achieve the perfect environment.The basics to creating this perfect environment are simple, firstly use the spray bottle to give the inside of the propagator a good misting of fresh water and then leave for 5-10 minutes for the temperature and humidity levels to settle, doing this will give you a true reading.

Now check the humidity. You want the humidity to be no less than 70% and no higher than 90%. If you find that it is way above that then open the ports on the top of the propagator to release some of the humidity.

If you find that it's not humid enough, say 40% then close the ports and mist with your spray bottle in order to increase and keep the humidity in. Have a play around with it, leaving it for 10 minutes at a time in order to give the levels time to settle before you check again.

It is a similar situation when trying to get the temperature to the right level.
if it is too hot in the propagator, say 34°C then increase the height of the light and vice versa if it is too cool say 14°C, just bring the light closer to the propagator in order to increase the temperature. It will take a little playing around with but it is well worth doing and getting right before you transfer the plantlings across.

Move the light further away to reduce the temperature inside the propagator.

Move light closer to increase the temperature inside the propagator.

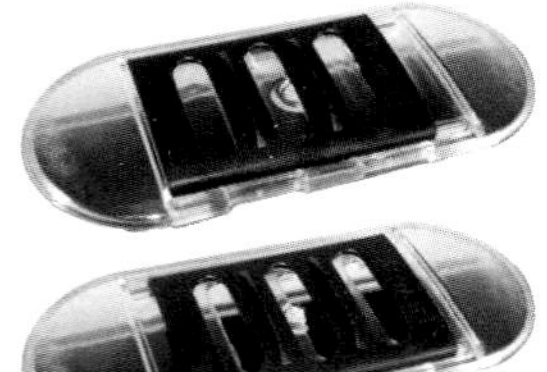

Vents closed. This will increase the humidity inside the propagator, but will also prevent any fresh air from getting to the plants.

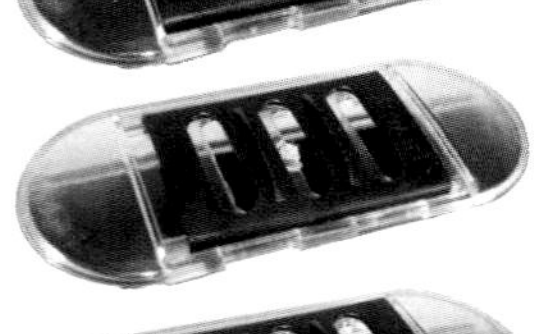

Vents partially opened. This is in the middle and thus will reduce the humidity inside the propagator and also give the plants a bit of fresh air. Ideally you need to let a little fresh air into the propagator to help the plants breathe.

Vents open. This will reduce the humidity greatly inside the propagator. It will also give the plants the most amount of fresh air, which is good for them.

The environment is very important at this stage as the plantlings are very susceptible to stress and can die very easily if they are not taken care of in the right way.

Remember that you get out what you put in, so it is good practice at this stage to put in as much effort in as you possibly can. Throughout each day the humidity will rise and fall and so will the temperatures. The more consistent and stable an environment that you can provide, the better the chance you have of your plantlings making it to the Vegetative stage and of them being strong.

Job done? Good! You're ready to transplant.

At this stage you will need to delicately take your transplanted seeds or freshly taken cuttings/clones and space them out evenly in your propagator as shown below. This makes sure that each transplanted cutting/clone gets an even spread of light thus improving the chances of survival.

It is important to note that the light needs to be on 24hrs a day 7 days a week until the plantlings are ready to come out of the propagator. The plants should be checked and sprayed with clean water once every day at least.

The bottom line is that the numbers never lie, if you can make the environment as stable as possible the better chance you will have of your plants being healthy and making it through to the Vegetative stage. Each time you check your plants you may need to adjust the lights height in order to increase or decrease the heat and open or close the propagators vents – to increase or decrease the humidity. The more you do this, the more you will learn to read the environment within the propagator.

For whatever reason if you do not have a temperature gauge or hygrometer then the rule of thumb is that the inside of the propagator should be slightly warmer than the average room temperature. In the case of humidity, there should be a misting of condensation on the inside of the propagator lid (the cloche) which when knocked should form droplets that run down the sides of the propagator. If there is no mist or condensation then the humidity is too low. In this event you will need to close the vents and or spray with the spray bottle. If the condensation is running down the sides

of the propagator lid without any force of you knocking the propagator, then this is a clear sign that it is too humid and you will need to open the vents. This strategy isn't really 100% fool proof but I find that generally it does work however my recommendation would still be to get the right equipment to help give you the precise temperatures and levels of humidity.

Sometimes the seedlings, cuttings and clones don't need any feed other than clean water. The feed should only be used as and when it's needed.

How do you know when it's needed?

Lightening in colour towards yellow means that your plantling needs more nutrients in its feed.
Your plantling should be a vibrant healthy green colour.

When the plantlings are this young, less is all ways more. If the leaves of the plant lighten towards a yellow colour it means that the plants need more feed. I would recommend as I stated earlier to use Formula-XL but at half strength. This can be applied through normal hand feeding or in the form of foliar spray. If using any of the other plant start feeds I would also half the dilution rate which the manufacturer states, just to be on the safe side. If the plant's leaves continue to lighten, increase the dosage of the feed in the dilution to the recommended rate.

For cuttings and clones you must remember that before they have roots they take in feed/liquid through the leaves so its good practice to keep them moist but not sodden until the roots start.

How long should your plants be in the propagator?........

Well, how long's a piece of string? Normally, if the environment is right it should take between 7 to 14 days. It will be different if you are propagating from seeds as opposed to cuttings/clones. To make it easier to understand I will go through each method individually.

From seed – unlike the cuttings/clones, the seed has a small root which is able to take in water and nutrients straight away. Therefore, it is essential that the medium in which you have transplanted the seed remains moist, it should not be water logged or left to go dry. If it is too dry the seedling will die and if it is too moist, the seedling will rot/suffocate.

The first visual signs of the plant's growth will be the seed leaves lifting out of the medium. Sometimes the leaves will still have the seed shell attached. If this happens then just leave it alone, it should fall off by itself naturally when ready. Remember that the seedling at this stage is very delicate and the smallest of shocks can kill it or have an adverse affect on the plant's life, so in other words, no touching!

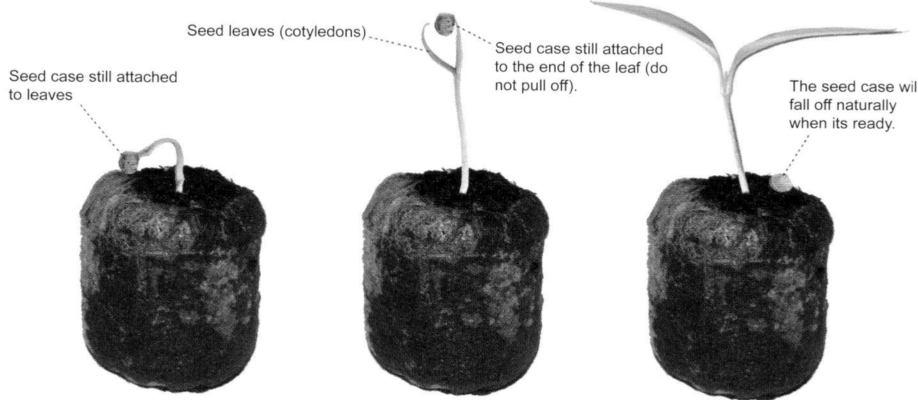
Seed case still attached to leaves
Seed leaves (cotyledons)
Seed case still attached to the end of the leaf (do not pull off).
The seed case will fall off naturally when its ready.

The first two leaves are called the cotyledons or the seed leaves and it is from the middle of the stem between these two leaves where the fresh growth of the main plant will emerge from.

From germination the plantlings should take no longer than 14-18 days to root through a 1 inch coco pellet/plug. Depending on which type of medium you have gone for this may take longer.

Fresh growth
Seed leaves (cotyledons)
Seed leaves (cotyledons)
roots

At the first sign of roots coming through the 1 inch medium, the plantlings need to be repotted. At no point should there be bare roots exposed to the light as this will stress the plant, stunt growth and potentially kill it.

For the first repotting I would recommend repotting them from a 1 inch block of medium into a 3 inch. So that's either a pot of at least 3 inch in diameter or as I have used, a 3 inch rockwool cube.

Not that I have here but I do advise that you should try and keep the medium the same all the way through, so if you used coco coir plug/pellets, stick to coco coir and if you use soil, stick with soil and so on through each transplantation. Make sure the medium that you are transplanting into is moist but not completely saturated.

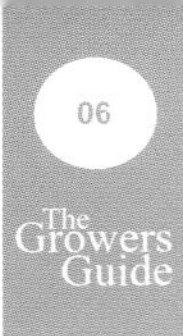

When transferring the rooted block into a larger block of medium be careful to try not to touch, bend or break the roots. The smaller block should fit tightly into the larger block. If there is any space inbetween the small block and larger block, take some excess from the side of the larger block and push it between the two to fill in the space.

Normally at this stage (if you haven't already) it is the right time to start to add some weak nutrient into the feed. I would recommend Formula-XL feed at a diluted rate.

Before the seedling can move on to the Vegetative stage of their lives they need to be strong enough to cope with more intense light and feeds. Based on this, I would recommend that they are not put into Veg until they either have three stages of nodes and/or have rooted through a 3 inch block. Normally both of these thing happen at pretty much the same time.

The other important thing to do before re-potting and transferring your plants into the Vegetative stage is to harden them off.

How do you harden your plants off?

The best and most effective way to harden off your plants is to remove the propagator's lid for increasing periods of time over three days. This will slowly get the

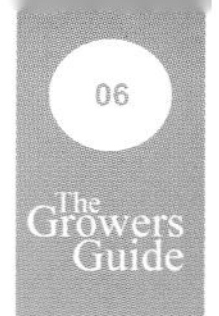

young plants used to life outside of the propagator. This is done in stages to try and reduce the amount of over all stress to the plants when they are transferred into the Vegetative stage.

I have found the most effective stress free way of doing this is over a 3 day period.

Day 1 - take the lid off the propagator (while the lights are on) for 6 hours.

Day 2 - take the lid off the propagator (while the lights are on) for 12 hours.

Day 3 - take the lid off the propagator (while the lights are on) for 24 hours.

After this is done the plants are ready to be re-potted and moved into the next stage of their life.

For the first re-pot I would suggest using a 3.5 litre pot. This will give the plants a chance to stretch their roots and settle into the medium that they will be spending the rest of their lives in.

When filling the pots up with coco it is best to leave a centimetre gap at the top of the pot. This will help you reduce spillage when watering. When all of the coco is in the pot you will need to make a hole for the rooted plant to fit into. In order to get the hole the right shape and dimension I use a spare rockwool cube of the same size. As you can see from the above image this will give you the correct shaped space ready for the transplantation. The coco around the hole should be lightly pressed so it just holds its shape as above. If pressed too firmly you will essentially push all of the air out of the coco and it will not leave adequate space for the roots to grow freely. As soon as all the above is ready you will need to add in the Mycorrhizae.

Follow the guidelines which are on the label of the Mycorrhizae which you will be using. If you have gone with my suggestion of Plant Success Great White Mycorrhizae there should be a small application spoon in each pot to help measure the right amount.

The idea is to lightly sprinkle the Mycorrhizae in and around the hole you have made ready for transplantation.

When transplanting the fresh rooted rockwool into the coco it is important to remember that the roots will be exposed and thus be very vulnerable. As discussed earlier in the book, roots do not like the light, so the faster they can be transplanted the better. Bearing this in mind it is also important that you take great care not to break any of the roots as you are transplanting into the coco. When the rockwool is in the coco the top of the rockwool cube should be level with the surface of the coco as shown in the image below.

From cuttings/clones - The main difference with cuttings and clones as opposed to seeds is that when they first go into the propagator they have no roots. This means that they absorb all of the nutrients they need through the leaves, so before the rooting gel works its magic it is important to keep the humidity inside the propagator up as much as possible. Doing this will ensure that there is enough available moisture for the plantlings to feed on until the roots are established. At no time should you let the propagator dry out or the humidity fall below 40%.

It is also good practice to pour a little water into the bottom of the propagator in order to encourage root growth.

As soon as your cuttings have been taken, they are ready to go into the propagator. The first 12-24 hours after they have been taken they will be standing up looking strong, after that they will wilt. To what extremes they wilt will all depend on the strength of the plant, if cuttings have been taken correctly and put into a suitable environment, the wilt period should last no longer than 24hrs. If they haven't started to stand up after 24hrs you have some real problems. On the next page are 3 images of some cuttings which I have taken in order to show you to what to expect.

6 hours after being taken from the mother plant. All cuttings are standing up straight and look healthy.

36 hours after being taken from the mother plant and as you can see the plantlings have wilted to the point that they look dead.

48 hours after being taken from the mother plant and as you can see they have picked back up.

After your plants have recovered from the wilt phase they should stay standing up for the rest of their lives. From here on in the rule of thumb is that as long as the plants are standing up its ok; if they wilt or lie down you are in trouble.

The medium in which you have put the cuttings/clones into should not be left to completely dry out but saying that you don't want it oversaturated either. A good and easy way to make sure that you are not over watering them is to water them via the tray. By feeding them via the tray the benefit is two fold, the first benefit is that it will encourage the downward growth of roots. The second benefit is that after the medium has already been pre-soaked it will replenish the moisture it needs from the bottom/tray. It's important to note that when re-feeding via the bottom/tray that you should throw away any old feed left in the tray.

In the next few weeks after the wilt period not much will change above ground. All the hard work is happening under the surface. The first thing to happen is that the the cut which was soaked in the rooting gel will form a callus, as seen in the image to the right. After this has formed the roots should start to grow from and around this callus. It will take a while for the first roots to start.... but when they do, they should grow fast and strong.

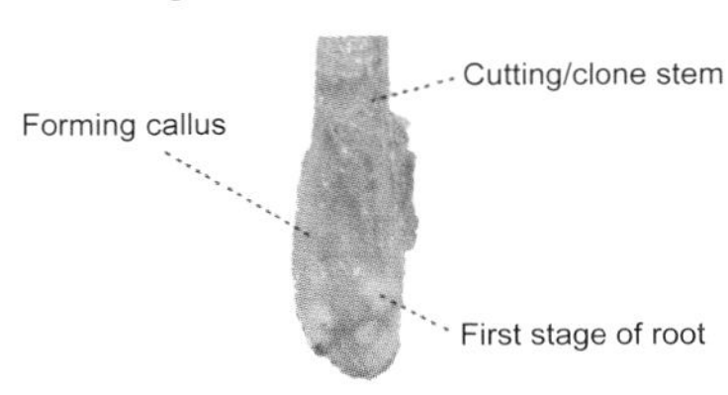

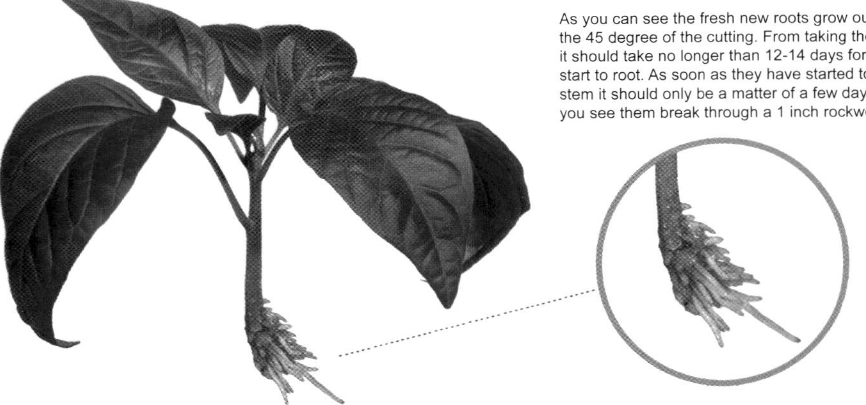

As you can see the fresh new roots grow out from the 45 degree of the cutting. From taking the cuttings it should take no longer than 12-14 days for them to start to root. As soon as they have started to root at the stem it should only be a matter of a few days before you see them break through a 1 inch rockwool cube.

At the first sign of the roots showing through the 1 inch medium it will need to be re-potted. For this first re-potting I would recommend upsizing from a 1 inch block into a 3 inch block of rockwool or medium. If you are going to transfer the cutting straight into a pot I would use a 3 litre one.

It is important that you do not leave any roots exposed to the light in any way shape or form. Roots don't like light. Leaving the roots exposed at any time will stress the plant, stunt its growth and in extreme case's potentially kill it.

As I have stated before a few times, you should if possible stick to the same medium at every stage of the plant's life. So if you originally put your cutting into rockwool it should be transplanted/repotted into rockwool at each stage of its life.

When transferring the rooted cutting/ clone from it's 1 inch block into a 3 inch, be careful to try and not touch, break or heavily bend any roots which are showing through. The smaller block should fit nice and snugly into the larger block. A great tip at this point is to twist the smaller block as you insert it into the larger block. This will reduce the amount of root stress/breakages.

As you put the smaller block into the larger block remember to twist it.

Normally at this stage (if you haven't already) it is the the right time to start to add some weak nutrient into the feed. I would recommend Formula-XL feed at a diluted rate.

Feeding your plants now at a diluted rate will help them feed faster, but remember at this early stage of their lives they are very delicate, so less is always more.

All plants (even if the same species) are different and grow at different speeds and rates. Before the cuttings can move on to the Vegetative stage they need to be strong enough to cope with the more intense light and feeds. I would recommend that they are not put into Veg until they either have three stages of nodes or have rooted through a 3 inch block of medium. Normally if everything has been followed correctly then this should happen at around the same time.

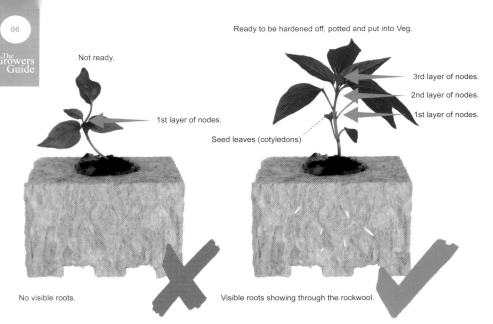

Ready to be hardened off, potted and put into Veg.

Not ready.

3rd layer of nodes.

2nd layer of nodes.

1st layer of nodes.

1st layer of nodes.

Seed leaves (cotyledons)

No visible roots.

Visible roots showing through the rockwool.

As soon as there are roots poking out of the 3 inch medium they will need to be re-potted again but before re-potting and transferring your plants into the Vegetative stage they will need to be “hardened off”.

How do you harden a plant off?

This following section is the same for cuttings as it is for seeds. The best and most effective way to harden off your plants is to remove the propagator’s lid for increasing periods of time over 3 days. This will slowly get the young plantlings used to life outside of the propagator. It’s best done in stages to try and reduce the amount of over all stress to the plants when they are transferred into the Vegetative stage.

I have found that the most effective, stress free way of doing this is over a 3 day period.

Day 1 - take the lid off the propagator (while the lights are on) for 6 hours.

Day 2 - take the lid off the propagator (while the lights are on) for 12 hours.

Day 3 - take the lid off the propagator (while the lights are on) for 24 hours.

After this is done the plants are ready to be re-potted and moved into the next stage of their life.

They will now need to be re-potted. For this first re-pot I would suggest a 3 to 3.5 litre pot. This will give the plant a chance to stretch its roots and settle into the medium that it will be spending the rest of its life in. It's important at this stage to not re-pot straight into a much larger pot, or the pot you ultimately want to end up in. To get the most out of your pots and root mass I always find it best to go up in pot sizes as close to 10 litres at a time as possible.

When filling the pots up with Dutch pro's PRO SOIL/AARDE LIGHT MIX it is best to leave a centimetre gap at the top of the pot, this will help you reduce spillage when watering. When all of the soil is in the pot you will have to make a hole for the rooted plant to fit into. In order to get the hole right shape and size dimensions I use a spare rockwool cube of the same size. As you can see from the below image this will give you the correct shaped space ready for the transplantation. The soil around the hole should be lightly pressed so it just holds its shape as above. If pressed too firmly you will essentially push all of the air out of the soil and it will not leave adequate space for the roots to grow freely. As soon as all the above is ready you will need to add in the Mycorrhizae.

Follow the guidelines which are on the label of the Mycorrhizae which you will be using. If you have gone with my suggestion of Plant Success Great White Mycorrhizae there should be a small application spoon in each pot to help measure the right amount.

Gently insert the rooted rockwool into the Mycorrhizae dusted hole you have already prepared.

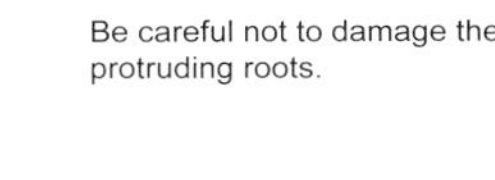

Be careful not to damage the protruding roots.

5.5 litre black square to round pot.

The idea is to lightly sprinkle the Mycorrhizae in and around the hole you have made ready for transplantation.

When transplanting the fresh rooted rockwool into the coco it is important to remember that the roots will be exposed and thus be very vulnerable. As discussed earlier in the book, roots do not like the light, so the faster they can be transplanted the better. Bearing this in mind it is also important that you take great care not to break any of the roots as you are transplanting into the coco. When the rockwool is in the coco the top of the rockwool cube should be level with the surface of the coco as shown in the image below.

The top of the rockwool should be level with the top of the soil.

Make sure there are no gaps between the rockwool and the soil, if there is then gently push the soil towards the sides of the rockwool. Ideally you want the top of the rockwool to be level with the top of the soil.

Your plants are now ready to go into the next stage.

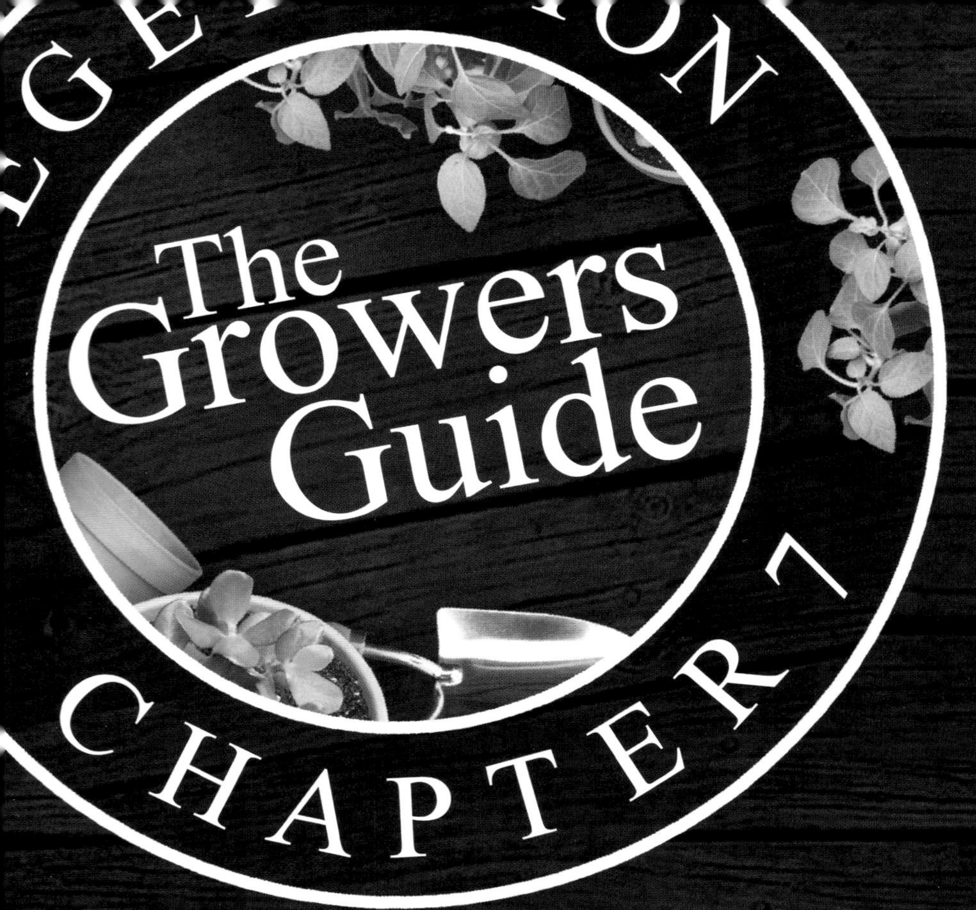

Vegetation

Simply put, Vegetation is the growth period which the plant goes through. It is a very important stage as it is when the plant is taking in all it needs to grow as strong as possible in order to produce the best fruits it can. To use the phrase "you reap what you sow" the more effort you put in at this point then the greater the rewards will be. In this chapter we will look step by step at how to set up your grow room properly for Vegetation. There is a breakdown of everything you need, why you need it and how it works. This chapter also covers the importance of light height within your growing environment and the factors of temperature and humidity, explaining how and why this can make a big difference to your crop. We are one of the first books to take the products currently available in hydroponic stores here in the UK and show you from beginning to end how to put together and set up your growing environment.

Vegetation/Vegetative Cycle – light cycle – lights on 18hrs, off 6hrs – time period 1 - 4 weeks.

In order to get the most out of your plants you will now have to change the light cycle to 18hrs on – 6 hrs off. This will put your plants into the Vegetation stage of their lives. You will also need to change the kind of light that you use and the environment which the plants are in.

For the benefit of the book, to keep things as easy as possible and to teach you the basics I will be looking to explain the Vegetative and the Flowering stages of the plant using what I would call a "single setup".

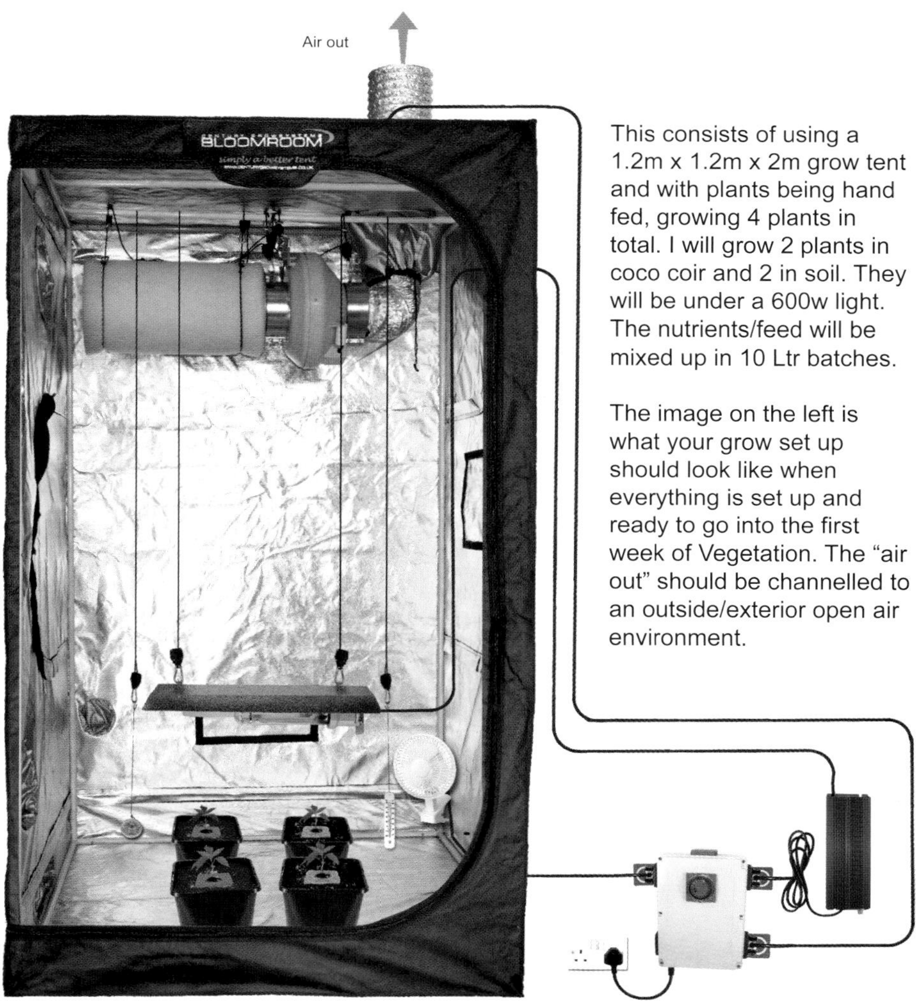

This consists of using a 1.2m x 1.2m x 2m grow tent and with plants being hand fed, growing 4 plants in total. I will grow 2 plants in coco coir and 2 in soil. They will be under a 600w light. The nutrients/feed will be mixed up in 10 Ltr batches.

The image on the left is what your grow set up should look like when everything is set up and ready to go into the first week of Vegetation. The "air out" should be channelled to an outside/exterior open air environment.

Equipment

The basic equipment you will need for the Vegetative stage is;

- **HID light/Dual spectrum light**
- **Protective eyewear**
- **Contactor – timer**
- **Oscillating fan**
- **Grow tent**
- **Ventilation kit (fan-filter-ducting-clamps)**
- **Feed/nutrient range + Mycorrhizae**
- **Medium - Coco coir/Soil**
- **E.C meter and pH meter/test kit**
- **Temperature gauge, Hygrometer, Equipment hangers**
- **Larger plant pots**
- **Saucers/catchment tray**

All of which can be purchased from your local hydroponic shop.

HID light/dual spectrum light – Now that your plant is ready to move into the Vegetative stage of its life it needs both a change to the kind of light used and to the light cycle itself (18hrs lights on – 6 hrs lights off).

The trick with growing indoors is to try and mimic the best possible conditions which the plant would have had if it was growing in its natural habitat. In the plants natural habitat and over its normal lifecycle of 12 months it will be subject to the four different seasons of the year which all bring light waves in different strengths.
By changing the indoor light and its polarity we trick the plant into thinking the season has changed and thus push the plant into the next stage of its lifecycle. By combining this with the correct amount of nutrients, water and stimulants we can compress a plants normal lifecycle of 12 months into 3 months, sometimes even shorter!

12 month season cycle

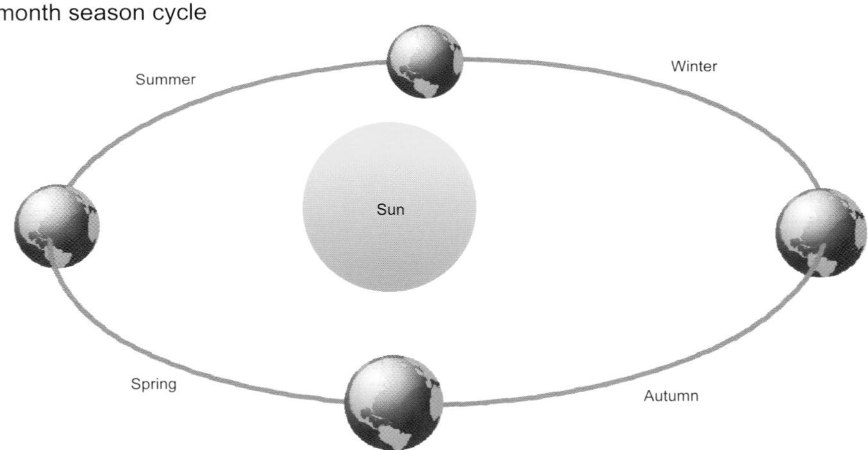

The light that you will need to change over to using for this stage comes in three parts;

1. **The shade**
2. **The ballast**
3. **The bulb**

1. Shades – are a matter of personal taste or preference, there are 100's out there of all shapes and sizes claiming all sorts of benefits and advantages. For the purposes of the book and to keep things as simple as possible we will be using a dutch barn hammertone shade. This is one of the most basic, no fuss, reliable and well performing shades on the market. It can be used with 250w – 400w – and 600w bulbs and ballasts.

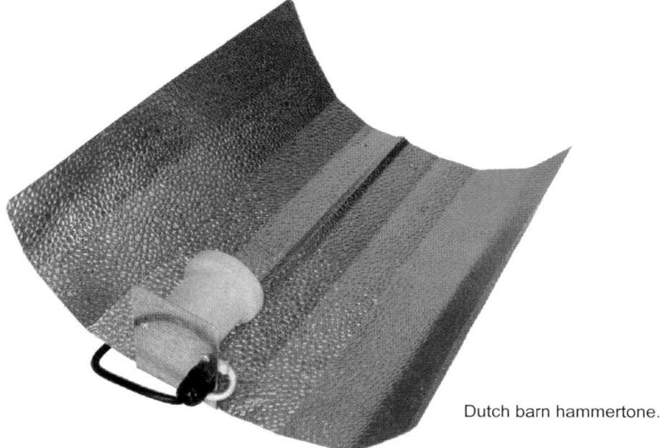

Dutch barn hammertone.

The Ballast – these are mostly available in three different wattages. 250w, 400w and 600w. The higher the wattage of the ballast, the higher the lumen and parr output becomes. The higher the lumen and parr the plant receives, the faster the plant can grow and thus the bigger the yield. The side effect to the plant of the increase in power is a dramatic rise in heat which the bulb gives off.

I have always used 600w lights and always will. So I would recommend you start as you mean to go on and go 600w all the way.

There are two types of ballasts on the market.

a. Non magnetic or "Digital" as they are more commonly known.
b. Magnetic

Both come in 250w – 400w and 600 fixed wattages however due to recent technical advances in the hydroponics world most of the digitals ballasts on today's market are 600w dimmable.

a, Non metallic/digital dimmable 600w - What this means is that they are 600w digital non metallic ballasts, which can be turned/dimmed down.

(please note that this ballast is a 600w so you should always use a 600w bulb even if you have them turned down all the time). They also have a boost setting which is preset at 660w (10% extra, which the plants love in the last week of Flower). Please be aware though that having the ballast on the 660w power boost will shorten the overall life of your bulb.

Digital 600w ballast.

If you can afford it I would recommend digital ballasts all the way. They give you the most control, run at the true wattages, use less electricity, have a small start up volt drain, run cooler than metallic ballasts and can be dimmed down (perfect for unexpected super hot days) or turned up (which is great to get the most out of the plants in the last week). All of these features do come at a cost however and they are the most expensive ballasts on the market, which can put a lot of people off.

There is also the i-Sun Pro 2 from Century Growsystems. This bad boy is the first of its kind, rather than having the standard pre set wattages it has a variable dial. This means that the ballast can be set at any wattage from 250W to 660W in increments of 10 watts, allowing it to be set at 260W - 270W - 280W - 290W - 300W - 310W - 320W all the way up to 660W. In doing this the ballast user has full control. It also has a built in digital timer (which can be bypassed if needed).

b, Metallic – there are two different styles of metallic ballasts on the market today. The first is the "resin cased ballast" which is normally the cheapest. They are mass produced and very popular, however as is the nature of the mass produced market you will find that there are a lot of cheaper brands out there which do not produce the true wattages stated. If you are going to go down the resin cased ballast route, my recommendation would be to buy a well known branded ballast.

600w magnetic ballast.

600w vented resin cased magnetic ballast.

The second style of metallic ballast is the "metal cased ballast". As it says on the tin they are metal cased, tend to have better internal components in them, run cooler than the resin ballasts and as a result are mid ranged in price. They are strong reliable and normally come with a longer warranty than the resin or digital ballasts.

The important thing to keep in mind when using metallic ballasts is that they do have a larger start up volt drain than non-metallic/digital ballasts.

What does this mean?

A magnetic ballast works by sending a large pulse of electricity to the bulb to initially ignite it. After the bulb has been initially ignited it then chokes the amount of electricity to the bulb at the right wattage. Without the ballast the bulb would keep drawing electricity until it overloads itself. When this happens it will have a large draw on the start-up voltage which can blow a fuse in most households. The way around this is to use a contactor.

Inside a 600w Magnetic Ballast.

Capacitor
Ballast, this is what chokes the electricity to the bulb at the right wattage.
Igniter, this sends the right electric pulse to the arc in order to initially light the lamp.

A true 600w ballast actually runs at around 655w - 660w this is to compensate for the watts which are lost through heat in the ballast and in the length of cable to the shade. This is something to bear in mind when purchasing your shades. The normal cable length which is taken into consideration when designing the wattage output for a ballast is 3m. If you have a cable length any longer than 3m then this will reduce the watts to the bulb.

This point yet again emphasises how important it is to have a true wattage ballast. Wattage readers can be brought online and are a good thing to have to test your ballasts.

Let me put it like this, I bought a wattage reader and tested over 20 different ballasts from different companies and only 6 of them were running at true wattage. The other 14 I took back to the shop and exchanged for ballasts with a true wattage.

Please note: Never open up a ballast for any reason. If you think there is something wrong with it just return it to the shop.

Bulbs - it is important to match the wattage of the bulb to the wattage of the ballasts. For the Vegetative stage of the plant's lifecycle there are two bulb types you can use.

- **Metal halide bulb** – (Veg stage only)
- **Dual spectrum bulb** – (can be used for both Veg and Flower stages)

For the Flowering stage of the plant's life there are also two bulbs which can be used.

- **HPS bulb** – high pressure sodium (Flower stage only)
- **Dual spectrum bulb** – (can be used for both Veg and Flower stages)

All these bulbs are basically HID (High Intensity Discharge) bulbs and all essentially work in the same way.

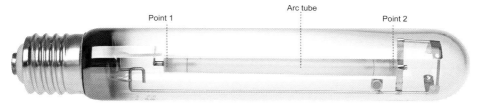

Dual spectrum lamp.

Inside the bulb there are two points between which an electrical charge is emitted. This is called the arc. The ballast initially sends out a large surge of electricity in order to connect the two points (like when lightning hits a church steeple, the two points being 1, the static cloud and 2, the churche's steeple). The ballast then chokes the level electrical charge to the bulb to the right wattage it is set up to produce. Either 250w – 400w – 600w – 1000w. Without the ballast/choke the arc would continue to draw electricity until it overloads itself.

Metal halide bulbs – are specifically used ONLY in the Vegetative stage of the plant's lifecycle. They give off a white blue light which is optimum for the Vegetative stage.

HPS (High pressure sodium) bulbs – are ONLY to be used in the Flowering stages of the plant's growth. They give off an orange/red spectrum which is ideal for the Flowering stage.

Dual spectrum bulbs – are a hybrid of the HPS flowering bulbs. They give off mainly an orange and red spectrum but also give off part of the blue spectrum. As they do this they can be used for the Vegetative and Flowering stages of the plant's lifecycle. One bulb does it all.

Metal halide lamp.

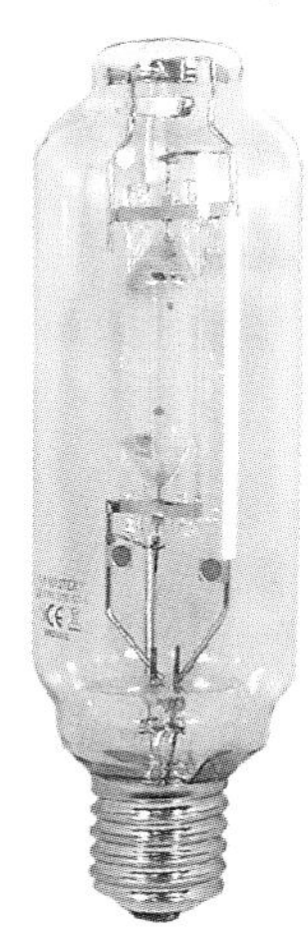

Combination light fixtures - These are commonly at the top end of the price bracket. They are basically the whole light fixture in one unit. The shade, ballast and lamp as shown in the image below. There are few different types/ styles and brands on the market to date but for my money there is only one clear choice; Gavita.

Gavita are the market leaders in this style of horticultural lighting system. They are strong, reliable, well made and worth every penny. A truly professional bit of kit. However, like I have already said they can be expensive. The two styles from the range that I have chosen to go through in a little more detail are the Gavita Pro 600 SE EU (which is below) and the Gavita Pro 600e SE EU (on the next page). These are also two of Gavitas biggest sellers, and for good reason.

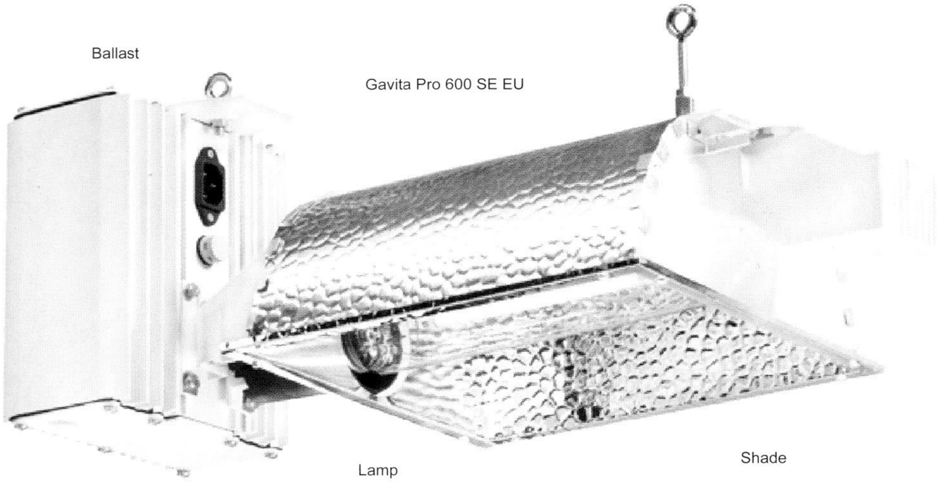

The Gavita Pro 600 is the first 240 Volt electronic ballast that powers the professional 600W 400V EL (electronic) lamps. These lamps have the highest PAR light output, improved spectrum and the best light maintenance (>95% PAR light over one year of use). Being the most efficient horticultural lamps available and the only lamps specifically developed for electronic ballasts this is the lamp of choice for Dutch professional greenhouse growers.

Having the ballast close to the lamp reduces the amount of EMI (RF interference). The complete fixture is easily mounted with two balanced eye bolts.

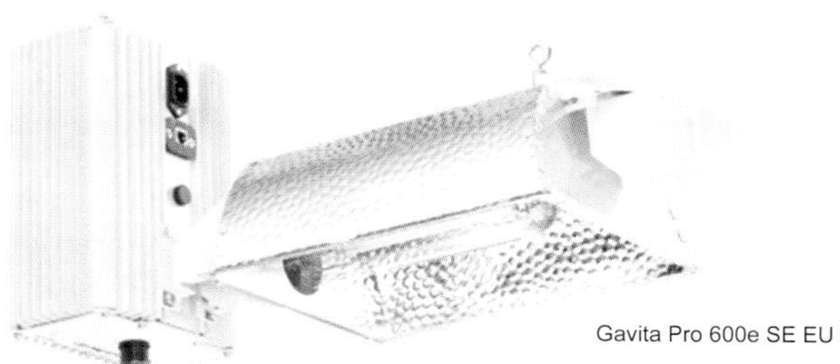

Gavita Pro 600e SE EU

Lighting control at your fingertips

The controller can switch all the interconnected fixtures on and off with its internal timer, adjust them to your required output level (in percentage or exact output power) and even simulate sunrise and sunset to gradually adjust the climate in your grow room when your lights go on or off. This electronic controller replaces expensive lighting timers and contactors while preventing ballast current in-rush when switching on your lights.

Two very important features are the autodim function and emergency shut-down. When the temperature in your grow room rises beyond the control level of your climate control your crop can be damaged beyond recovery. The temperature probe senses this and will automatically dim the lights to not overshoot your safe temperature, and maintain it. The display and warning LED indicate when this happens, and also indicate if this has happened while you were away so you can correct the problem. If for any reason your climate control completely fails and the temperature rises to unacceptable levels the system will perform an emergency shutdown of all connected equipment. The alarm contact of the controller can be connected to your alarm system for instant notification.

You can connect all your e-series fixtures to one controller.

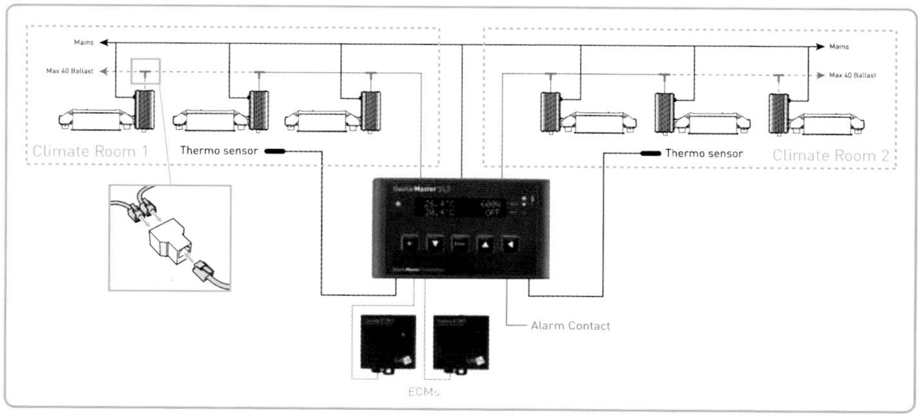

Protective eyewear - This is a commonly overlooked subject within indoor growing. There are a few brands out there at the low end and only really one at the top: Method Seven. I would highly recommend the purchase of a pair of quality protective glasses from the Method Seven range. With glasses you get what you pay for, so if you have a £10 pair of eyes then get a £10 pair of glasses. If however you value your vision, the clarity of colour, and your sight, then I suggest that you buy the best that you can afford.

Method Seven technology blends incredible colour-balancing for each of the standard grow lighting spectrums (HPS, metal halide, LED, sun) with exceptionally high quality lenses that provide the best in optical clarity. Additionally, Method Seven protection removes all harmful UV A/B rays like most others but additionally also removes harmful UVC rays which are filtered out of sunlight by the upper atmosphere, but pose a significant hazard under grow lighting.

Many growers suffer through unnecessary stress, fatigue, decreased yield, and even permanent eye injury from using sunglasses or cheaper knock-off grow room glasses. At best, even premium sunglasses attenuate (decrease) excess light in the grow room but do a horrible job of colour-balancing in indoor lighting environments, leading not only to discomfort and stress, but also to poor viewing and maintenance of your plants. Cheap grow room glasses do an okay job of colour-balancing, but typically have very poor optical quality and inadequate protection from UVC rays.

HPS lens

HPS lens clip-on

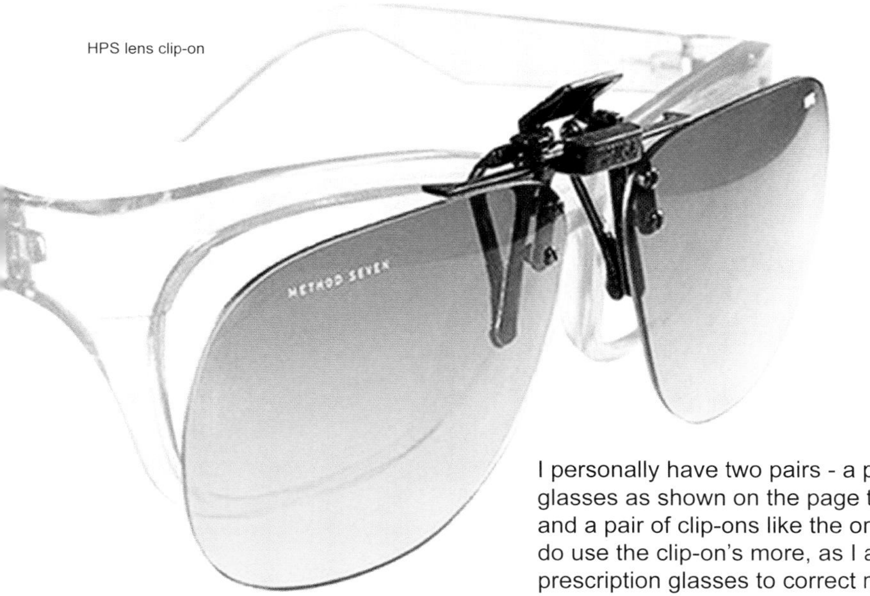

I personally have two pairs - a pair of full glasses as shown on the page to the left and a pair of clip-ons like the ones above. I do use the clip-on's more, as I already wear prescription glasses to correct my vision.

I keep mine clipped to the strap on the front of the tent door in the funky microfibre bag which came with them so I don't lose them and I always know where they are.

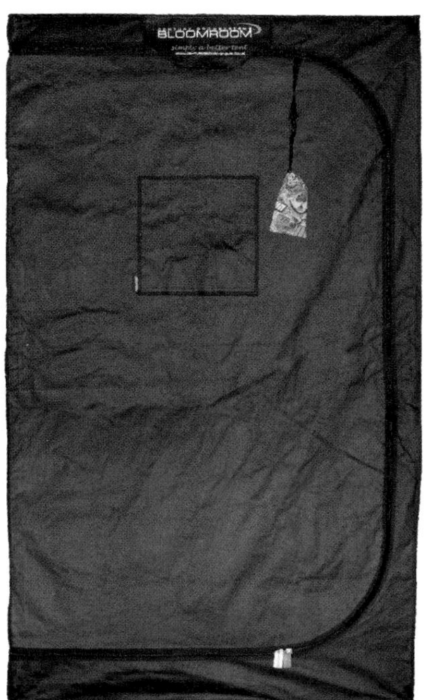

Method Seven Rendition HPS delivers "Perfect Colour" for the world's ultimate grow experience in the intense yellow spectrum and harsh conditions of HPS lighting. They deliver absolutely the highest available optical clarity and ability to absorb infrared (heat). These are THE best lenses for the professional working extended hours under HPS or the passionate hobbyist who simply wants the best. The "plus" silver coating option makes the Method Seven glass lens even better for working in high wattage environments or for crossover use outside. Plus, they just look cool. Their patent-pending formulation is manufactured with the highest quality German durable mineral glass to provide perfect colour, perfect clarity, and 100% UV protection.

Contactor & Timer – contactors spread the electrical discharge to reduce the chances of the main fuse blowing when the main strike up of the lamp/ballast happens. When using light kits of the above nature I would always recommend using a good quality contactor. The better contactors on the market have built in analogue timers. The benefit of this is that you don't have to have the timer at the wall where the contactor would be plugged in. Analogue timers at the wall tend to often fail completely, or drift.

Setting the timer is easy, the image here is set to 18hrs on and 6hrs off (18-6 vegetative light cycle). Where the pins are pushed into the middle = lights off. Where they are pushed away from the middle = lights on. The timer runs from the black triangle shown on the dial when powered up. Here is an example of how it works. Say its 12 o'clock midday, I would turn the dial to 12 (24 would be 12 at night) and then push 18 hrs worth of pins away from the middle (lights on) making sure that the last 6 are pushed into the middle (lights off).

Drifting is when an analogue timers "on and off" times become inaccurate. They drift due to the electrical surges that happen in the main electric loop. I've seen them drift out of time by over an hour in less than a week! Over the standard 3 month growing period this can dramatically throw the rest of your grow room out of sync.This drifting can be reduced by having an analogue timer in the contactor. Failing that you can use a digital timer. Digital timers have zero drift but can be complicated to set, especially if you don't read the instructions!!!

Oscillating fan – My recommendation would be to buy a clip on oscillating fan from your local hydroponics store. They are in the same price range as normal oscillating fans but have the added benefit of being able to clip on to poles and can easily be used upside down (unlike normal oscillating fans), which can be a huge benefit when space is an issue. The oscillating fan should be positioned as far away from the plants as possible. The idea of the oscillating fan is threefold.

The first is to take the warm air away from the plants, so cooling them in the process.

The second is to help move the gasses being emitted from the leaves away from the plant, this in turn helps move oxygen and carbon dioxide toward the leaves, assisting with the photosynthesis process.

The third is to shudder, or gently shake the plants. What this does is to increase the strength of the stems. As the plant is gently shook by the movement of the fan it slowly builds up a resistance in the stem and strengthens the whole plant making it firmer and more hardy.

Grow tents – come in all shapes and sizes, their inner lining normally being either silver or white. If you want a silver lining the best on the market is Century Growsystems Bloomroom and if you want a white lining I would recommend a Budbox Evolution. For the purposes of this setup I will be using a 1.2m x 1.2m x 2m Bloomroom grow tent from Century Growsystems.

With grow tents you get what you pay for. A good grow tent will last you for years if treated with respect. The main things to look for in a quality tent are a good "DR" which is the thickness of the tent material (higher the better), thick poles and GOOD ZIPS!

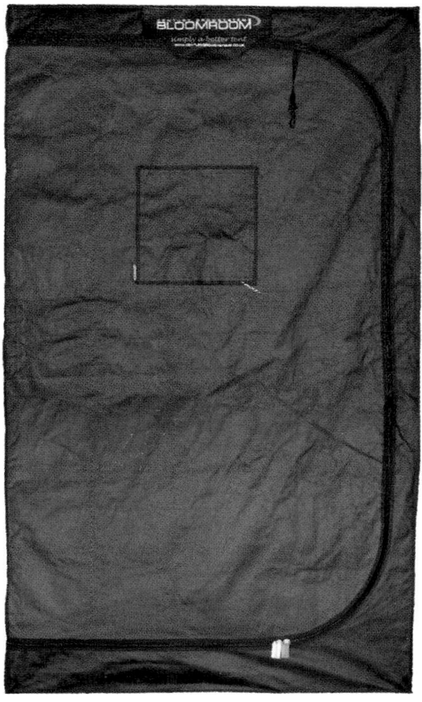

Bloomroom standard grow tent
1.2m x 1.2m x 2m

Homebox Evolution grow tent
1.2m x 1.2m x 2m

Equipment hangers – I recommend using ratchet hangers as they are strong, reliable and can hold the weight of anything you need to hang in a 1.2m x 1.2m x2m tent/growroom. Most of the major companies do them and you can pick a pack of 2 up for normally less than £5.

Be careful when screwing the lamp into the shade. It should be screwed in firmly and safely. Try not to directly touch the glass of the lamp as the grease on your hand will affect its efficiency. My tip would be to use the sleeve which the lamp comes in as a protective barrier to screw the lamp into the shade.

Above is the layout of how the lamp, shade, ballast and contactor should all go together.

The lamp screws into the shade and the shade is hung within the environment. The shade is then plugged into the ballast. The ballast is then plugged into the contactor. The timer on the contactor should then be set to the required settings and plugged into the wall socket with the main switch pressed to the off position. When everything is in place and ready to go, switch the socket on.

The cable from the dutch barn hammer tone is normally 5 metres, which is more than enough to reach from where the shade and lamp is hanging to the ballast which should be either on the floor or ideally hung vertically on the wall as shown in the image above.

The contactor will also be used to power the ventilation system and the oscillating fan as well as the light.

This will all run on the same time cycle.

Below is an image of how the light set up should look when in situ inside the tent.

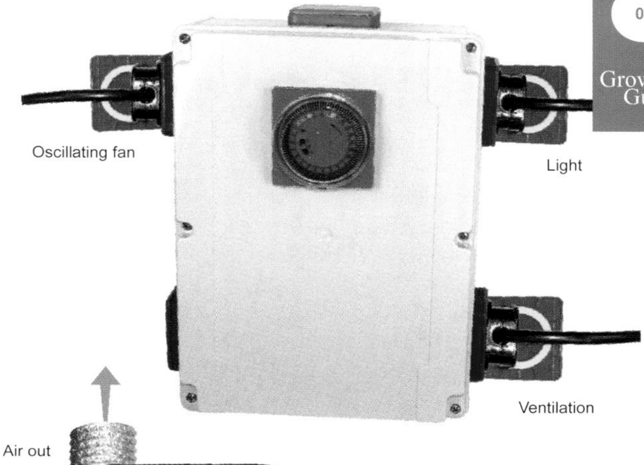

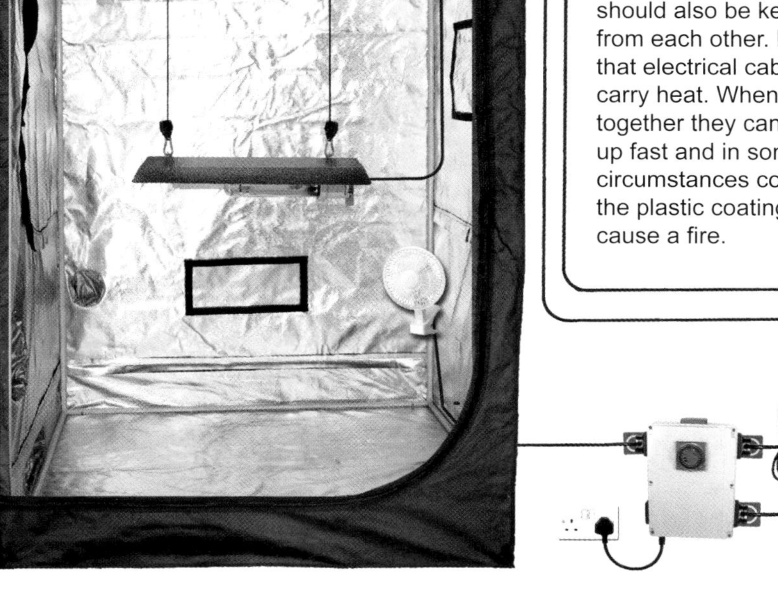

Ideally you should run the wires from both the light and the ventilation system through the upper part of the tent/grow room and down towards the ballast and contactor outside of the grow room.

The neater you can keep the wires the better. The wires should also be kept apart from each other. Don't forget that electrical cables also carry heat. When bunched together they can easily heat up fast and in some extreme circumstances could melt the plastic coating and cause a fire.

EC meter and PH meter/test kit – I have gone through EC meters and pH meter/test kits in the Nutrients section of the book. Just to recap, I would recommend HM digital for your EC reader and a simple chemical test kit for your pH.

Temperature gauge and Hygrometer – You can use the same ones as you used for Propagation, however if it were me, I would buy an all-in-one digital temperature and hygrometer gauge. They are pretty cheap and can be brought from any hydroponic store worth their salt. It is important to remember when taking the temperature and moisture readings that this should be taken at the top of the plants canopy. Canopy – meaning the top of the main mass of the plant/plants.

Temperature gauge

Hygrometer

Plant's canopy

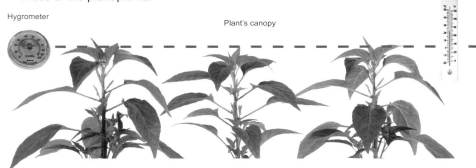

Ventilation kit (fan-filter-ducting-clamps) - A good air exchange is essential to a great environment. Most hydroponic shops will sell full ventilation kits depending on how much air you want to move and scrub (clean). In this case we are growing in a 1.2m x 1.2m x 2m space and so a 6" L1 RVK fan with a matched Dutch Touch filter is perfect. In order to connect the filter to the fan and from the fan to where you will be exhausting the scrubbed air too, ducting will need to be used. There are 3 main types of ducting.

Standard - which is just bog standard silver aluminium ducting.

Plastic coated - which is exactly the same as the standard but with black plastic, heat moulded around it.

Acoustic ducting - this is a dual layer of standard ducting with acoustic fibreglass sandwiched inbetween it. This stuff really keeps the noise down but is twice the price of the standard ducting. If you can afford it I would recommend the acoustic ducting.

It can get itchy and messy so make sure you wear gloves and ideally a face mask when handling it.

The last part of the ventilation kit is the clamps, or as they are more commonly known "J clamps". A lot of shops, in order to keep prices down and to make the ventilation kits more competitive sell tape with the kits instead of clamps. Tape might hold for a week or so but it's really not worth the hassle hoff. GET CLAMPS! When fitting the ducting, make sure that all the clamps are as tight as they can be, as loose clamps and ducting can cause whistling from the air movement.

As for fitting the ventilation kit into your grow tent, I would put the fan as close as you can to the filter. This will make sure that you get the most out of the filter as it will move and scrub the most amount of air possible.

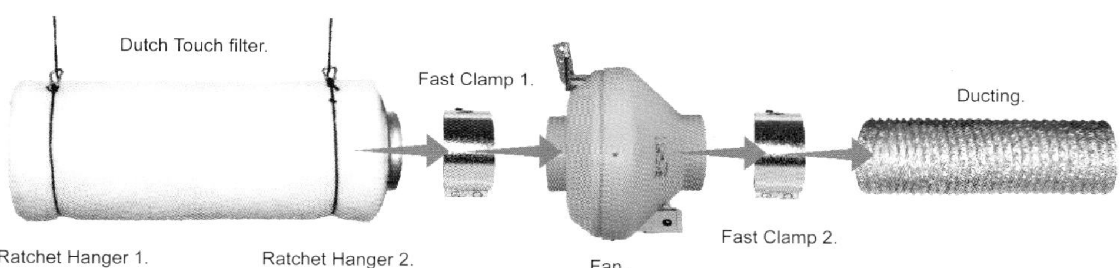

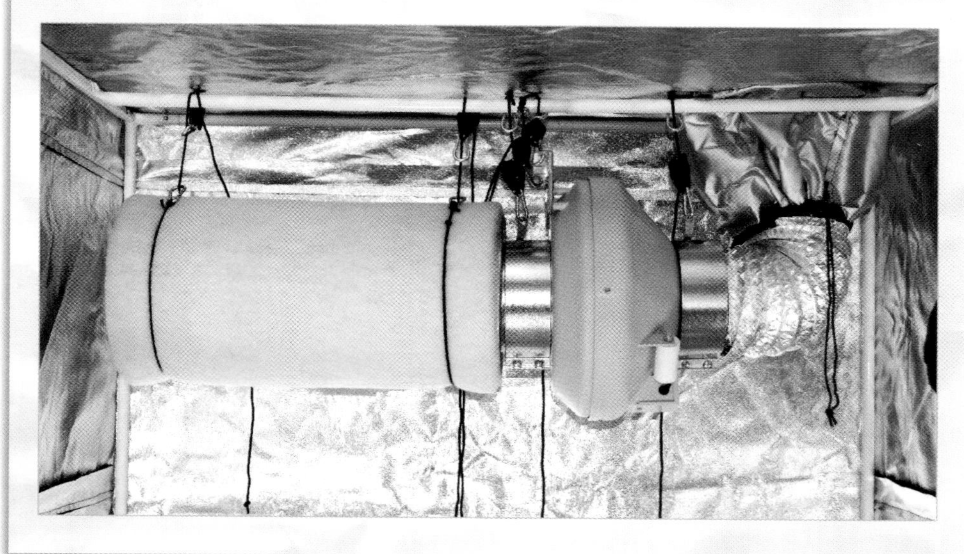

Above is how it should look all put together and in the grow room. It is positioned at the top, back of the tent. I have put the outwards air ducting through the top of the grow room. As you can see I have used ratchet hagers to secure the fan and the fast clamps in place. Be careful when setting up the main ventilation kit to not have the filter pushed all the way to the back or the side where it is touching the walls or side of the main tent/grow room. The filter should be free hanging with as much space around it as possible.

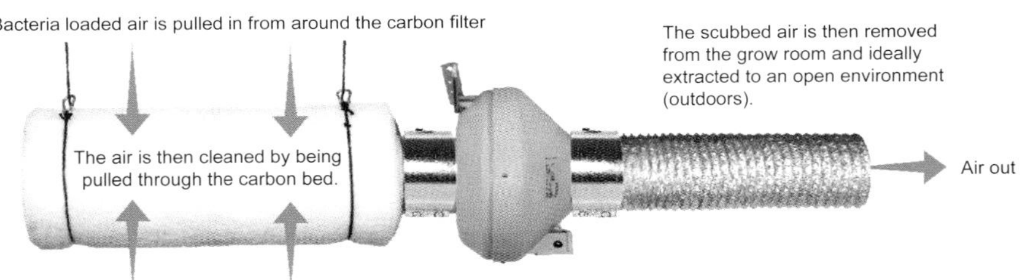

Bacteria loaded air is pulled in from around the carbon filter
The scubbed air is then removed from the grow room and ideally extracted to an open environment (outdoors).
The air is then cleaned by being pulled through the carbon bed.
Air out

The filter has a bed of carbon within it; the depth and the quality of this carbon can vary massively. The higher the quality of the carbon bed, the better. The fan will pull air through the carbon within the filter. As it does this it will scrub the air removing any bacteria.

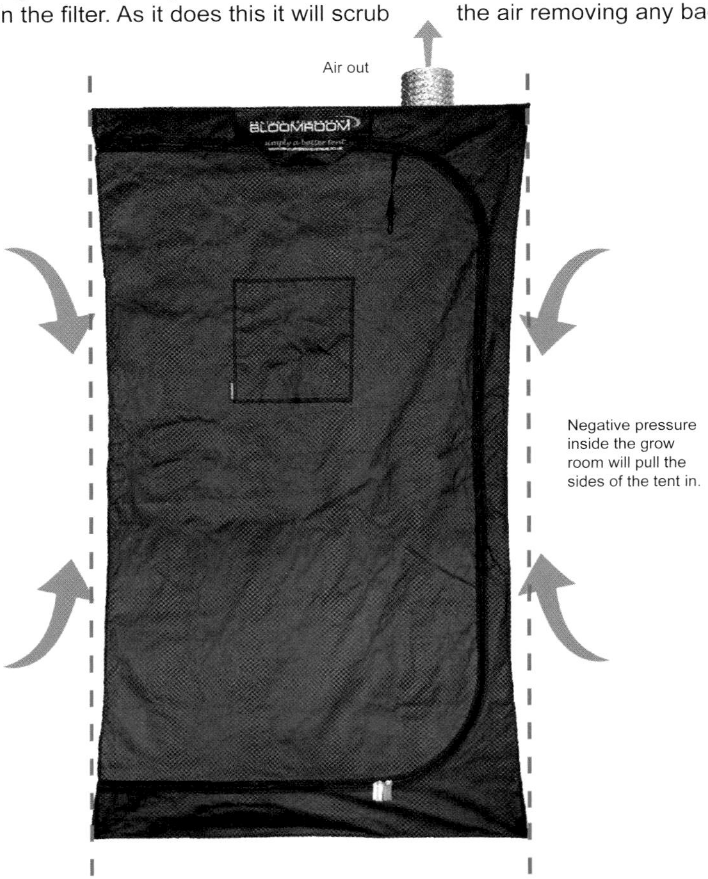

Air out

Negative pressure inside the grow room will pull the sides of the tent in.

When the ventilation system is in the tent and turned on it should make the grow room /tent suck in at the sides slightly. This is commonly known as internal negative pressure. By opening and closing the various vents and openings in the tent you should be able to achieve the right amount of negative pressure within. This will ensure that all of the air leaving the grow room will have been passed through the filter and thus be scrubbed/cleaned.

Right ok, so we have gone through everything you need to start up a basic grow room for the Vegetative cycle. What we need to do now is to get it all ready for the plants.

When the set up is complete it should look something like this below.

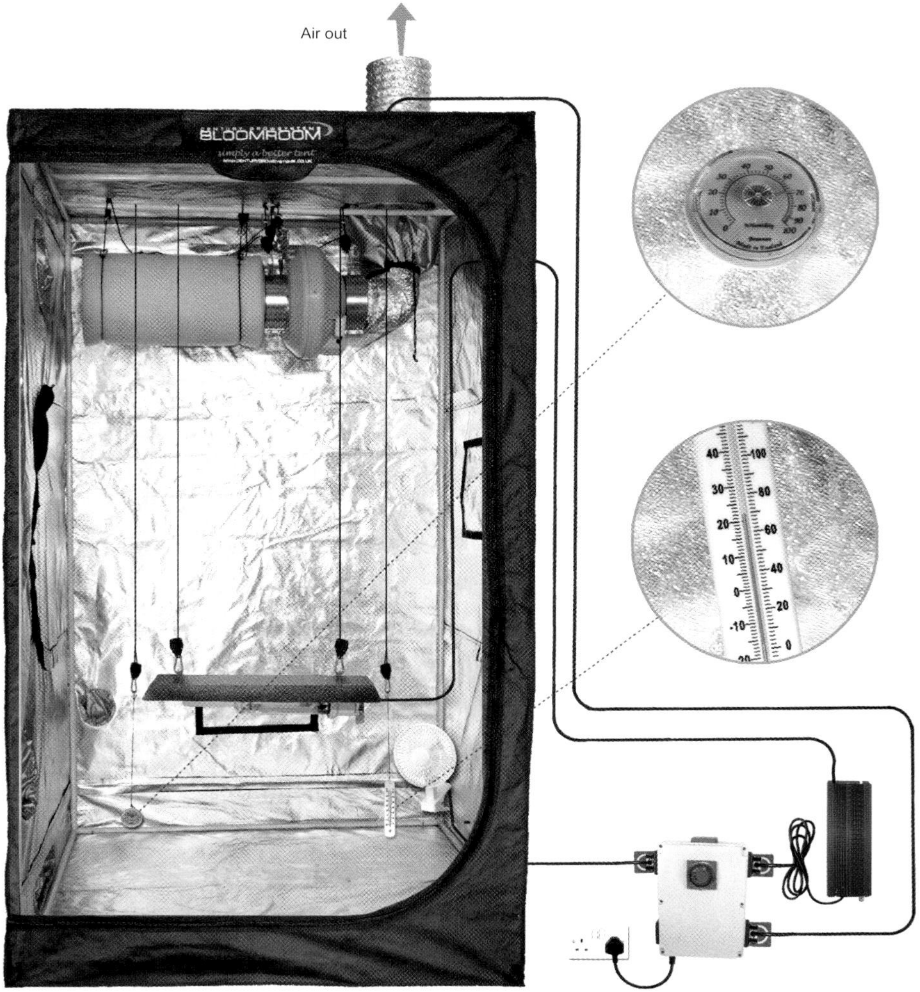

Air out

Just as when you were setting up the plants for the Propagation stage it is good practice to get everything ready and set up a good week before the plants are ready to go in. This will give you the chance to work out any unforeseen problems, get the environment right and generally get your head around what's what and where it goes. A dry run if you will.

Environment, environment, environment. I can't stress how important getting the environment right is.

All the conditions inside your grow room such as the temperature, humidity, and light strength need to be at their optimum level for them to work effectively together to create the perfect environment for your plants. Remember that we are trying to mimic the plants natural outdoor environment, inside and this is no easy feat. It only takes one element to be at the wrong level to knock your whole grow room out of sync.
I will go through the exact conditions that you are looking to achieve in more detail below. I must at this point, re-iterate however, how important it is that you take your time with this stage of the process, making sure that you fully understand what it is that you are trying to achieve and why.

The environment is fundamentally what you need to get right here. Without the plant being in the tent at this dry run stage I would take the temperature and the humidity levels from the centre of the tent. This will give you a good base line reading for the environment of the tent.

The temperature when the lights are on should ideally be between 24˚c and 27˚c. Any hotter than 30˚c and it's too hot (at 32˚c and above the plant will go into shock and deteriorate very quickly). Any lower than 19˚c and its way too cold (at 15˚c and below the plant will also go into shock and deteriorate very quickly).

The temperature at the point where the level is being taken can primarily be raised or lowered depending on the height of the light. The closer the light is the hotter it will be and thus the higher/further away the light source is, the cooler it will become. This will take a little bit of adjusting to get right but ideally you want the light closer to the plant than further away. The ideal distance between the plants and the light should be 1 foot – (12 inches).

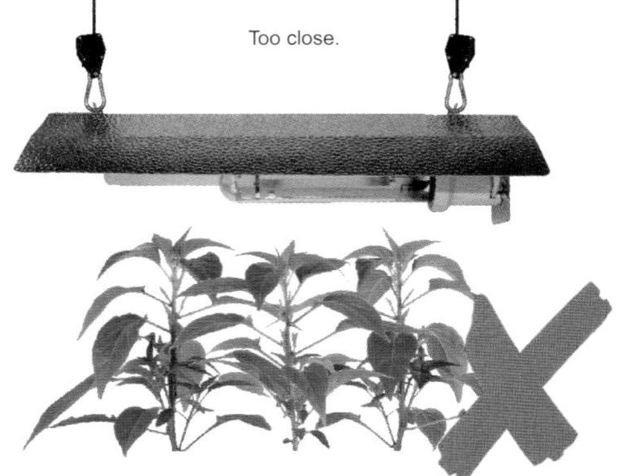

This distance ensures that the plant gets the maximum amount of lumen and par available without the top of the plant shadowing the overall mass of it.

Lumens decrease exponentially with the distance they travel. As you can see by this simple diagram, that from the source of the light the 1 lumen is a 1/16 of what it was at the distance of 1 foot.

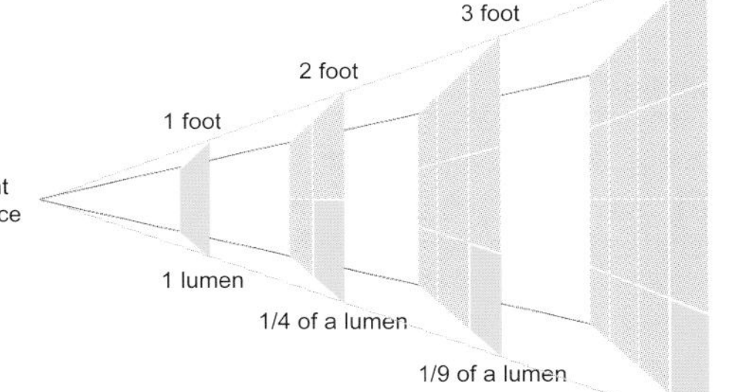

To get the light this close to the plant without the aid of an air cooled shade can be a challenge. This is where the position of the oscillating fan can come into play. As you can see in the image below, placing the oscillating fan in the right place at the right distance can dramatically cool the canopy of the main plant. What the oscillating fan does is to take the heat which the bulb is directly producing away from the main canopy and spread it around the grow tent. I have also positioned the out-take filter at the top of the tent so when it's on it will take the warmer air being blown away from the bulb out of the grow tent first and thus cool the whole grow tent at a steady rate. This will also make sure that there is a good air exchange, which is essential to the plant's health. The light and the oscillating fan will obviously need to be moved as the plant grows in order to maintain the correct distance.

Doing the dry run a week before should give you enough tinkering time to get things right.

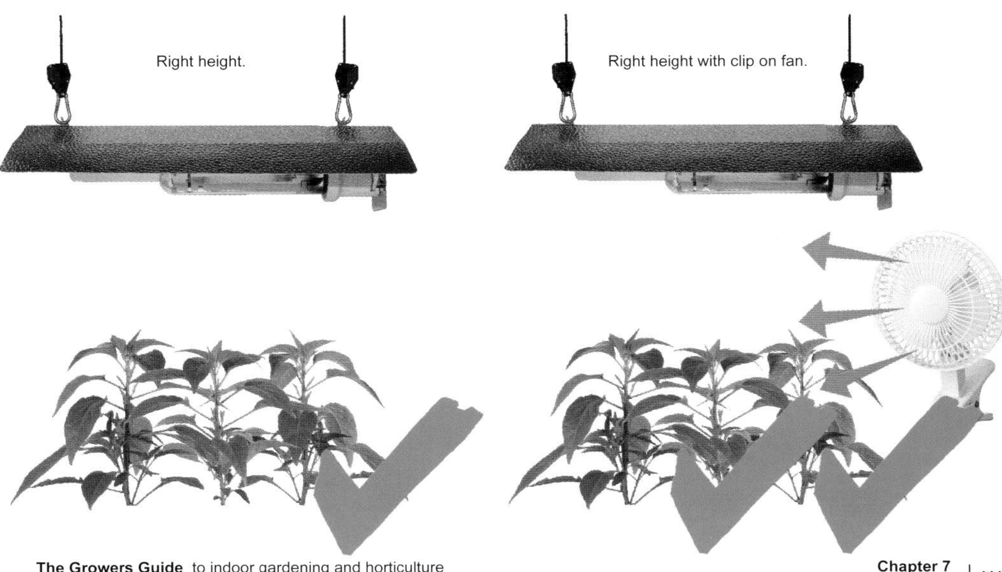

Larger Plant pots - The next sized plant pot that you will need is a 15 ltr square to round pot. They are called "square to round" as they are square at the top and round at the bottom. Pots come in all shapes and colours however you will find that plant pots used in an indoor growing environment are normally black, this is because a black pot is less translucent than any other colour pot and so keeps the plant's root system in the darkest environment possible; which is what we want. When re-potting into a larger pot the same method should be used as you followed when you potted your rock wool cube into your first plant pot. When filling the pots up with fresh medium it is best to leave between a centimetre and an inch gap at the top, this will help to reduce spillage when watering. When all of the medium is in the pot you will have to make a hole in which to fit the rooted plant. In order to achieve the correct shape and size of hole you can use a spare 5.5ltr pot. Push the 5.5 ltr pot into your 15ltr pot and then press the medium around the hole lightly so that it holds its shape, do not press too firmly however as doing this can essentially push all of the air out of the medium and can leave it too dense for any new roots to grow freely. As soon as all of the above is ready you will need to add in your mycorrhizae before the plant is transferred, this should be done following the same method as when you were potting the plant for the first time.

Feed/nutrient range and mycorrhizae - We have gone through the feed range and how you prepare it ready for use in the Vegetation/Grow stage in Chapter 2 "Understanding water and nutrients" To recap for the Veg stage however you will need the following

- **Plagron cocos a**
- **Plagron cocos b**
- **Plagron pure enzym**
- **Dutch pro Take Root**
- **Plant Magic Evolution**
- **Great White Mycorrhizae**

Just a reminder here that the Evolution spray should be applied every 5 days when the lights go off.

Plant Success Great White.

Plagron cocos a.

Plagron cocos b.

Plagron pure enzym.

Dutch pro Take Root.

Plant Magic Evolution.

Pot Saucers/Catchment tray - You may also need plant pot saucers and or a catchment tray for any over feeding run off which may have occurred whilst watering.

Standard Garland tray.

How long should you Veg for?

You can Veg for anywhere from 1 to 4 weeks. Well technically speaking you can keep a plant in the Vegetative stage for as long as you like. For the purposes of the book we will be "Vegging" the plant in the grow tent for a full 4 weeks. Should you however decide to "Veg" for less simply follow the flower chapter from where you wish.

While you are in the Vegetation/Grow stage of the plant's life it is good practice to follow a 3 day check list as follows;

- Check the top and the underside of leaves for insects and insect damage.
- "Dead leaf" each plant. ie, remove any dead or dying leaves.
- Check the plants for toxicity from overnutrition. This is normally indicated by the curling inwards of leaves. It can also discolour the very end of each leaf blade.
- Check for signs of undernutrition. This will be shown by either lightening of the plant (normally at the top first) or droopy leaves.
- Turn each plant 90° to get the most out of the light.
- Make sure your growing environment and growing equipment is clean.
- Check the temperature and the humidity are at the correct level.
- Make sure the light is the optimal distance away from the plants.

We will now go through the next 4 weeks of Veg/Grow, week by week so you know what to expect and when.

Vegetation/Grow

Week 1 - As this is the first week in the Vegetation light cycle the plants have a few new things to get used to. A new type of light, a different light cycle. a new environment, a new pot in a different medium and a whole new nutrient rich feed. Taking all the above into consideration it will take a while for the plants to settle in and overcome the stresses of these new changes.

As soon as the plants are put into the Vegetation/Grow stage "week 1" the feeding schedule begins.

Coco Coir

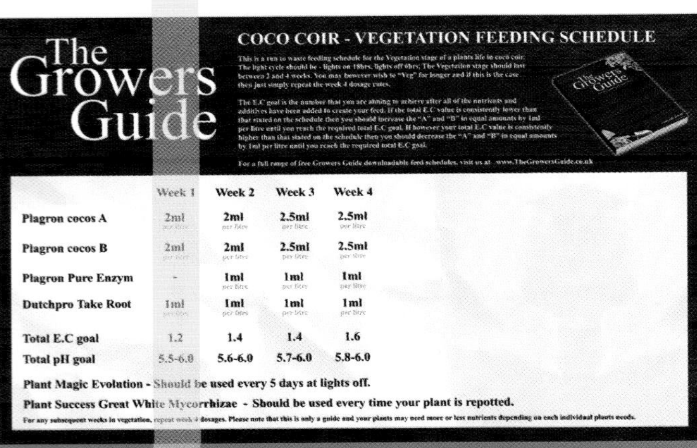

The Growers Guide

COCO COIR - VEGETATION FEEDING SCHEDULE

This is a run to waste feeding schedule for the Vegetation stage of a plants life in coco coir. The light cycle should be - lights on 18hrs, lights off 6hrs. The Vegetation stage should last between 2 and 4 weeks. You may however wish to "Veg" for longer and if this is the case then just simply repeat the week 4 dosage rates.

The E.C goal is the number that you are aiming to achieve after all of the nutrients and additives have been added to create your feed. If the total E.C value is consistently lower than that stated on the schedule then you should increase the "A" and "B" in equal amounts by 1ml per litre until you reach the required total E.C goal. If however your total E.C value is consistently higher than that stated on the schedule then you should decrease the "A" and "B" in equal amounts by 1ml per litre until you reach the required total E.C goal.

For a full range of free Growers Guide downloadable feed schedules, visit us at www.TheGrowersGuide.co.uk

	Week 1	Week 2	Week 3	Week 4
Plagron cocos A	2ml per litre	2ml per litre	2.5ml per litre	2.5ml per litre
Plagron cocos B	2ml per litre	2ml per litre	2.5ml per litre	2.5ml per litre
Plagron Pure Enzym	-	1ml per litre	1ml per litre	1ml per litre
Dutchpro Take Root	1ml per litre	1ml per litre	1ml per litre	1ml per litre
Total E.C goal	1.2	1.4	1.4	1.6
Total pH goal	5.5-6.0	5.6-6.0	5.7-6.0	5.8-6.0

Plant Magic Evolution - Should be used every 5 days at lights off.

Plant Success Great White Mycorrhizae - Should be used every time your plant is repotted.

For any subsequent weeks in vegetation, repeat week 4 dosages. Please note that this is only a guide and your plants may need more or less nutrients depending on each individual plants needs.

VEGETATION FEEDING SCHEDULE

welcome to the revolution.

I have highlighted the correct week on both the coco coir and soil feeding schedules to avoid any confusion.

We will be mixing the nutrients up in batches of 10 litres as we have already gone through in the "Understanding water and nutrients" chapter.

The plants first feed in this stage should see you completely saturate all of the medium which the plant is now in.

Soil

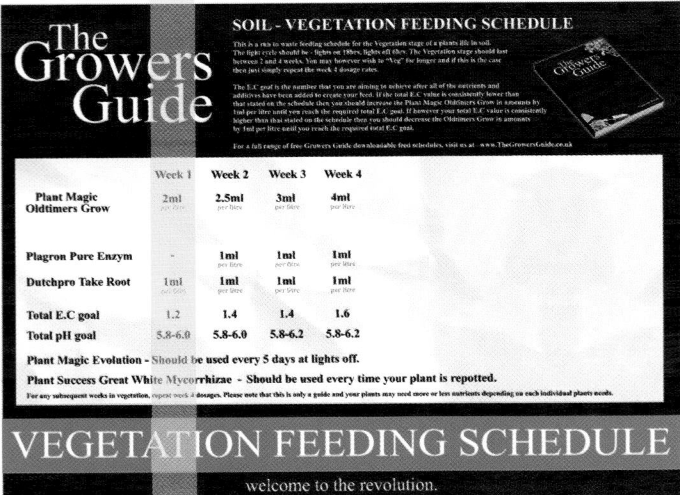

The Growers Guide

SOIL - VEGETATION FEEDING SCHEDULE

This is a run to waste feeding schedule for the Vegetation stage of a plants life in soil. The light cycle should be - lights on 18hrs, lights off 6hrs. The Vegetation stage should last between 2 and 4 weeks. You may however wish to "Veg" for longer and if this is the case then just simply repeat the week 4 dosage rates.

The E.C goal is the number that you are aiming to achieve after all of the nutrients and additives have been added to create your feed. If the total E.C value is consistently lower than that stated on the schedule then you should increase the Plant Magic Oldtimers Grow in amounts by 1ml per litre until you reach the required total E.C goal. If however your total E.C value is consistently higher than that stated on the schedule then you should decrease the Oldtimers Grow in amounts by 1ml per litre until you reach the required total E.C goal.

For a full range of free Growers Guide downloadable feed schedules, visit us at www.TheGrowersGuide.co.uk

	Week 1	Week 2	Week 3	Week 4
Plant Magic Oldtimers Grow	2ml per litre	2.5ml per litre	3ml per litre	4ml per litre
Plagron Pure Enzym	-	1ml per litre	1ml per litre	1ml per litre
Dutchpro Take Root	1ml per litre	1ml per litre	1ml per litre	1ml per litre
Total E.C goal	1.2	1.4	1.4	1.6
Total pH goal	5.8-6.0	5.8-6.0	5.8-6.2	5.8-6.2

Plant Magic Evolution - Should be used every 5 days at lights off.

Plant Success Great White Mycorrhizae - Should be used every time your plant is repotted.

For any subsequent weeks in vegetation, repeat week 4 dosages. Please note that this is only a guide and your plants may need more or less nutrients depending on each individual plants needs.

VEGETATION FEEDING SCHEDULE

welcome to the revolution.

The idea is that all the medium is saturated but no feed (or as little as possible) comes out of the bottom of the plant pot. This is a skill in itself and will take a few feeds to get right. Be sure to feel the weight of the plant, pot and medium before watering and then again after watering. This will give you a feel for how much weight difference there is between a completely dry plant pot and a fully saturated one. The difference as you will feel is considerable. Doing this each time, you will quickly learn how much feed/moisture is in the plant and whether you feel it needs to be fed (and roughly how much) or not. It is crucial to remember that every plant is different and will have different needs at different times, the trick is to get to know each plants individual needs. One of the most asked questions for growers starting out is....

How often should I be feeding my plants?

The answer is simple. Whenever they need it! The trick is to know when they need to be fed. Lifting the plant pot will give you a good indication. It is also important to water them in the right way. When watering a plant the feed should be poured in a circular motion around the main stem making sure that the medium around the plant is saturated evenly. This will ensure a good growth rate and shape around the whole of the plant.

As you can see from the start to the end of week 1 there really isn't that much visual difference. Don't worry, this is normal as the plants are settling into their new environment.

Start of week 1

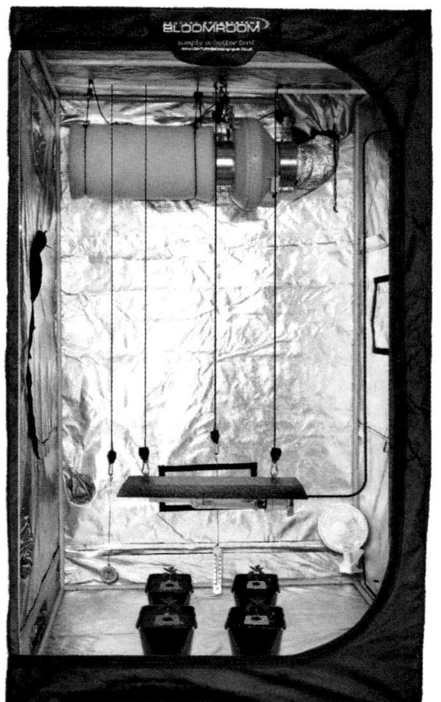

Coco Soil

End of week 1

Coco Soil

Vegetation/Grow

Week 2 - Entering into week 2 the plants will be settled and now used to their new environment. As a result of this, throughout the week you will start to see new lateral and horizontal growth. Under the new regime of energy-rich light and being fed a nutrient-rich feed you will also see a noticeable difference in their colour. They should become a fresh vibrant (almost glowing) healthy green.

This is around the time you will need to start your 3 day health checks on the plant.

Coco Coir

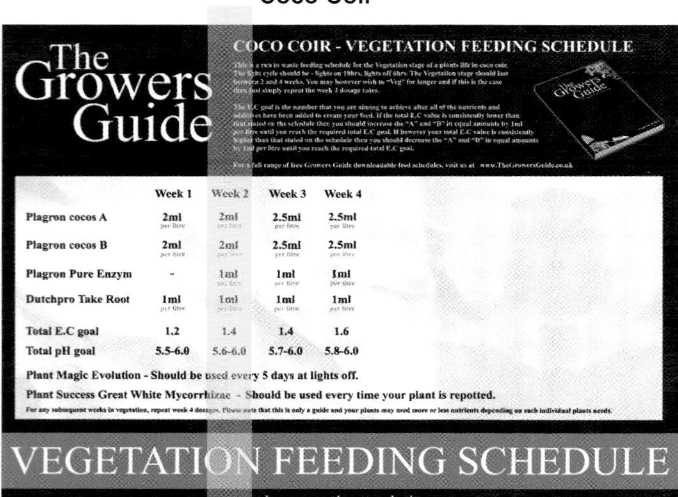

The Growers Guide

COCO COIR - VEGETATION FEEDING SCHEDULE

This is a run to waste feeding schedule for the Vegetation stage of a plants life in coco coir. The light cycle should be - lights on 18hrs, lights off 6hrs. The Vegetation stage should last between 2 and 4 weeks. You may however wish to "Veg" for longer and if this is the case then just simply repeat the week 4 dosage rates.

The E.C goal is the number that you are aiming to achieve after all of the nutrients and additives have been added to create your feed. If the total E.C value is consistently lower than that stated on the schedule then you should increase the "A" and "B" in equal amounts by 1ml per litre until you reach the required total E.C goal. If however your total E.C value is consistently higher than that stated on the schedule then you should decrease the "A" and "B" in equal amounts by 1ml per litre until you reach the required total E.C goal.

For a full range of free Growers Guide downloadable feed schedules, visit us at www.TheGrowersGuide.co.uk

	Week 1	Week 2	Week 3	Week 4
Plagron cocos A	2ml per litre	2ml per litre	2.5ml per litre	2.5ml per litre
Plagron cocos B	2ml per litre	2ml per litre	2.5ml per litre	2.5ml per litre
Plagron Pure Enzym	-	1ml per litre	1ml per litre	1ml per litre
Dutchpro Take Root	1ml per litre	1ml per litre	1ml per litre	1ml per litre
Total E.C goal	1.2	1.4	1.4	1.6
Total pH goal	5.5-6.0	5.6-6.0	5.7-6.0	5.8-6.0

Plant Magic Evolution - Should be used every 5 days at lights off.

Plant Success Great White Mycorrhizae - Should be used every time your plant is repotted.

For any subsequent weeks in vegetation, repeat week 4 dosages. Please note that this is only a guide and your plants may need more or less nutrients depending on each individual plants needs.

VEGETATION FEEDING SCHEDULE

welcome to the revolution.

Soil

The Growers Guide

SOIL - VEGETATION FEEDING SCHEDULE

This is a run to waste feeding schedule for the Vegetation stage of a plants life in soil. The light cycle should be - lights on 18hrs, lights off 6hrs. The Vegetation stage should last between 2 and 4 weeks. You may however wish to "Veg" for longer and if this is the case then just simply repeat the week 4 dosage rates.

The E.C goal is the number that you are aiming to achieve after all of the nutrients and additives have been added to create your feed. If the total E.C value is consistently lower than that stated on the schedule then you should increase the Plant Magic Oldtimers Grow in amounts by 1ml per litre until you reach the required total E.C goal. If however your total E.C value is consistently higher than that stated on the schedule then you should decrease the Oldtimers Grow in amounts by 1ml per litre until you reach the required total E.C goal.

For a full range of free Growers Guide downloadable feed schedules, visit us at www.TheGrowersGuide.co.uk

	Week 1	Week 2	Week 3	Week 4
Plant Magic Oldtimers Grow	2ml per litre	2.5ml per litre	3ml per litre	4ml per litre
Plagron Pure Enzym	-	1ml per litre	1ml per litre	1ml per litre
Dutchpro Take Root	1ml per litre	1ml per litre	1ml per litre	1ml per litre
Total E.C goal	1.2	1.4	1.4	1.6
Total pH goal	5.8-6.0	5.8-6.0	5.8-6.2	5.8-6.2

Plant Magic Evolution - Should be used every 5 days at lights off.

Plant Success Great White Mycorrhizae - Should be used every time your plant is repotted.

For any subsequent weeks in vegetation, repeat week 4 dosages. Please note that this is only a guide and your plants may need more or less nutrients depending on each individual plants needs.

VEGETATION FEEDING SCHEDULE

welcome to the revolution.

I have highlighted the correct week (week 2) on both the coco coir and soil feeding schedules to avoid any confusion.

Like week 1 and as we will be doing for the entirety of the grow, we will be mixing the nutrients up in batches of 10 litres as we have already gone through in the "Understanding water and nutrients" chapter. If you have any feed left over from week 1's ratios, this will need to be discarded and a fresh batch containing the week 2 ratios will need to be mixed up ready for their next feed.

It is easy at this stage to start to get carried away with the feeding/watering of your plants as you can start to see growth almost on a

day-to-day level. The medium that the plants are in should not be continuously fully saturated. This will lead to overwatering/feeding and will have a double, negative effect on your plant's growth, the first effect being on the roots. If overwatered they can become sodden and easily susceptible to rot and disease. The second is that the roots will not work as hard as they should or could under the right conditions.

Ideally coco should be 70% wet to 30% dry. What this means is that the coco should be left until 70% of it is dry and then is re-hydrated with feed/nutrient mix so that it is 100% saturated. Complete saturation is the point at which the medium cannot hold anymore liquid and run off will occur.

Ideally soil should have the ratio of 60% wet to 40% dry. This is different to the coco as the soil is less absorbent but already contains a certain amount of nutrient elements which the roots can extract at a drier ratio.

It's always a good thing to remember that what we are trying to do is to fool the plants into thinking that they are in the best natural home environment for them. Plants have evolved over millions of years to feed and take up liquid primarily when it rains. Thus they will naturally benefit more when there are drier and wetter spells.

Start of week 2

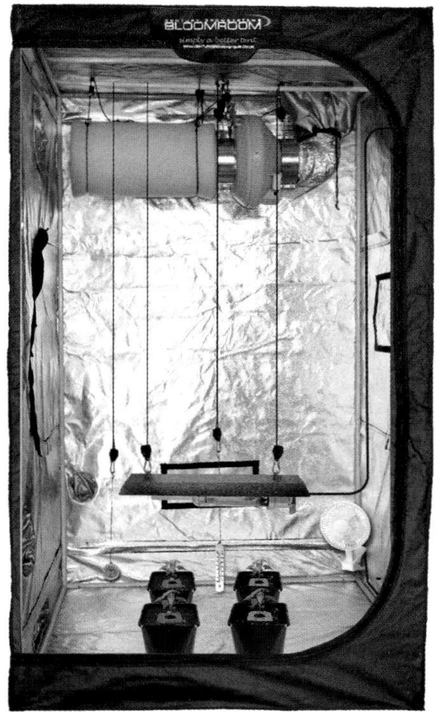

Coco Soil

End of week 2

Coco Soil

Vegetation/Grow

Week 3 - This is where the growth should be explosive throughout the week. You should expect to see your plants double in height and mass. Make sure you are carrying out your 3 day plant check list; checking for infection, disease and insects. As the plants are growing so rapidly in a humid environment they will become very attractive to hungry pests. At this stage you may also need to adjust the ventilation ports on your tent accordingly to counteract the plant's mass growing in the tent. As the plant takes up more mass inside the tent there will be less space and this may have an effect on the temperature and the humidity.

Coco Coir

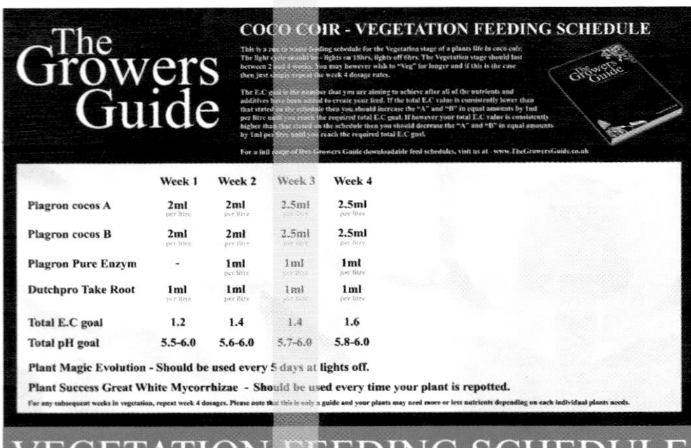

The Growers Guide

COCO COIR - VEGETATION FEEDING SCHEDULE

This is a run to waste feeding schedule for the Vegetation stage of a plants life in coco coir. The light cycle should be - lights on 18hrs, lights off 6hrs. The Vegetation stage should last between 2 and 4 weeks. You may however wish to "Veg" for longer and if this is the case then just simply repeat the week 4 dosage rates.

The E.C goal is the number that you are aiming to achieve after all of the nutrients and additives have been added to create your feed. If the total E.C value is consistently lower than that stated on the schedule then you should increase the "A" and "B" in equal amounts by 1ml per litre until you reach the required total E.C goal. If however your total E.C value is consistently higher than that stated on the schedule then you should decrease the "A" and "B" in equal amounts by 1ml per litre until you reach the required total E.C goal.

For a full range of free Growers Guide downloadable feed schedules, visit us at - www.TheGrowersGuide.co.uk

	Week 1	Week 2	Week 3	Week 4
Plagron cocos A	2ml per litre	2ml per litre	2.5ml per litre	2.5ml per litre
Plagron cocos B	2ml per litre	2ml per litre	2.5ml per litre	2.5ml per litre
Plagron Pure Enzym	-	1ml per litre	1ml per litre	1ml per litre
Dutchpro Take Root	1ml per litre	1ml per litre	1ml per litre	1ml per litre
Total E.C goal	1.2	1.4	1.4	1.6
Total pH goal	5.5-6.0	5.6-6.0	5.7-6.0	5.8-6.0

Plant Magic Evolution - Should be used every 5 days at lights off.

Plant Success Great White Mycorrhizae - Should be used every time your plant is repotted.

For any subsequent weeks in vegetation, repeat week 4 dosages. Please note that this is only a guide and your plants may need more or less nutrients depending on each individual plants needs.

VEGETATION FEEDING SCHEDULE

welcome to the revolution.

Soil

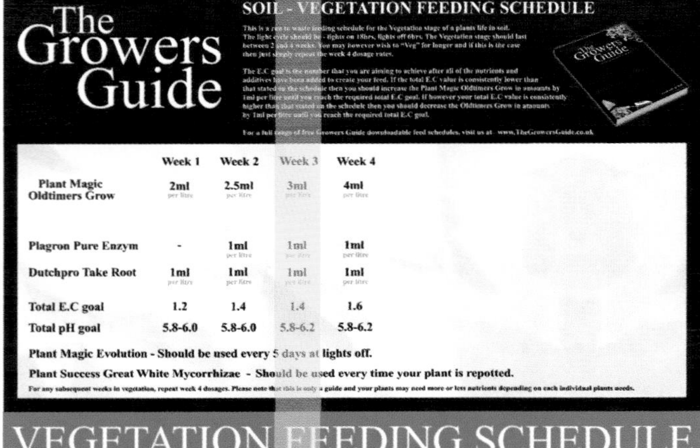

The Growers Guide

SOIL - VEGETATION FEEDING SCHEDULE

This is a run to waste feeding schedule for the Vegetation stage of a plants life in soil. The light cycle should be - lights on 18hrs, lights off 6hrs. The Vegetation stage should last between 2 and 4 weeks. You may however wish to "Veg" for longer and if this is the case then just simply repeat the week 4 dosage rates.

The E.C goal is the number that you are aiming to achieve after all of the nutrients and additives have been added to create your feed. If the total E.C value is consistently lower than that stated on the schedule then you should increase the Plant Magic Oldtimers Grow in amounts by 1ml per litre until you reach the required total E.C goal. If however your total E.C value is consistently higher than that stated on the schedule then you should decrease the Oldtimers Grow in amounts by 1ml per litre until you reach the required total E.C goal.

For a full range of free Growers Guide downloadable feed schedules, visit us at - www.TheGrowersGuide.co.uk

	Week 1	Week 2	Week 3	Week 4
Plant Magic Oldtimers Grow	2ml per litre	2.5ml per litre	3ml per litre	4ml per litre
Plagron Pure Enzym	-	1ml per litre	1ml per litre	1ml per litre
Dutchpro Take Root	1ml per litre	1ml per litre	1ml per litre	1ml per litre
Total E.C goal	1.2	1.4	1.4	1.6
Total pH goal	5.8-6.0	5.8-6.0	5.8-6.2	5.8-6.2

Plant Magic Evolution - Should be used every 5 days at lights off.

Plant Success Great White Mycorrhizae - Should be used every time your plant is repotted.

For any subsequent weeks in vegetation, repeat week 4 dosages. Please note that this is only a guide and your plants may need more or less nutrients depending on each individual plants needs.

VEGETATION FEEDING SCHEDULE

welcome to the revolution.

I have highlighted the correct week on both the coco coir and soil feeding schedules.If you have any feed left over from week 2's ratios, this will need to be discarded and a fresh batch containing the week 3 ratios will need to be mixed up ready for their next feed.

Hopefully by this stage you are starting to get a feel for how often your plants need feeding. As your plants go through week 3's rapid growth rate the amount of feeding times should rise rapidly as well.

Remember to not overfeed. It is important for you to keep to the coco and soil, wet to dry ratios as closely as possible. This will ensure that the plants as a whole are working as hard as they can to grow as fast as they can. The growth on the plants shown below right (end of week 3) has been so great and so fast that I have chosen to re-pot them into the next size pot needed. We have gone through the re-potting procedure earlier in this chapter, just remember to be as careful and as delicate as possible. As soon as the plants have been repotted they will all then need to be fed in order to wet/saturate the new medium within the new larger pot. This will encourage the continued rapid growth of the plant, its root system and reduce any stress which the plant might have encountered while re-potting.

I have noticed that one of the leaves close to the base of the plant has started to turn yellow, why is this?

As the plants increase in height and mass they will inevitably cut light out from reaching the lower extremities. As the leaf is unable to maintain the level of photosynthesis needed, it will slowly start to die. The plant will become aware of this and stop sending the leaf reserve energy from its store, as the leaf is not producing as much energy as some of the top leaves which are directly under the light source. In order to stop the plant suffering any stress these leaves should be removed.

Start of week 3

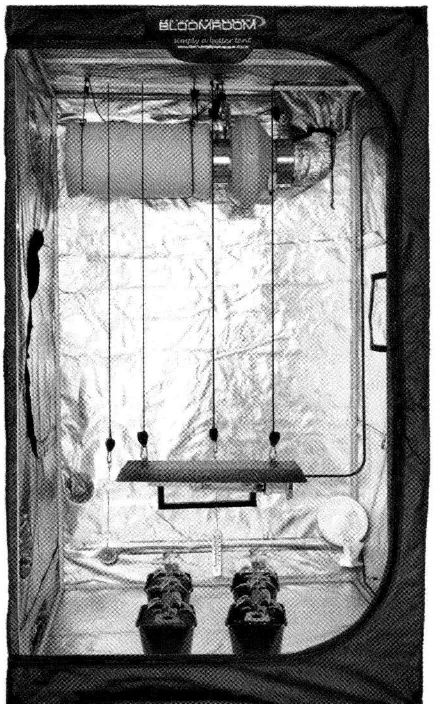

Coco Soil

End of week 3

Coco Soil

Vegetation/Grow

Week 4 - is the last week of the Vegetation/Grow stage of the plant's life. In this week the plants should triple, if not quadruple in size. As we have increased the size of the plant pot and thus the medium the plant sits in it will exponentially increase the amount of feed/nutrients available to the plant. The plants should also show signs of opening out at the top of the canopy. This is due to the internode spacing becoming closer and closer and as the plant grows larger each branch actively seeks out the best space in the growing environment in order to get the most sunlight or in this case artificial light.

Coco Coir

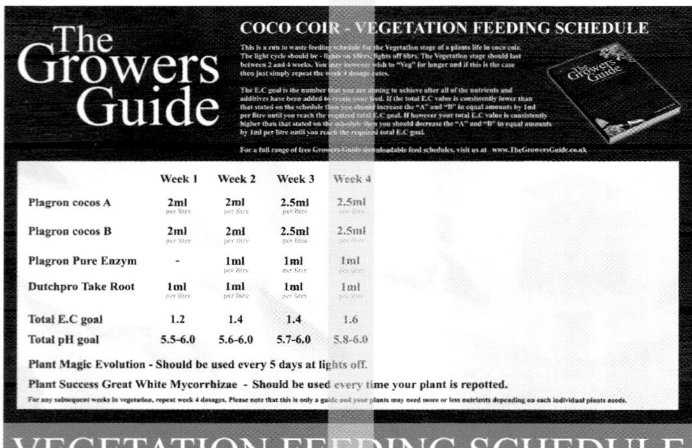

The Growers Guide

COCO COIR - VEGETATION FEEDING SCHEDULE

This is a run to waste feeding schedule for the Vegetation stage of a plants life in coco coir. The light cycle should be - lights on 18hrs, lights off 6hrs. The Vegetation stage should last between 2 and 4 weeks. You may however wish to "Veg" for longer and if this is the case then just simply repeat the week 4 dosage rates.

The E.C goal is the number that you are aiming to achieve after all of the nutrients and additives have been added to create your feed. If the total E.C value is consistently lower than that stated on the schedule then you should increase the "A" and "B" in equal amounts by 1ml per litre until you reach the required total E.C goal. If however your total E.C value is consistently higher than that stated on the schedule then you should decrease the "A" and "B" in equal amounts by 1ml per litre until you reach the required total E.C goal.

For a full range of free Growers Guide downloadable feed schedules, visit us at www.TheGrowersGuide.co.uk

	Week 1	Week 2	Week 3	Week 4
Plagron cocos A	2ml per litre	2ml per litre	2.5ml per litre	2.5ml per litre
Plagron cocos B	2ml per litre	2ml per litre	2.5ml per litre	2.5ml per litre
Plagron Pure Enzym	-	1ml per litre	1ml per litre	1ml per litre
Dutchpro Take Root	1ml per litre	1ml per litre	1ml per litre	1ml per litre
Total E.C goal	1.2	1.4	1.4	1.6
Total pH goal	5.5-6.0	5.6-6.0	5.7-6.0	5.8-6.0

Plant Magic Evolution - Should be used every 5 days at lights off.

Plant Success Great White Mycorrhizae - Should be used every time your plant is repotted.

For any subsequent weeks in vegetation, repeat week 4 dosages. Please note that this is only a guide and your plants may need more or less nutrients depending on each individual plants needs.

VEGETATION FEEDING SCHEDULE

welcome to the revolution.

I have highlighted the correct week on both the coco coir and soil feeding schedules. As always If you have any feed left over from week 3's ratios, this will need to be discarded and a fresh batch containing the week 4 ratios will need to be mixed up ready to use.

When the plants are growing this fast it is easy to get carried away and increase the E.C of the feed or the amount of times they are being fed. Try to keep as close to the coco and soil wet to dry ratios as possible.

If the plant starts to lighten at the top, this is a sign that it can in fact handle a higher E.C ratio. Remember the feeding schedule is only a guide. A good guide........don't get

Soil

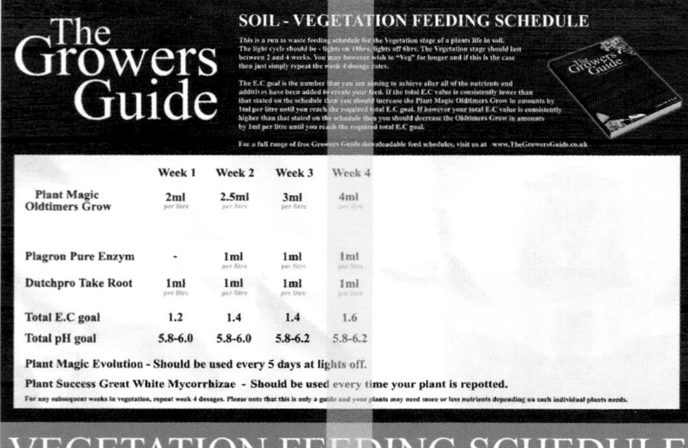

The Growers Guide

SOIL - VEGETATION FEEDING SCHEDULE

This is a run to waste feeding schedule for the Vegetation stage of a plants life in soil. The light cycle should be - lights on 18hrs, lights off 6hrs. The Vegetation stage should last between 2 and 4 weeks. You may however wish to "Veg" for longer and if this is the case then just simply repeat the week 4 dosage rates.

The E.C goal is the number that you are aiming to achieve after all of the nutrients and additives have been added to create your feed. If the total E.C value is consistently lower than that stated on the schedule then you should increase the Plant Magic Oldtimers Grow in amounts by 1ml per litre until you reach the required total E.C goal. If however your total E.C value is consistently higher than that stated on the schedule then you should decrease the Oldtimers Grow in amounts by 1ml per litre until you reach the required total E.C goal.

For a full range of free Growers Guide downloadable feed schedules, visit us at www.TheGrowersGuide.co.uk

	Week 1	Week 2	Week 3	Week 4
Plant Magic Oldtimers Grow	2ml per litre	2.5ml per litre	3ml per litre	4ml per litre
Plagron Pure Enzym	-	1ml per litre	1ml per litre	1ml per litre
Dutchpro Take Root	1ml per litre	1ml per litre	1ml per litre	1ml per litre
Total E.C goal	1.2	1.4	1.4	1.6
Total pH goal	5.8-6.0	5.8-6.0	5.8-6.2	5.8-6.2

Plant Magic Evolution - Should be used every 5 days at lights off.

Plant Success Great White Mycorrhizae - Should be used every time your plant is repotted.

For any subsequent weeks in vegetation, repeat week 4 dosages. Please note that this is only a guide and your plants may need more or less nutrients depending on each individual plants needs.

VEGETATION FEEDING SCHEDULE

welcome to the revolution.

me wrong, but a guide nevertheless. As I've said before and I will say again and again, all plants are different and will sometimes require more (or less) than the plants around it.

Plant lightening at the top.

When increasing the E.C do so slowly at each feed. The current E.C in week 4 should be 1.6 in order to not over-fertilize the plant and send it into nute lock or over toxicity. I would increase the E.C by 0.1 at a time. If after feeding, the leaves of the plant start to curl then this is the first sign of over fertilization, which means your E.C is too high. If this does happen then the best thing to do is to feed the affected plant just with water. This will gently flush the plant of toxicity and reduce the E.C of the feed/nutrients still left within the medium. As the top of the plant spreads out, naturally the lower part of the plant will receive less light. As it does this (like in week 3) there might be yellowing of some of the lower/bottom leaves. These yellowing leaves need to be removed.

That's the end of week 4 "Veg". Your plants should be now ready to move on to the Flowering stage of their lives. If you want to keep your plants in the Vegetative stage for longer than the 4 weeks that we have looked at here then just repeat week four feed/nutrient dosage rates.

Start of week 4

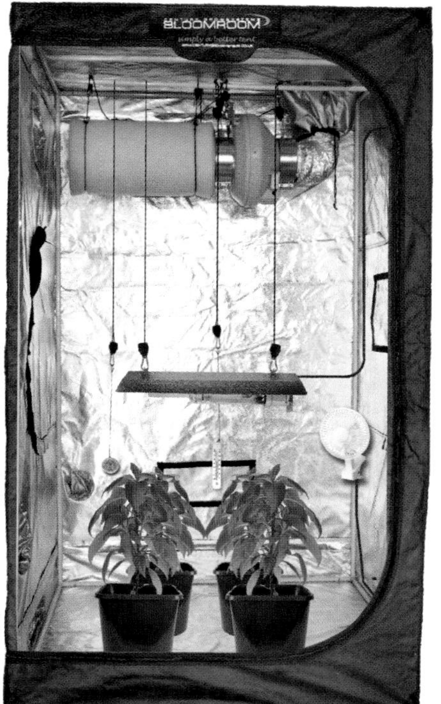

Coco Soil

End of week 4

Coco Soil

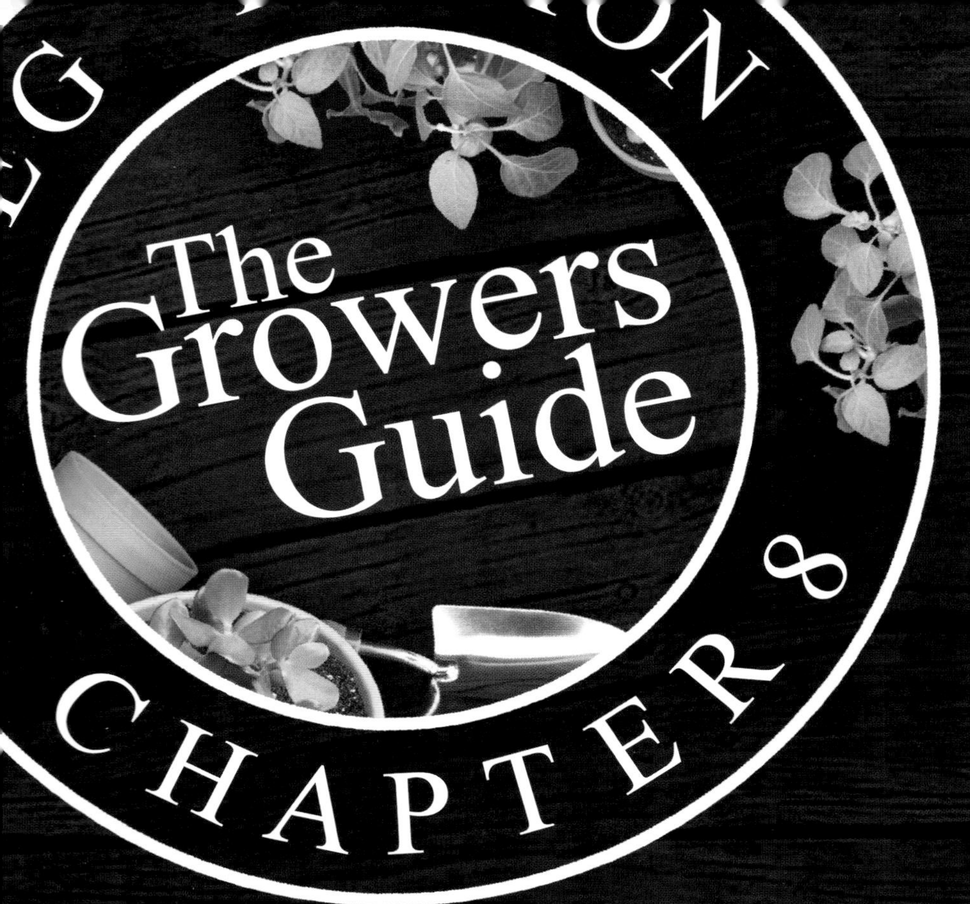

Flowering

In this chapter we will look at what the plants need when they are put into the Flowering phase by the changing of the light cycle. We will cover how to prepare your growing environment for the Flowering period, including using light timers and how to set them. I will show you how to care for and maintain your fruiting plants including what to feed them and when to feed them and also what you should expect to see on a week-to-week basis.

Flower/Flower cycle – light cycle – lights on 12hrs, off 12hrs – time period 8+ weeks.

Whilst not possible for all plants, the plants which we are focusing on can be put into the Flowering stage by the changing of their light cycle. Light cycle meaning – the length of time that the lights in your grow room are on and off over a 24 hour period.

The Flower light cycle is 12 hours lights on, 12 hours lights off. If you are using a dual spectrum lamp you will need to adjust your light cycle to that above, If you have, however, been using a vegetate only lamp such as a metal halide or vegetate CFL you will now need to replace this with a dual spectrum or a specific flowering lamp.

The equipment you need for the Flowering stage is very minimal as we will be using most of the same equipment which was used in the Vegetative stage.

You will need the following equipment for the Flowering stage;

Equipment

- **Dual spectrum lamp/specific flowering lamp**
- **Larger plant pots**
- **Intake fan kit**
- **Dehumidifier**
- **Flowering feed/nutrient range**

Dual spectrum lamp/specific flowering lamp – Now that your plants are ready to move into the Flower stage you may need to change the lamp. If you have used a dual spectrum bulb for the Vegetative stage of the plant's life then you don't have to change the lamp just the light cycle.

When the plant is moved into the Flowering stage of its life it is best to give it the most effective flowering part of the light spectrum.

Dual spectrum lamps - are a hybrid of HPS flowering bulbs. They give off mainly an orange and red spectrum but also give off part of the blue spectrum. As they do this they can be used for both the Vegetative and Flowering stages of the plant's lifecycle. One bulb does it all.

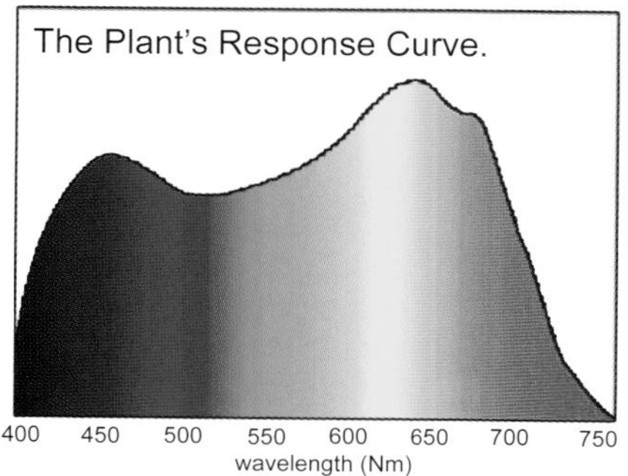

As you can see a dual spectrum lamp hits both the Veg peak and the Flower peak making it the best all round lamp on the market to date.

600W Dual spectrum lamp's output spectrum.

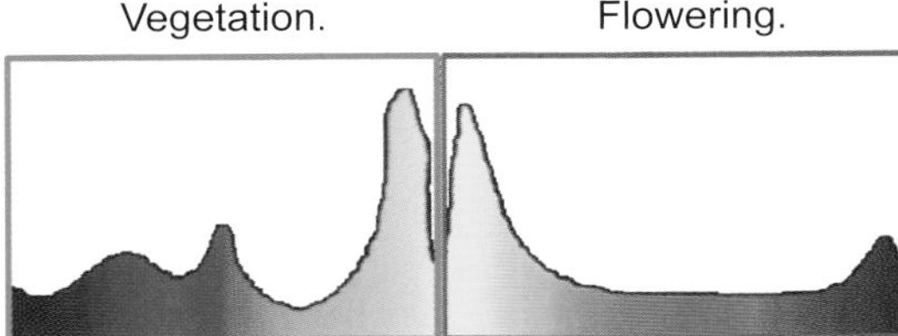

Specific flowering lamps – Are tailored especially for the Flowering stage of the plant's life and should only be used in the Flowering stage. These lamps are great to use but can overstretch the height of plants while in use. My recommendation to you would be to use a dual spectrum lamp.

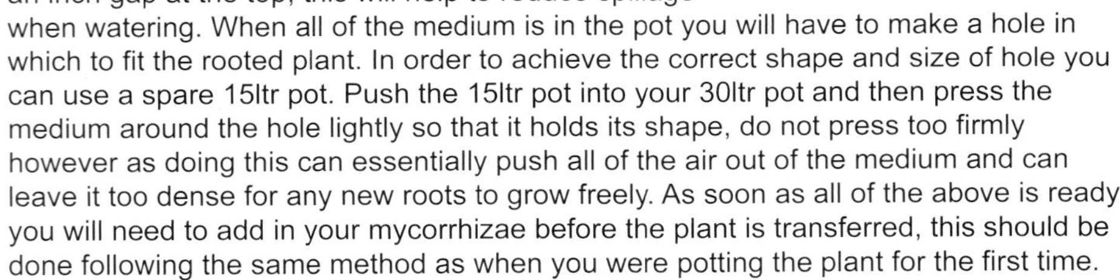

Larger plant pots - The next sized plant pot that you will need is a 30ltr round pot. Pots come in all shapes and colours however you will find that plant pots used in an indoor growing environment are normally black, this is because a black pot is less translucent than any other colour pot and so keeps the plant's root system in the darkest environment possible which is what we want. When re-potting into a larger pot the same method should be used as that which you followed when you potted your rock wool cube into your first plant pot. When filling the pots up with fresh medium it is best to leave between a centimetre and an inch gap at the top, this will help to reduce spillage when watering. When all of the medium is in the pot you will have to make a hole in which to fit the rooted plant. In order to achieve the correct shape and size of hole you can use a spare 15ltr pot. Push the 15ltr pot into your 30ltr pot and then press the medium around the hole lightly so that it holds its shape, do not press too firmly however as doing this can essentially push all of the air out of the medium and can leave it too dense for any new roots to grow freely. As soon as all of the above is ready you will need to add in your mycorrhizae before the plant is transferred, this should be done following the same method as when you were potting the plant for the first time.

Intake fan kit - As your plants get larger the space in the tent will be reduced at an alarming rate. As this happens you will find that the over all internal temperature of the tent will increase. The first method of combating this is to add an intake fan. For this we will be using a 4" RVK fan. It is the same brand of fan which is being used in the ventilation system, just a smaller spigot size and it is lower in power, thus it will not move as much air as the outtake fan. This is an important point as it is crucial to keep

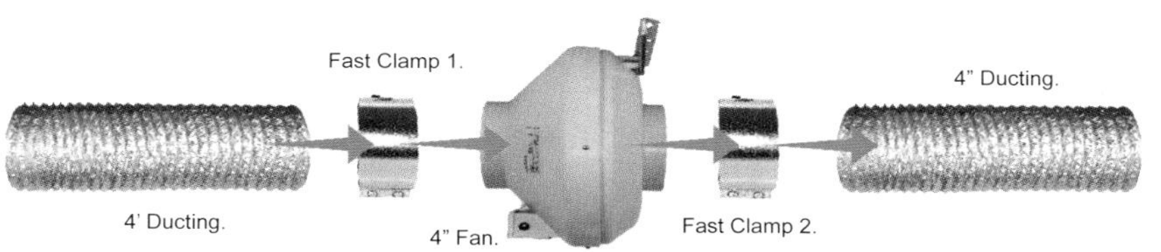

the tent under a negative pressure. The intake system is put together as shown above. It will take some adjusting to get the correct temperature inside the tent when setting this up and of course it will need re-adjusting as the plants grow and the space inside the tent gets smaller and smaller. The rule of thumb is, the longer the ducting to the fan and from the fan into the tent, then the further the air has to travel and therefore less of it is pulled into the tent. In contrast, the shorter the ducting from the fresh air source to the fan and from the fan into the growing tent, then the less distance the air has to travel and the cooler the tent will be. In a nut shell, the shorter the ducting the cooler the tent; the longer the ducting, then the warmer the tent will be.

The fresh air intake should be brought into the tent at the lowest point furthest away from the outtake filter. This will help with air movement throughout the entire grow room and will also help keep the roots cool.

The intake fan should only be switched on to manage the temperature while the lights are on and so it can be plugged into the last socket left on the contactor.

Air out should ideally be taken out to an open environment (outside).

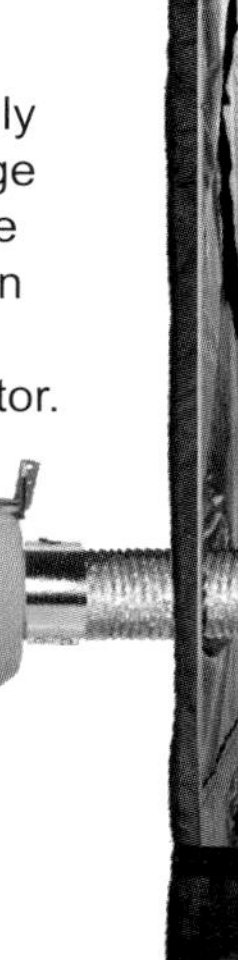

Clean fresh air should ideally be brought in from an open environment (outdoors).

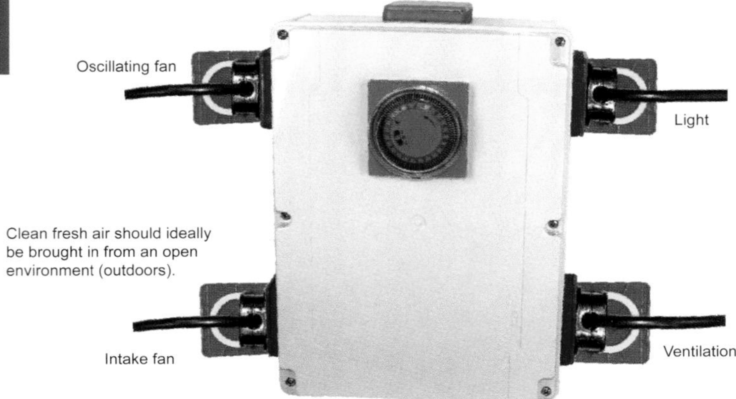

Dehumidifier - A dehumidifier will take the water out of the air, these can be expensive but you do get what you pay for. Ideally you should get a dehumidifier with a digital setting, this will ensure that the humidity stays at a constant. This will need to be plugged into a socket without a timer as it should be on 24hrs a day.

Feed/nutrient range and mycorrhizae - We have gone through the feed range and how you prepare it ready for use in the Flowering/Bloom stage in Chapter 2 "Understanding water and nutrients" To recap for the Flowering stage however you will need the following

- **Plagron cocos a**
- **Plagron cocos b**
- **Plagron pure enzym**
- **Dutch pro Explode**
- **Bio Green PK 13/14**
- **Great White Mycorrhizae**

Plant Success Great White.

Plagron cocos a.

Plagron cocos b.

Plagron pure enzym.

Dutch pro Explode.

Bio Green PK 13/14.

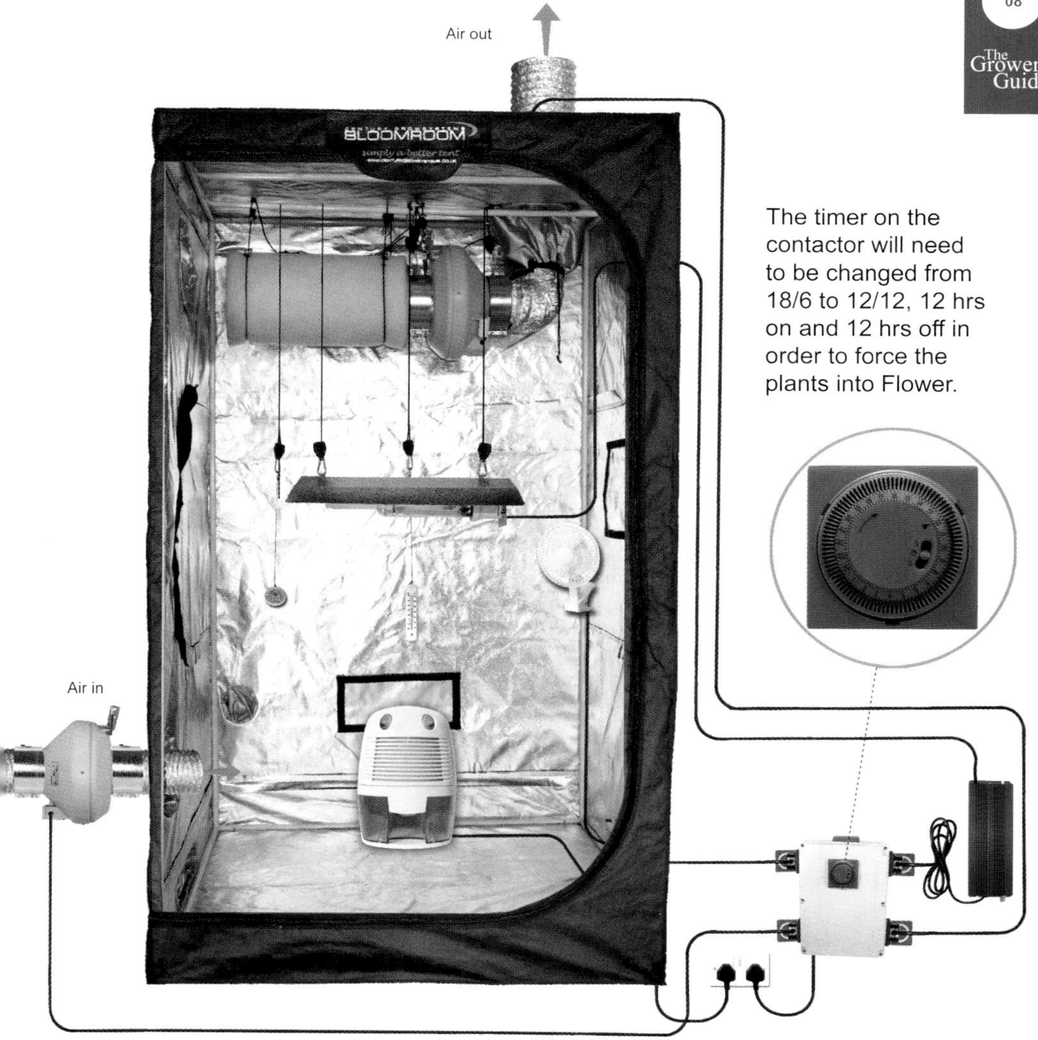

Air out

BLOOMROOM

simply a better tent

Air in

The timer on the contactor will need to be changed from 18/6 to 12/12, 12 hrs on and 12 hrs off in order to force the plants into Flower.

Depending on your grow room's environment you may find it hard to decrease the humidity levels to below 40%; the easy option is to use a dehumidifier. Although they are expensive, if you are struggling with bringing humidity levels down then it's a quick easy fix. As I've mentioned before they can be bought with a digital setting, which is great as it will give you a constant humidity level. The humidifier needs to be at an easy to reach location at the bottom of the grow room. The water tray (which collects the moisture out of the air) will need to be emptied as and when it fills up. Above is an image of how all the new additions need to be set up. As you can see the dehumidifier is plugged straight into a socket without a timer as it will be on 24hrs a day. The intake fan however is plugged into the contactor as it will be on the same cycle as the lights and the outtake fan/filter kit.

The temperature of the grow room in the Flower cycle should be a few degrees higher than in the Vegetative stage.

The temperature when the lights are on should ideally be between 26°C and 29°C. Any hotter than 31°C and it's too hot (at 32°C and above the plant will go into shock and deteriorate very quickly). Any lower than 19°C and it's way too cold (at 15°C and below the plant will also go into shock and deteriorate very quickly).

In an ideal world the temperature difference from lights on and lights off should be no greater than 10 degrees.

The temperature at the point where the level is being taken can primarily be raised or lowered by the height of the light. The closer the light, the hotter it will be and thus the higher/further away the light source is, the cooler it will become. This will take a little bit of adjusting to get right. Ideally you want the light closer to the plant than further away. The ideal distance between the plants and the light should be 1 foot – (12 inches).

This distance ensures that the plant gets the maximum amount of lumen and par available without the top of the plant shadowing the overall mass. To get the light this close to the plant without the aid of an air cooled shade can be a challenge. This is where the position of the oscillating fan can come into play.

As you can see in the image on the left, placing the oscillating fan in the right place at the right distance can dramatically cool the canopy of the main plant. What the oscillating fan does is to take the heat which the bulb is directly producing away from the main canopy and spread it around the grow tent. In the example I have shown on the last page I have also positioned the outtake filter at the opposing side of the oscillating fan so that when it is switched on it will take the warmer air being blown away from the bulb out of the grow tent first and thus cool the whole grow tent at a steady rate. This will also make sure that there is a good air exchange, which is essential for the plant's health.

How long should you Flower for?

The answer to that one is simple, no less than 8 weeks! The Flowering stage is separated into 2 stages the reproduction stage (the first 4 weeks) and the fruit stage (the second 4 weeks) totalling 8 weeks. Some plants take longer to flower so as a rule I always say that the Flowering stage is 8 weeks plus. Any additional weeks after the standard 8 weeks schedule should be a replicate of week 8. Thus the environment and the nutrients should be should be the same as they were in week 8.

While you're in the Flowering/Bloom stage of the plants life it is good practice to follow a three day check list. The list is as follows;

- Check the top and the under side of leaves for insects and insect damage.
- "Dead leaf" each plant. ie, remove any dead or dying leaves.
- Check plant for toxicity from overnutrition. This is normally indicated by the curling inwards of leaves. It can also discolour the very end of each leaf blade.
- Check for signs of undernutrition. This will be shown in either lightening of the plant (normally at the top first) or droopy leaves.
- Turn each plant 90° to get the most out of the light.
- Make sure that your growing environment and growing equipment is clean.
- Check that the temperature and the humidity is right.
- Make sure that the light is the optimal distance away from the plants.

We will now go through the next 8 weeks in Flower/Bloom, week-by-week so you know what to expect and when.

Flower/Bloom

Week 1 - As this is the first week in the flowering light cycle the plants have a few new things to get used to. Possibly a new type of light, a different light cycle and a new range of nutrients. Taking all of the above into consideration it will take a while for the plants to settle in and overcome the stresses of these new changes.

As soon as the plants are put into the Flowering/Bloom stage, "week 1" of the new feeding schedule begins. I have highlighted the correct week on both the coco coir and soil feeding schedules to avoid any confusion.

Coco Coir

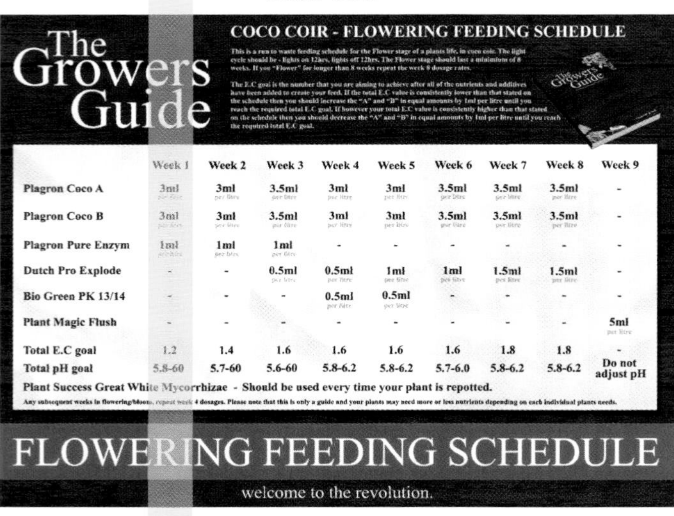

COCO COIR - FLOWERING FEEDING SCHEDULE

This is a run to waste feeding schedule for the Flower stage of a plants life, in coco coir. The light cycle should be - lights on 12hrs, lights off 12hrs. The Flower stage should last a minimum of 8 weeks. If you "Flower" for longer than 8 weeks repeat the week 8 dosage rates.

The E.C goal is the number that you are aiming to achieve after all of the nutrients and additives have been added to create your feed. If the total E.C value is consistently lower than that stated on the schedule then you should increase the "A" and "B" in equal amounts by 1ml per litre until you reach the required total E.C goal. If however your total E.C value is consistently higher than that stated on the schedule then you should decrease the "A" and "B" in equal amounts by 1ml per litre until you reach the required total E.C goal.

	Week 1	Week 2	Week 3	Week 4	Week 5	Week 6	Week 7	Week 8	Week 9
Plagron Coco A	3ml per litre	3ml per litre	3.5ml per litre	3ml per litre	3ml per litre	3.5ml per litre	3.5ml per litre	3.5ml per litre	-
Plagron Coco B	3ml per litre	3ml per litre	3.5ml per litre	3ml per litre	3ml per litre	3.5ml per litre	3.5ml per litre	3.5ml per litre	-
Plagron Pure Enzym	1ml per litre	1ml per litre	1ml per litre	-	-	-	-	-	-
Dutch Pro Explode	-	-	0.5ml per litre	0.5ml per litre	1ml per litre	1ml per litre	1.5ml per litre	1.5ml per litre	-
Bio Green PK 13/14	-	-	-	0.5ml per litre	0.5ml per litre	-	-	-	-
Plant Magic Flush	-	-	-	-	-	-	-	-	5ml per litre
Total E.C goal	1.2	1.4	1.6	1.6	1.6	1.6	1.8	1.8	-
Total pH goal	5.8-60	5.7-60	5.6-60	5.8-6.2	5.8-6.2	5.7-6.0	5.8-6.2	5.8-6.2	Do not adjust pH

Plant Success Great White Mycorrhizae - Should be used every time your plant is repotted.

Any subsequent weeks in flowering/bloom, repeat week 4 dosages. Please note that this is only a guide and your plants may need more or less nutrients depending on each individual plants needs.

FLOWERING FEEDING SCHEDULE

welcome to the revolution.

Soil

The Growers Guide

SOIL - FLOWERING FEEDING SCHEDULE

This is a run to waste feeding schedule for the Flower stage of a plants life, in soil. The light cycle should be - lights on 12hrs, lights off 12hrs. The Flower stage should last a minimum of 8 weeks. If you "Flower" for longer than 8 weeks repeat the week 8 dosage rates.

The E.C goal is the number that you are aiming to achieve after all of the nutrients and additives have been added to create your feed. If the total E.C value is consistently lower than that stated on the schedule then you should increase the Oldtimer Bloom in amounts by 1ml per litre until you reach the required total E.C goal. If however your total E.C value is consistently higher than that stated on the schedule then you should decrease the Oldtimers Bloom in equal amounts by 1ml per litre until you reach the required total E.C goal.

	Week 1	Week 2	Week 3	Week 4	Week 5	Week 6	Week 7	Week 8	Week 9
Plant Magic Oldtimers Bloom	3ml per litre	3.5ml per litre	3.5ml per litre	4ml per litre	3.5ml per litre	3.5ml per litre	3ml per litre	2ml per litre	-
Plagron Pure Enzym	1ml per litre	1ml per litre	1ml per litre	-	-	-	-	-	-
Dutch Pro Explode	-	-	0.5ml per litre	0.5ml per litre	1ml per litre	1ml per litre	1.5ml per litre	1.5ml per litre	-
Bio Green PK 13/14	-	-	-	0.5ml per litre	0.5ml per litre	-	-	-	-
Plant Magic Flush	-	-	-	-	-	-	-	-	5ml per litre
Total E.C goal	1.4	1.4	1.4	1.6	1.8	1.8	1.6	1.6	-
Total pH goal	5.8-6.2	5.7-6.2	5.6-6.0	5.5-6.0	5.8-6.2	5.7-6.2	5.6-6.2	5.5-6.0	Do not adjust pH

Plant Success Great White Mycorrhizae - Should be used every time your plant is repotted.

Any subsequent weeks in flowering/bloom, repeat week 4 dosages. Please note that this is only a guide and your plants may need more or less nutrients depending on each individual plants needs.

FLOWERING FEEDING SCHEDULE

welcome to the revolution.

Once again we shall be mixing the nutrients up in batches of 10 litre quantities as we have been doing in the Vegetative stage.

The plants first feed in the Flowering/Bloom stage should completely saturate the entirety of the medium in which the plant is now in, as it should do with each and every feed moving forward.

When feeding/watering your plants remember to water the whole surface area of the top of the medium in a circular motion around the main stem of the plant as this will help saturate all of the roots below evenly. The amount of people that water their plants in the wrong way is unbelievable, so often I have seen people watering their plants in the same corner or side of the pot each time, which I'm sure is a mix of laziness and/or ignorance. The moral of the story is; don't be lazy as what you put in you will get out, you want to ensure you are watering as many of the roots as possible.

In the first week of Flower the plants will continue to grow in all directions they have done in week 4 of the Vegetation stage. By the end of week 1 of Flower they will start to fight for the light. This is shown by the plants leaning towards the light, you may notice that a few of the branches will start to stretch above the majority of the canopy trying to get more light than the others. This early stage of the plant stretching is natural and is nothing to worry about (as long as it is not putting the rest of the plants into shadow). If this happens you need to gently bend the stretching branch down so it is level with the rest of the canopy.

Start of week 1

Coco Soil

End of week 1

Coco Soil

Flower/Bloom

Week 2 - As we move into week 2 of Flower, the plants will continue to grow in all directions. By this stage they should have settled into the new light cycle and adjusted to any environmental changes that you may have had to implement. It is vital throughout the Flowering stage that you religiously carry out the 3 day checks on your plants. I have highlighted the correct week on both the coco coir and soil feeding schedules to avoid any confusion.

Coco Coir

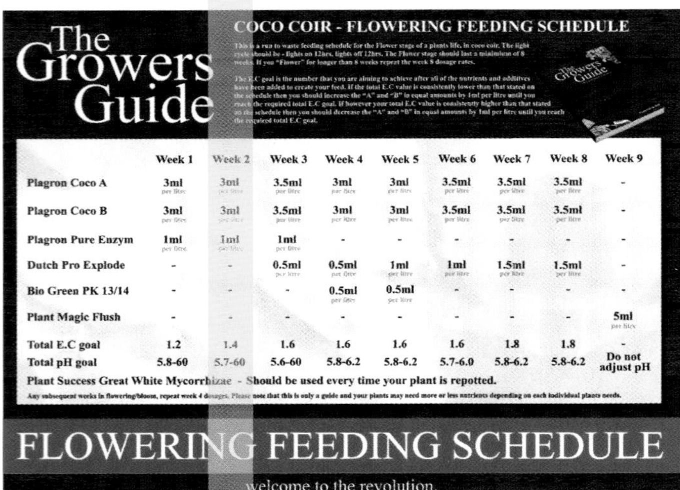

The Growers Guide

COCO COIR - FLOWERING FEEDING SCHEDULE

This is a run to waste feeding schedule for the Flower stage of a plants life, in coco coir. The light cycle should be - lights on 12hrs, lights off 12hrs. The Flower stage should last a minimum of 8 weeks. If you "Flower" for longer than 8 weeks repeat the week 8 dosage rates.

The E.C goal is the number that you are aiming to achieve after all of the nutrients and additives have been added to create your feed. If the total E.C value is consistently lower than that stated on the schedule then you should increase the "A" and "B" in equal amounts by 1ml per litre until you reach the required total E.C goal. If however your total E.C value is consistently higher than that stated on the schedule then you should decrease the "A" and "B" in equal amounts by 1ml per litre until you reach the required total E.C goal.

	Week 1	Week 2	Week 3	Week 4	Week 5	Week 6	Week 7	Week 8	Week 9
Plagron Coco A	3ml per litre	3ml per litre	3.5ml per litre	3ml per litre	3ml per litre	3.5ml per litre	3.5ml per litre	3.5ml per litre	-
Plagron Coco B	3ml per litre	3ml per litre	3.5ml per litre	3ml per litre	3ml per litre	3.5ml per litre	3.5ml per litre	3.5ml per litre	-
Plagron Pure Enzym	1ml per litre	1ml per litre	1ml per litre	-	-	-	-	-	-
Dutch Pro Explode	-	-	0.5ml per litre	0.5ml per litre	1ml per litre	1ml per litre	1.5ml per litre	1.5ml per litre	-
Bio Green PK 13/14	-	-	-	0.5ml per litre	0.5ml per litre	-	-	-	-
Plant Magic Flush	-	-	-	-	-	-	-	-	5ml per litre
Total E.C goal	1.2	1.4	1.6	1.6	1.6	1.6	1.8	1.8	-
Total pH goal	5.8-60	5.7-60	5.6-60	5.8-6.2	5.8-6.2	5.7-6.0	5.8-6.2	5.8-6.2	Do not adjust pH

Plant Success Great White Mycorrhizae - Should be used every time your plant is repotted.

Any subsequent weeks in flowering/bloom, repeat week 4 dosages. Please note that this is only a guide and your plants may need more or less nutrients depending on each individual plants needs.

FLOWERING FEEDING SCHEDULE

welcome to the revolution.

Soil

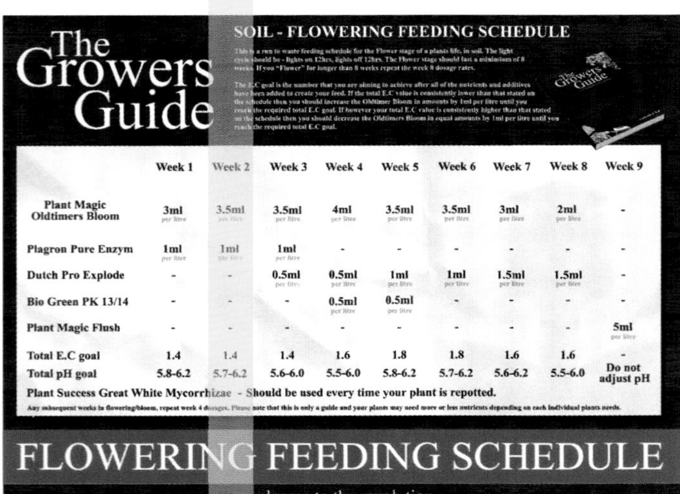

The Growers Guide

SOIL - FLOWERING FEEDING SCHEDULE

This is a run to waste feeding schedule for the Flower stage of a plants life, in soil. The light cycle should be - lights on 12hrs, lights off 12hrs. The Flower stage should last a minimum of 8 weeks. If you "Flower" for longer than 8 weeks repeat the week 8 dosage rates.

The E.C goal is the number that you are aiming to achieve after all of the nutrients and additives have been added to create your feed. If the total E.C value is consistently lower than that stated on the schedule then you should increase the Oldtimer Bloom in amounts by 1ml per litre until you reach the required total E.C goal. If however your total E.C value is consistently higher than that stated on the schedule then you should decrease the Oldtimers Bloom in equal amounts by 1ml per litre until you reach the required total E.C goal.

	Week 1	Week 2	Week 3	Week 4	Week 5	Week 6	Week 7	Week 8	Week 9
Plant Magic Oldtimers Bloom	3ml per litre	3.5ml per litre	3.5ml per litre	4ml per litre	3.5ml per litre	3.5ml per litre	3ml per litre	2ml per litre	-
Plagron Pure Enzym	1ml per litre	1ml per litre	1ml per litre	-	-	-	-	-	-
Dutch Pro Explode	-	-	0.5ml per litre	0.5ml per litre	1ml per litre	1ml per litre	1.5ml per litre	1.5ml per litre	-
Bio Green PK 13/14	-	-	-	0.5ml per litre	0.5ml per litre	-	-	-	-
Plant Magic Flush	-	-	-	-	-	-	-	-	5ml per litre
Total E.C goal	1.4	1.4	1.4	1.6	1.8	1.8	1.6	1.6	-
Total pH goal	5.8-6.2	5.7-6.2	5.6-6.0	5.5-6.0	5.8-6.2	5.7-6.2	5.6-6.2	5.5-6.0	Do not adjust pH

Plant Success Great White Mycorrhizae - Should be used every time your plant is repotted.

Any subsequent weeks in flowering/bloom, repeat week 4 dosages. Please note that this is only a guide and your plants may need more or less nutrients depending on each individual plants needs.

FLOWERING FEEDING SCHEDULE

welcome to the revolution.

We will again be mixing the nutrients up in batches of 10 litre quantities as we have done in the first week of the Flowering stage.

Always remember that the feed charts shown are only a guide and that the strength of the feed should be decreased and increased with each plant when required. The key to becoming a good grower is to keenly observe your plants and learn to read them, as they will give you all the signs that you need.

It is also essential at this point to check that your light is at the correct distance away from the canopy of the plants as the plant's growth can be so extreme that you may need to move the position of your light on a daily basis. When moving your light, remember that you also need to move your oscillating fan so that it is in line with the space between the light and the canopy of the plants. This will ensure that you have maximum air movement around your growing environment.

You may also need to continue to tie down any rogue branches that are making a run for the light. The canopy of the plants should be as level as possible as shown.

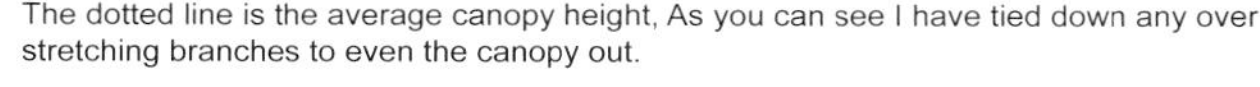
The dotted line is the average canopy height, As you can see I have tied down any over stretching branches to even the canopy out.

Start of week 2

End of week 2

Coco Soil

Coco Soil

Flower/Bloom

Week 3 - This is where the growth should be explosive throughout the week and you should expect to see your plants double in height and mass. Make sure you are carrying out your 3 day plant check list, checking for infection, disease and insects. As the plants are growing so rapidly in a closed, protected and humid environment they will become very attractive to hungry pests who thrive in such conditions, so at this stage you may also need to adjust the openings on your tent in order to control the humidity and temperature. This is because, as the plant's mass grows inside the tent you will inevitably be left with less space and this may cause an increase in the temperature and humidity, which in turn will attract more pests.

Coco Coir

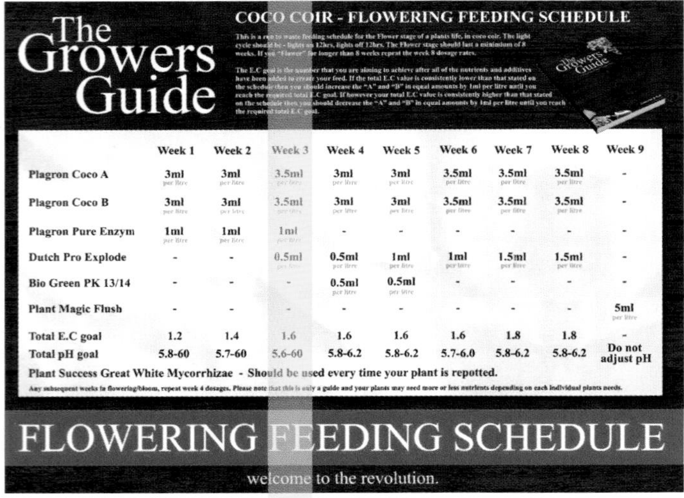

The Growers Guide

COCO COIR - FLOWERING FEEDING SCHEDULE

This is a run to waste feeding schedule for the Flower stage of a plants life, in coco coir. The light cycle should be - lights on 12hrs, lights off 12hrs. The Flower stage should last a minimium of 8 weeks. If you "Flower" for longer than 8 weeks repeat the week 8 dosage rates.

The E.C goal is the number that you are aiming to achieve after all of the nutrients and additives have been added to create your feed. If the total E.C value is consistently lower than that stated on the schedule then you should increase the "A" and "B" in equal amounts by 1ml per litre until you reach the required total E.C goal. If however your total E.C value is consistently higher than that stated on the schedule then you should decrease the "A" and "B" in equal amounts by 1ml per litre until you reach the required total E.C goal.

	Week 1	Week 2	Week 3	Week 4	Week 5	Week 6	Week 7	Week 8	Week 9
Plagron Coco A	3ml per litre	3ml per litre	3.5ml per litre	3ml per litre	3ml per litre	3.5ml per litre	3.5ml per litre	3.5ml per litre	-
Plagron Coco B	3ml per litre	3ml per litre	3.5ml per litre	3ml per litre	3ml per litre	3.5ml per litre	3.5ml per litre	3.5ml per litre	-
Plagron Pure Enzym	1ml per litre	1ml per litre	1ml per litre	-	-	-	-	-	-
Dutch Pro Explode	-	-	0.5ml per litre	0.5ml per litre	1ml per litre	1ml per litre	1.5ml per litre	1.5ml per litre	-
Bio Green PK 13/14	-	-	-	0.5ml per litre	0.5ml per litre	-	-	-	-
Plant Magic Flush	-	-	-	-	-	-	-	-	5ml per litre
Total E.C goal	1.2	1.4	1.6	1.6	1.6	1.6	1.8	1.8	-
Total pH goal	5.8-60	5.7-60	5.6-60	5.8-6.2	5.8-6.2	5.7-6.0	5.8-6.2	5.8-6.2	Do not adjust pH

Plant Success Great White Mycorrhizae - Should be used every time your plant is repotted.

Any subsequent weeks in flowering/bloom, repeat week 4 dosages. Please note that this is only a guide and your plants may need more or less nutrients depending on each individual plants needs.

FLOWERING FEEDING SCHEDULE

welcome to the revolution.

Soil

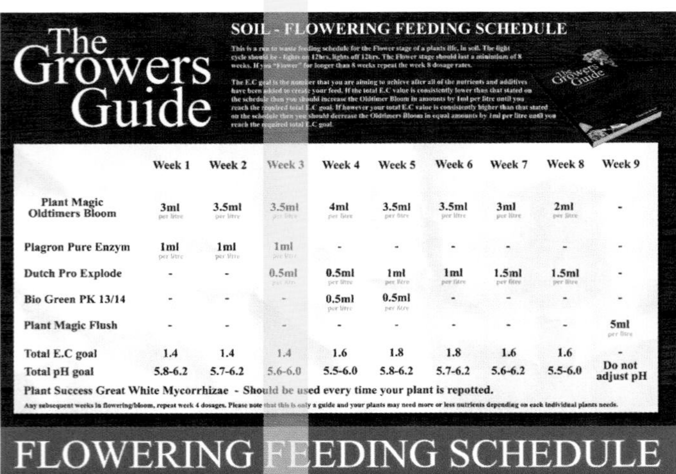

The Growers Guide

SOIL - FLOWERING FEEDING SCHEDULE

This is a run to waste feeding schedule for the Flower stage of a plants life, in soil. The light cycle should be - lights on 12hrs, lights off 12hrs. The Flower stage should last a minimium of 8 weeks. If you "Flower" for longer than 8 weeks repeat the week 8 dosage rates.

The E.C goal is the number that you are aiming to achieve after all of the nutrients and additives have been added to create your feed. If the total E.C value is consistently lower than that stated on the schedule then you should increase the Oldtimer Bloom in amounts by 1ml per litre until you reach the required total E.C goal. If however your total E.C value is consistently higher than that stated on the schedule then you should decrease the Oldtimers Bloom in equal amounts by 1ml per litre until you reach the required total E.C goal.

	Week 1	Week 2	Week 3	Week 4	Week 5	Week 6	Week 7	Week 8	Week 9
Plant Magic Oldtimers Bloom	3ml per litre	3.5ml per litre	3.5ml per litre	4ml per litre	3.5ml per litre	3.5ml per litre	3ml per litre	2ml per litre	-
Plagron Pure Enzym	1ml per litre	1ml per litre	1ml per litre	-	-	-	-	-	-
Dutch Pro Explode	-	-	0.5ml per litre	0.5ml per litre	1ml per litre	1ml per litre	1.5ml per litre	1.5ml per litre	-
Bio Green PK 13/14	-	-	-	0.5ml per litre	0.5ml per litre	-	-	-	-
Plant Magic Flush	-	-	-	-	-	-	-	-	5ml per litre
Total E.C goal	1.4	1.4	1.4	1.6	1.8	1.8	1.6	1.6	-
Total pH goal	5.8-6.2	5.7-6.2	5.6-6.0	5.5-6.0	5.8-6.2	5.7-6.2	5.6-6.2	5.5-6.0	Do not adjust pH

Plant Success Great White Mycorrhizae - Should be used every time your plant is repotted.

Any subsequent weeks in flowering/bloom, repeat week 4 dosages. Please note that this is only a guide and your plants may need more or less nutrients depending on each individual plants needs.

FLOWERING FEEDING SCHEDULE

welcome to the revolution.

I have highlighted the correct week on both the coco coir and soil feeding schedules. If you have any feed left over from week 2's ratios, this will need to be discarded and a fresh batch containing the week 3 ratios will need to be mixed up ready for their next feed.

Hopefully by this stage you are starting to get a feel for how often your plants need feeding. As your plants go through week 3's rapid growth rate, you should see the amount of feeding times increase as well.

It is important to not overfeed your plants, but equally, it is vital for you to keep to the coco and soil wet-to-dry ratios as closely as you possibly can without overfeeding as this will ensure that the plants as a whole are working as hard as possible. Due to the massive growth of the plants they will now need to be repotted into the final size of pot which is the 30ltr round black pot that we spoke about earlier in this chapter. The plants will spend the rest of their lives in this pot so it is vital that this re-potting is done well.

Due to the size and the weight of the plants this will be the most difficult re-potting to get right. The plants will be heavy at both the top and the bottom so when handling them its best to keep them in a vertical position. The key to getting this procedure right is preparation. Prepare the 30ltr pots in exactly the same manner as we have done when previously repotting. Make sure that when the potting hole is ready, that it is sprinkled with Plant Success Great White Mycorrhizae. This will ensure that the roots make the most out of the nutrients which they will be fed. The medium around the new plant should be pressed firmly to a point that it is stable horizontally. You may have to add some more medium to the top of the pot after pressing what you already have around the freshly potted plant and root mass. Repeat the process with all of your plants and return them back into their growing environment and then water as per the feeding schedule.

Start of week 3

Coco Soil

End of week 3

Coco Soil

Flower/Bloom

Week 4 - signifies the start of a new chapter in the plant's life. The Flowering stage is separated into 2 phases. The first stage is where we will be adding a PK 13/14 into the nutrient feed. This addition will chemically tell the plant that it needs to start the second phase. This final stage is where the plant will start to shut down all horizontal, lateral and root growth. By doing this the plant will then send the majority of it's energy and efforts to the growing and swelling of the fruits. From the time that you begin feeding the plant with this added PK 13/14, it should take no more than a week to start to see the effects.

Coco Coir

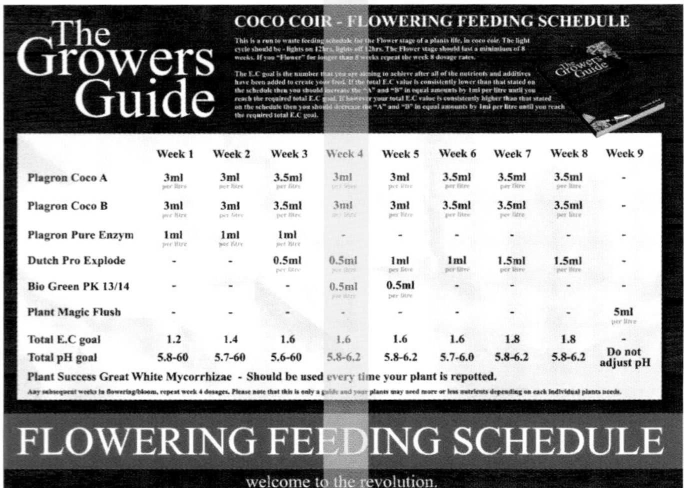

The Growers Guide

COCO COIR - FLOWERING FEEDING SCHEDULE

This is a run to waste feeding schedule for the Flower stage of a plants life, in coco coir. The light cycle should be - lights on 12hrs, lights off 12hrs. The Flower stage should last a minimum of 8 weeks. If you "Flower" for longer than 8 weeks repeat the week 8 dosage rates.

The E.C goal is the number that you are aiming to achieve after all of the nutrients and additives have been added to create your feed. If the total E.C value is consistently lower than that stated on the schedule then you should increase the "A" and "B" in equal amounts by 1ml per litre until you reach the required total E.C goal. If however your total E.C value is consistently higher than that stated on the schedule then you should decrease the "A" and "B" in equal amounts by 1ml per litre until you reach the required total E.C goal.

	Week 1	Week 2	Week 3	Week 4	Week 5	Week 6	Week 7	Week 8	Week 9
Plagron Coco A	3ml per litre	3ml per litre	3.5ml per litre	3ml per litre	3ml per litre	3.5ml per litre	3.5ml per litre	3.5ml per litre	-
Plagron Coco B	3ml per litre	3ml per litre	3.5ml per litre	3ml per litre	3ml per litre	3.5ml per litre	3.5ml per litre	3.5ml per litre	-
Plagron Pure Enzym	1ml per litre	1ml per litre	1ml per litre	-	-	-	-	-	-
Dutch Pro Explode	-	-	0.5ml per litre	0.5ml per litre	1ml per litre	1ml per litre	1.5ml per litre	1.5ml per litre	-
Bio Green PK 13/14	-	-	-	0.5ml per litre	0.5ml per litre	-	-	-	-
Plant Magic Flush	-	-	-	-	-	-	-	-	5ml per litre
Total E.C goal	1.2	1.4	1.6	1.6	1.6	1.6	1.8	1.8	-
Total pH goal	5.8-60	5.7-60	5.6-60	5.8-6.2	5.8-6.2	5.7-6.0	5.8-6.2	5.8-6.2	Do not adjust pH

Plant Success Great White Mycorrhizae - Should be used every time your plant is repotted.

Any subsequent weeks in flowering/bloom, repeat week 4 dosages. Please note that this is only a guide and your plants may need more or less nutrients depending on each individual plants needs.

FLOWERING FEEDING SCHEDULE

welcome to the revolution.

Soil

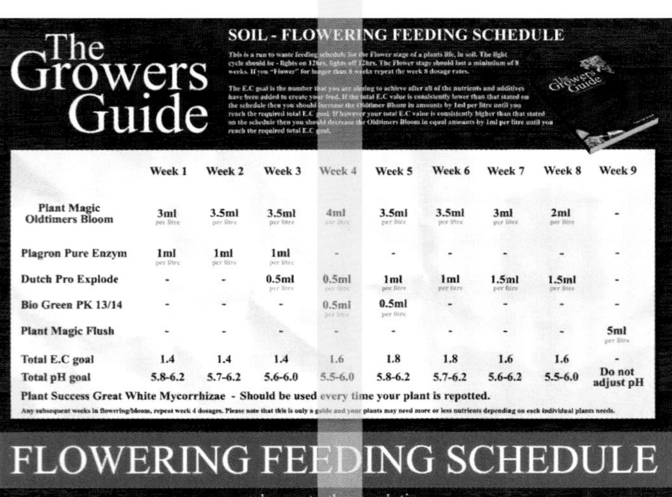

The Growers Guide

SOIL - FLOWERING FEEDING SCHEDULE

This is a run to waste feeding schedule for the Flower stage of a plants life, in soil. The light cycle should be - lights on 12hrs, lights off 12hrs. The Flower stage should last a minimum of 8 weeks. If you "Flower" for longer than 8 weeks repeat the week 8 dosage rates.

The E.C goal is the number that you are aiming to achieve after all of the nutrients and additives have been added to create your feed. If the total E.C value is consistently lower than that stated on the schedule then you should increase the Oldtimer Bloom in amounts by 1ml per litre until you reach the required total E.C goal. If however your total E.C value is consistently higher than that stated on the schedule then you should decrease the Oldtimers Bloom in equal amounts by 1ml per litre until you reach the required total E.C goal.

	Week 1	Week 2	Week 3	Week 4	Week 5	Week 6	Week 7	Week 8	Week 9
Plant Magic Oldtimers Bloom	3ml per litre	3.5ml per litre	3.5ml per litre	4ml per litre	3.5ml per litre	3.5ml per litre	3ml per litre	2ml per litre	-
Plagron Pure Enzym	1ml per litre	1ml per litre	1ml per litre	-	-	-	-	-	-
Dutch Pro Explode	-	-	0.5ml per litre	0.5ml per litre	1ml per litre	1ml per litre	1.5ml per litre	1.5ml per litre	-
Bio Green PK 13/14	-	-	-	0.5ml per litre	0.5ml per litre	-	-	-	-
Plant Magic Flush	-	-	-	-	-	-	-	-	5ml per litre
Total E.C goal	1.4	1.4	1.4	1.6	1.8	1.8	1.6	1.6	-
Total pH goal	5.8-6.2	5.7-6.2	5.6-6.0	5.5-6.0	5.8-6.2	5.7-6.2	5.6-6.2	5.5-6.0	Do not adjust pH

Plant Success Great White Mycorrhizae - Should be used every time your plant is repotted.

Any subsequent weeks in flowering/bloom, repeat week 4 dosages. Please note that this is only a guide and your plants may need more or less nutrients depending on each individual plants needs.

FLOWERING FEEDING SCHEDULE

welcome to the revolution.

We will be adding Bio Green's PK13/14 for the next two weeks (weeks 4 and 5) just to make sure that the plants have had enough time to take the chemical change on board.

The people that are closely following this book may ask, Isn't Dutch Pro "Explode" also a PK booster? The answer to that one is simple, Yes but I do however like to add "straight" PK 13/14 on top also, as I believe it pushes the plants into the second phase of flowering faster.

This week you will also have to tie down any rogue branches that are making a bee line for the light and out running the majority of the rest of the canopy.

There is a technique known as "snapping" or "bruising" which is very widely used within the hydroponics world. The basic principle of this technique is to bring the stem which is growing out of control back down in line with the rest of your grow room. This is done by gently bending the stem so that minimal breakage or a bruise is created. The idea is that the damage created will heal and the plant will recover, but that as a result the plant will now grow at more of an angle horizontally instead of vertically and will stay level with the rest of the canopy. Personally, however, I would not recommend doing this, as while it can work, if not done properly it can have devastating results to your plants and their fruits. It will stress the plants out and in my book that's never a good thing. The most effective way is to tie the branches down to a lower point of the grow room using a gardening twine. While this can be more time consuming, it is guaranteed not to stress your plant out and as a result the plant can then concentrate on what it should be doing, opposed to having to fix or heal bruises and breaks.

By the end of week 4 the plant's growth should be noticeably slowing. Don't forget your 3 day checks and to move your light and oscillating fan when needed.

Start of week 4

Coco Soil

End of week 4

Coco Soil

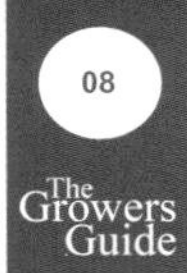

Flower/Bloom

Week 5 – Moving into week 5, your plants should now be completely settled in after their re-potting a few weeks ago and the overall vertical and horizontal growth should be slowing to a complete halt by the end of this week. You may also find that the branches which have been tied down have bent back around towards the light but as long as they are level with the majority of the rest of the canopy they will be fine. If any have exceeded the canopy then they will need to be re-tied.

Coco Coir

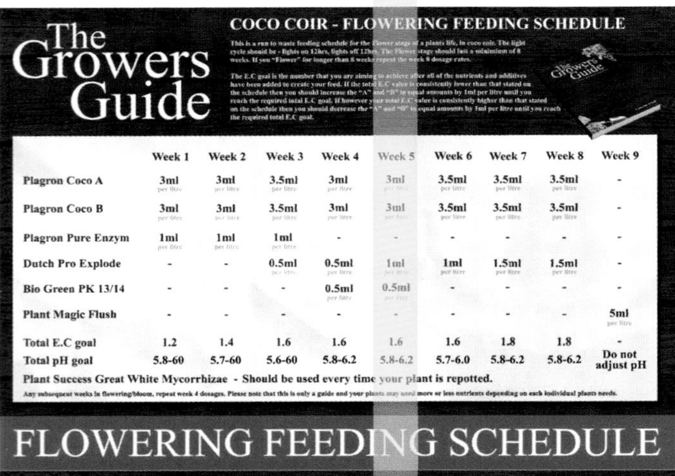

The Growers Guide

COCO COIR - FLOWERING FEEDING SCHEDULE

This is a run to waste feeding schedule for the Flower stage of a plants life, in coco coir. The light cycle should be - lights on 12hrs, lights off 12hrs. The Flower stage should last a minimum of 8 weeks. If you "Flower" for longer than 8 weeks repeat the week 8 dosage rates.

The E.C goal is the number that you are aiming to achieve after all of the nutrients and additives have been added to create your feed. If the total E.C value is consistently lower than that stated on the schedule then you should increase the "A" and "B" in equal amounts by 1ml per litre until you reach the required total E.C goal. If however your total E.C value is consistently higher than that stated on the schedule then you should decrease the "A" and "B" in equal amounts by 1ml per litre until you reach the required total E.C goal.

	Week 1	Week 2	Week 3	Week 4	Week 5	Week 6	Week 7	Week 8	Week 9
Plagron Coco A	3ml per litre	3ml per litre	3.5ml per litre	3ml per litre	3ml per litre	3.5ml per litre	3.5ml per litre	3.5ml per litre	-
Plagron Coco B	3ml per litre	3ml per litre	3.5ml per litre	3ml per litre	3ml per litre	3.5ml per litre	3.5ml per litre	3.5ml per litre	-
Plagron Pure Enzym	1ml per litre	1ml per litre	1ml per litre	-	-	-	-	-	-
Dutch Pro Explode	-	-	0.5ml per litre	0.5ml per litre	1ml per litre	1ml per litre	1.5ml per litre	1.5ml per litre	-
Bio Green PK 13/14	-	-	-	0.5ml per litre	0.5ml per litre	-	-	-	-
Plant Magic Flush	-	-	-	-	-	-	-	-	5ml per litre
Total E.C goal	1.2	1.4	1.6	1.6	1.6	1.6	1.8	1.8	-
Total pH goal	5.8-60	5.7-60	5.6-60	5.8-6.2	5.8-6.2	5.7-6.0	5.8-6.2	5.8-6.2	Do not adjust pH

Plant Success Great White Mycorrhizae - Should be used every time your plant is repotted.

Any subsequent weeks in flowering/bloom, repeat week 4 dosages. Please note that this is only a guide and your plants may need more or less nutrients depending on each individual plants needs.

FLOWERING FEEDING SCHEDULE

welcome to the revolution.

Soil

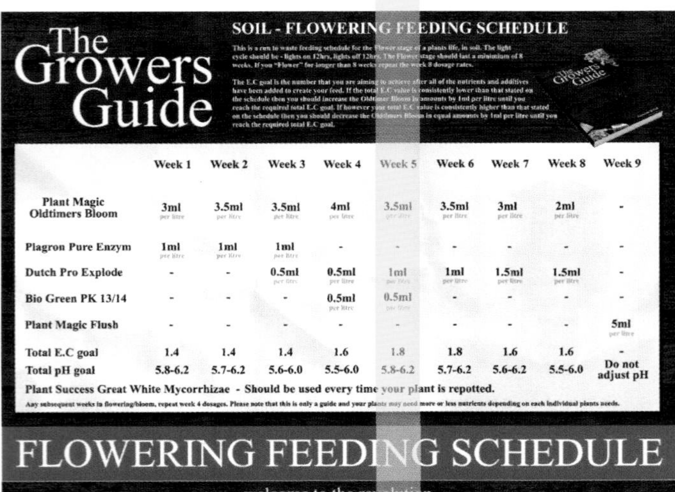

The Growers Guide

SOIL - FLOWERING FEEDING SCHEDULE

This is a run to waste feeding schedule for the Flower stage of a plants life, in soil. The light cycle should be - lights on 12hrs, lights off 12hrs. The Flower stage should last a minimum of 8 weeks. If you "Flower" for longer than 8 weeks repeat the week 8 dosage rates.

The E.C goal is the number that you are aiming to achieve after all of the nutrients and additives have been added to create your feed. If the total E.C value is consistently lower than that stated on the schedule then you should increase the Oldtimer Bloom in amounts by 1ml per litre until you reach the required total E.C goal. If however your total E.C value is consistently higher than that stated on the schedule then you should decrease the Oldtimers Bloom in equal amounts by 1ml per litre until you reach the required total E.C goal.

	Week 1	Week 2	Week 3	Week 4	Week 5	Week 6	Week 7	Week 8	Week 9
Plant Magic Oldtimers Bloom	3ml per litre	3.5ml per litre	3.5ml per litre	4ml per litre	3.5ml per litre	3.5ml per litre	3ml per litre	2ml per litre	-
Plagron Pure Enzym	1ml per litre	1ml per litre	1ml per litre	-	-	-	-	-	-
Dutch Pro Explode	-	-	0.5ml per litre	0.5ml per litre	1ml per litre	1ml per litre	1.5ml per litre	1.5ml per litre	-
Bio Green PK 13/14	-	-	-	0.5ml per litre	0.5ml per litre	-	-	-	-
Plant Magic Flush	-	-	-	-	-	-	-	-	5ml per litre
Total E.C goal	1.4	1.4	1.4	1.6	1.8	1.8	1.6	1.6	-
Total pH goal	5.8-6.2	5.7-6.2	5.6-6.0	5.5-6.0	5.8-6.2	5.7-6.2	5.6-6.2	5.5-6.0	Do not adjust pH

Plant Success Great White Mycorrhizae - Should be used every time your plant is repotted.

Any subsequent weeks in flowering/bloom, repeat week 4 dosages. Please note that this is only a guide and your plants may need more or less nutrients depending on each individual plants needs.

FLOWERING FEEDING SCHEDULE

welcome to the revolution.

The canopy should now be pretty much covering the whole of the width of the tent as shown in the images to the right. When the canopy is this dense it will have an adverse effect on the lower leaves of the plant, the bottom line being that without the light the leaves will die. Any leaves which do start to show signs of dying (normally apparent from the lightening/yellowing in colour) should be removed as soon as possible in order to reduce the plant from wasting energy by trying to keep the leaves alive and because of the overall stress which this can cause to the plant.

The 2 main causes of leaves lightening/yellowing at this stage are a lack of light and the use of

nutrient solution that is too weak which results in the plant being under-fed. To ensure that your nutrient solution (feed) is not too weak, you need to be consistent when making it up. It is very easy to get a bit lazy a few weeks in and add the wrong amount of a certain element to your feed, so you should always take your time and check your dosage levels. It is good practice to keep a diary of how much of each solution you are adding, especially if you are deviating from the feed charts provided. By doing this it ensures that you do not forget or confuse the amounts that you have been using. The rule of thumb is that if leaves are yellowing on an individual basis at the base of the plant then this is normally as a result of "lack of light" (and thus they should be removed). If the leaves at the top/new growth parts of the plant are yellowing as a whole, it is usually due to the plant being under-fed. By under-fed, I do not mean under-watered I mean that the nutrient solution that you are feeding them is too weak, either because it is being made up incorrectly as just discussed or because of the individual needs of the plant as looked at in Week 4 of the Vegetation chapter.

Coming to the end of week 5 the vertical and horizontal growth has now all but stopped. You may also notice flowering sites starting to appear prominently all over the plants.

Start of week 5

Coco Soil

End of week 5

Coco Soil

Flower/Bloom

Week 6 – entering into week 6 all growth is now completely concentrated towards the growth of the fruits and the flowering sites. Over the next 7 days you will notice that each fruit site will start to develop and the fruits growing from these points should be hard to the touch. The plants may also now start to release a stronger odour as the fruit and the flowers develop, this is completely natural and the filter which we have installed at the start of the process will come into it's own as it should scrub all bacteria from the air. The inside of the grow tent therefore should smell of the fruits/ plants which you are growing but there should be no smell outside the grow room as there should be no odour/ bacteria leaving the closed environment. If there is an odour outside the grow room then the first thing to do would be to check if you have any gaps in the ducting from the filter, fan or to the outside environment which you are extracting too.

As you can see by the feeding schedule, we are now only feeding the plant with Plagrons cocos a, Plagrons cocos b and Dutch pro's Explode. You may be tempted to add more nutrients or add a different booster etc, but you really don't have to. Using a stronger feed here is not always the best

Coco Coir

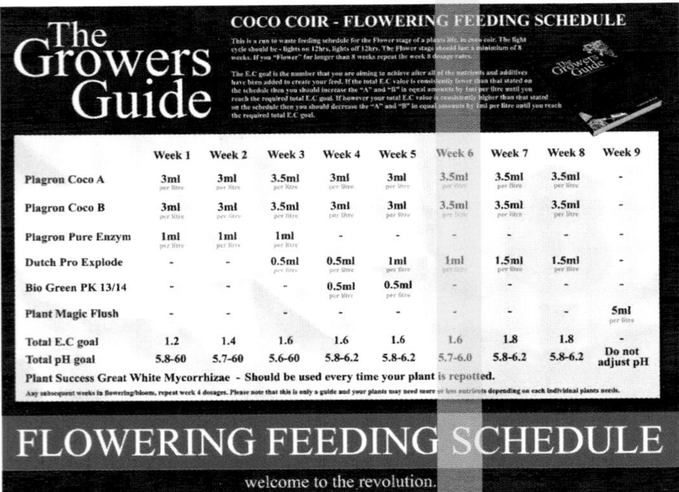

The Growers Guide

COCO COIR - FLOWERING FEEDING SCHEDULE

This is a run to waste feeding schedule for the Flower stage of a plants life, in coco coir. The light cycle should be - lights on 12hrs, lights off 12hrs. The Flower stage should last a minimium of 8 weeks. If you "Flower" for longer than 8 weeks repeat the week 8 dosage rates.

The E.C goal is the number that you are aiming to achieve after all of the nutrients and additives have been added to create your feed. If the total E.C value is consistently lower than that stated on the schedule then you should increase the "A" and "B" in equal amounts by 1ml per litre until you reach the required total E.C goal. If however your total E.C value is consistently higher than that stated on the schedule then you should decrease the "A" and "B" in equal amounts by 1ml per litre until you reach the required total E.C goal.

	Week 1	Week 2	Week 3	Week 4	Week 5	Week 6	Week 7	Week 8	Week 9
Plagron Coco A	3ml per litre	3ml per litre	3.5ml per litre	3ml per litre	3ml per litre	3.5ml per litre	3.5ml per litre	3.5ml per litre	-
Plagron Coco B	3ml per litre	3ml per litre	3.5ml per litre	3ml per litre	3ml per litre	3.5ml per litre	3.5ml per litre	3.5ml per litre	-
Plagron Pure Enzym	1ml per litre	1ml per litre	1ml per litre	-	-	-	-	-	-
Dutch Pro Explode	-	-	0.5ml per litre	0.5ml per litre	1ml per litre	1ml per litre	1.5ml per litre	1.5ml per litre	-
Bio Green PK 13/14	-	-	-	0.5ml per litre	0.5ml per litre	-	-	-	-
Plant Magic Flush	-	-	-	-	-	-	-	-	5ml per litre
Total E.C goal	1.2	1.4	1.6	1.6	1.6	1.6	1.8	1.8	-
Total pH goal	5.8-60	5.7-60	5.6-60	5.8-6.2	5.8-6.2	5.7-6.0	5.8-6.2	5.8-6.2	Do not adjust pH

Plant Success Great White Mycorrhizae - Should be used every time your plant is repotted.

Any subsequent weeks in flowering/bloom, repeat week 4 dosages. Please note that this is only a guide and your plants may need more or less nutrients depending on each individual plants needs.

FLOWERING FEEDING SCHEDULE

welcome to the revolution.

Soil

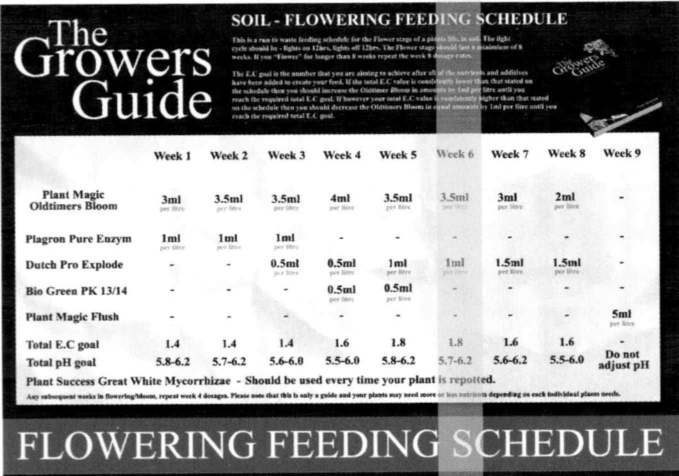

The Growers Guide

SOIL - FLOWERING FEEDING SCHEDULE

This is a run to waste feeding schedule for the Flower stage of a plants life, in soil. The light cycle should be - lights on 12hrs, lights off 12hrs. The Flower stage should last a minimium of 8 weeks. If you "Flower" for longer than 8 weeks repeat the week 8 dosage rates.

The E.C goal is the number that you are aiming to achieve after all of the nutrients and additives have been added to create your feed. If the total E.C value is consistently lower than that stated on the schedule then you should increase the Oldtimer Bloom in amounts by 1ml per litre until you reach the required total E.C goal. If however your total E.C value is consistently higher than that stated on the schedule then you should decrease the Oldtimers Bloom in equal amounts by 1ml per litre until you reach the required total E.C goal.

	Week 1	Week 2	Week 3	Week 4	Week 5	Week 6	Week 7	Week 8	Week 9
Plant Magic Oldtimers Bloom	3ml per litre	3.5ml per litre	3.5ml per litre	4ml per litre	3.5ml per litre	3.5ml per litre	3ml per litre	2ml per litre	-
Plagron Pure Enzym	1ml per litre	1ml per litre	1ml per litre	-	-	-	-	-	-
Dutch Pro Explode	-	-	0.5ml per litre	0.5ml per litre	1ml per litre	1ml per litre	1.5ml per litre	1.5ml per litre	-
Bio Green PK 13/14	-	-	-	0.5ml per litre	0.5ml per litre	-	-	-	-
Plant Magic Flush	-	-	-	-	-	-	-	-	5ml per litre
Total E.C goal	1.4	1.4	1.4	1.6	1.8	1.8	1.6	1.6	-
Total pH goal	5.8-6.2	5.7-6.2	5.6-6.0	5.5-6.0	5.8-6.2	5.7-6.2	5.6-6.2	5.5-6.0	Do not adjust pH

Plant Success Great White Mycorrhizae - Should be used every time your plant is repotted.

Any subsequent weeks in flowering/bloom, repeat week 4 dosages. Please note that this is only a guide and your plants may need more or less nutrients depending on each individual plants needs.

FLOWERING FEEDING SCHEDULE

welcome to the revolution.

option. One of the biggest mistakes which people make at this point is to think, "well things are looking good now, I bet if I add more nutrients I will get a better/bigger result". Wrong! Keep as close as possible to the E.C goal stated on the feeding schedule that I have provided . If you exceed the E.C to a margin that the plants can't handle, all you will do is poison your plants and lock them out. Or as its commonly known give them "nute lock". This as I have explained before will essentially shut the plant down from taking in any more nutrients/feed, to try and prevent the plant from poisoning itself. The tell tale signs of overfertilisation are very clear if you know what you are looking for. The first sign of this is what is commonly know as tip burn. This is when the very tips of the leaves will turn brown and another more extreme sign is the inward curling of the leaves.

Tip Burn.

Start of week 6

Coco Soil

End of week 6

Coco Soil

Flower/Bloom

Week 7 – Things in the grow room should now look really good. The humidity shouldn't have increased but if you find that it has a little, just carry out some checks to see if you can pinpoint the problem. It will probably be something that can be easily resolved and secured, such as a few loose small holes around the unused ventilation ports in the tents, which could be bringing in moisture rich air from the environment just outside the grow tent. The fruits should now be looking on the larger side of big and be taking in nearly 10ltrs of feed every 24hrs. At this stage it is crucial that you manage the tying up of your plants properly as over the next week the fruits will continue to swell in size and weight, making the top of the plant far heavier than the bottom. When tying up you should use a natural gardening twine which will not give off any unwanted chemicals or residues within the grow tent. Due to the shortened lifecycle of the plant and the use of the correct nutrients to accelerate the growth, each fruit/ branch if not completely horizontal should and will bend by the weight of its own fruit, as the fruit will far exceed the weight and strength of the stem/branch. You may also notice the yellowing of some of the leaves sporadically around

Coco Coir

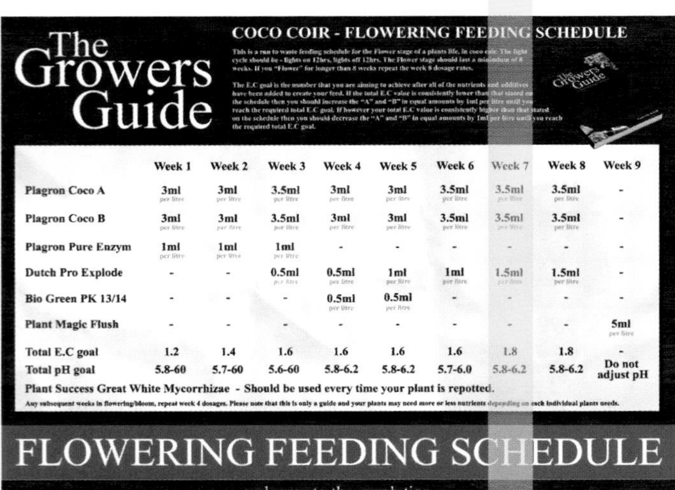

The Growers Guide

COCO COIR - FLOWERING FEEDING SCHEDULE

This is a run to waste feeding schedule for the Flower stage of a plants life, in coco coir. The light cycle should be - lights on 12hrs, lights off 12hrs. The Flower stage should last a minimum of 8 weeks. If you "Flower" for longer than 8 weeks repeat the week 8 dosage rates.

The E.C goal is the number that you are aiming to achieve after all of the nutrients and additives have been added to create your feed. If the total E.C value is consistently lower than that stated on the schedule then you should increase the "A" and "B" in equal amounts by 1ml per litre until you reach the required total E.C goal. If however your total E.C value is consistently higher than that stated on the schedule then you should decrease the "A" and "B" in equal amounts by 1ml per litre until you reach the required total E.C goal.

	Week 1	Week 2	Week 3	Week 4	Week 5	Week 6	Week 7	Week 8	Week 9
Plagron Coco A	3ml per litre	3ml per litre	3.5ml per litre	3ml per litre	3ml per litre	3.5ml per litre	3.5ml per litre	3.5ml per litre	-
Plagron Coco B	3ml per litre	3ml per litre	3.5ml per litre	3ml per litre	3ml per litre	3.5ml per litre	3.5ml per litre	3.5ml per litre	-
Plagron Pure Enzym	1ml per litre	1ml per litre	1ml per litre	-	-	-	-	-	-
Dutch Pro Explode	-	-	0.5ml per litre	0.5ml per litre	1ml per litre	1ml per litre	1.5ml per litre	1.5ml per litre	-
Bio Green PK 13/14	-	-	-	0.5ml per litre	0.5ml per litre	-	-	-	-
Plant Magic Flush	-	-	-	-	-	-	-	-	5ml per litre
Total E.C goal	1.2	1.4	1.6	1.6	1.6	1.6	1.8	1.8	-
Total pH goal	5.8-60	5.7-60	5.6-60	5.8-6.2	5.8-6.2	5.7-6.0	5.8-6.2	5.8-6.2	Do not adjust pH

Plant Success Great White Mycorrhizae - Should be used every time your plant is repotted.

Any subsequent weeks in flowering/bloom, repeat week 4 dosages. Please note that this is only a guide and your plants may need more or less nutrients depending on each individual plants needs.

FLOWERING FEEDING SCHEDULE

welcome to the revolution.

Soil

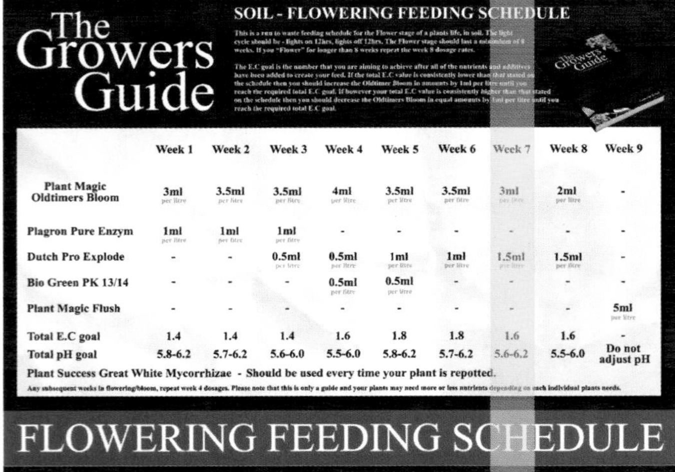

The Growers Guide

SOIL - FLOWERING FEEDING SCHEDULE

This is a run to waste feeding schedule for the Flower stage of a plants life, in soil. The light cycle should be - lights on 12hrs, lights off 12hrs. The Flower stage should last a minimum of 8 weeks. If you "Flower" for longer than 8 weeks repeat the week 8 dosage rates.

The E.C goal is the number that you are aiming to achieve after all of the nutrients and additives have been added to create your feed. If the total E.C value is consistently lower than that stated on the schedule then you should increase the Oldtimer Bloom in amounts by 1ml per litre until you reach the required total E.C goal. If however your total E.C value is consistently higher than that stated on the schedule then you should decrease the Oldtimers Bloom in equal amounts by 1ml per litre until you reach the required total E.C goal.

	Week 1	Week 2	Week 3	Week 4	Week 5	Week 6	Week 7	Week 8	Week 9
Plant Magic Oldtimers Bloom	3ml per litre	3.5ml per litre	3.5ml per litre	4ml per litre	3.5ml per litre	3.5ml per litre	3ml per litre	2ml per litre	-
Plagron Pure Enzym	1ml per litre	1ml per litre	1ml per litre	-	-	-	-	-	-
Dutch Pro Explode	-	-	0.5ml per litre	0.5ml per litre	1ml per litre	1ml per litre	1.5ml per litre	1.5ml per litre	-
Bio Green PK 13/14	-	-	-	0.5ml per litre	0.5ml per litre	-	-	-	-
Plant Magic Flush	-	-	-	-	-	-	-	-	5ml per litre
Total E.C goal	1.4	1.4	1.4	1.6	1.8	1.8	1.6	1.6	-
Total pH goal	5.8-6.2	5.7-6.2	5.6-6.0	5.5-6.0	5.8-6.2	5.7-6.2	5.6-6.2	5.5-6.0	Do not adjust pH

Plant Success Great White Mycorrhizae - Should be used every time your plant is repotted.

Any subsequent weeks in flowering/bloom, repeat week 4 dosages. Please note that this is only a guide and your plants may need more or less nutrients depending on each individual plants needs.

FLOWERING FEEDING SCHEDULE

welcome to the revolution.

the plant which is caused by a deficiency of magnesium. This is natural and should happen to a certain extent but if you do start to see large groups of yellowing leaves then I would advise adding a small amount of Plant Magic Cal Mag which can be bought in any hydroponic shop. Follow the dosage on the side of the bottle and if ever in doubt remember that less is always more, so just use half the recommended dosage at first to ensure that you do not "lock" the plant out where it shuts down all nutrient uptake, as we described earlier. Remember as always to do your 3 day checks and try to keep the canopy as level as you can in order to maximise the spread of light from the lamp evenly across the whole of the grow room.

Week 7 is the beginning of the final push for your fruits and this is where using the dimmable ballast will come into its own, as it has a boost switch which will give you 660w as opposed to the 600w which you will have been getting up until now. The plants will love this sudden increase of light and the fruit swelling will be exponential. This will however change the temperature of the grow room so you may need to adjust it accordingly.

Start of week 7

Coco Soil

End of week 7

Coco Soil

Flower/Bloom

Week 8 - This will be the last week in Flower before we begin the flushing process. However, some plants may need to be kept in the flowering stage longer due to their species/genetics. If this is the case then repeat the week 8 feeding schedule which I have highlighted in yellow for both coco coir and soil. This being the final week, it will be your last chance to feed your plants the nutrient rich solution which we have been doing throughout. It is also important at this stage, as with every other, that you do not get carried away/over excited and think that by increasing the strength of your feed that this will give you larger fruits. I have grown for many years and believe me less is always more, to lock your plants out at this late stage would be a disaster after all the hard work that you have put in so far, stick to the feed charts as close as you can and everything should be ok.

The fruits on the plants should now be starting to get firmer to the touch which means that they are almost ready to go into the flush stage. With the fruits being so firm they are also exceedingly heavy and as a result throughout the week you may have to re-tie some of the branches in order to keep the canopy as level as possible to maximise the light.

Coco Coir

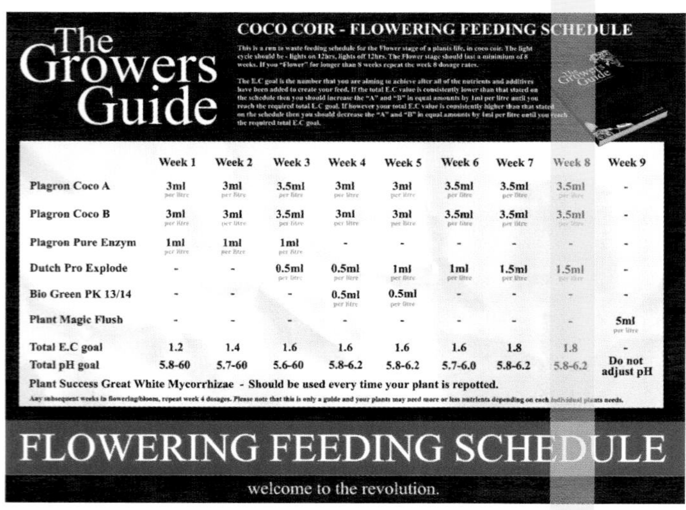

The Growers Guide

COCO COIR - FLOWERING FEEDING SCHEDULE

This is a run to waste feeding schedule for the Flower stage of a plants life, in coco coir. The light cycle should be - lights on 12hrs, lights off 12hrs. The Flower stage should last a minimium of 8 weeks. If you "Flower" for longer than 8 weeks repeat the week 8 dosage rates.

The E.C goal is the number that you are aiming to achieve after all of the nutrients and additives have been added to create your feed. If the total E.C value is consistently lower than that stated on the schedule then you should increase the "A" and "B" in equal amounts by 1ml per litre until you reach the required total E.C goal. If however your total E.C value is consistently higher than that stated on the schedule then you should decrease the "A" and "B" in equal amounts by 1ml per litre until you reach the required total E.C goal.

	Week 1	Week 2	Week 3	Week 4	Week 5	Week 6	Week 7	Week 8	Week 9
Plagron Coco A	3ml per litre	3ml per litre	3.5ml per litre	3ml per litre	3ml per litre	3.5ml per litre	3.5ml per litre	3.5ml per litre	-
Plagron Coco B	3ml per litre	3ml per litre	3.5ml per litre	3ml per litre	3ml per litre	3.5ml per litre	3.5ml per litre	3.5ml per litre	-
Plagron Pure Enzym	1ml per litre	1ml per litre	1ml per litre	-	-	-	-	-	-
Dutch Pro Explode	-	-	0.5ml per litre	0.5ml per litre	1ml per litre	1ml per litre	1.5ml per litre	1.5ml per litre	-
Bio Green PK 13/14	-	-	-	0.5ml per litre	0.5ml per litre	-	-	-	-
Plant Magic Flush	-	-	-	-	-	-	-	-	5ml per litre
Total E.C goal	1.2	1.4	1.6	1.6	1.6	1.6	1.8	1.8	-
Total pH goal	5.8-60	5.7-60	5.6-60	5.8-6.2	5.8-6.2	5.7-6.0	5.8-6.2	5.8-6.2	Do not adjust pH

Plant Success Great White Mycorrhizae - Should be used every time your plant is repotted.

Any subsequent weeks in flowering/bloom, repeat week 4 dosages. Please note that this is only a guide and your plants may need more or less nutrients depending on each individual plants needs.

FLOWERING FEEDING SCHEDULE

welcome to the revolution.

Soil

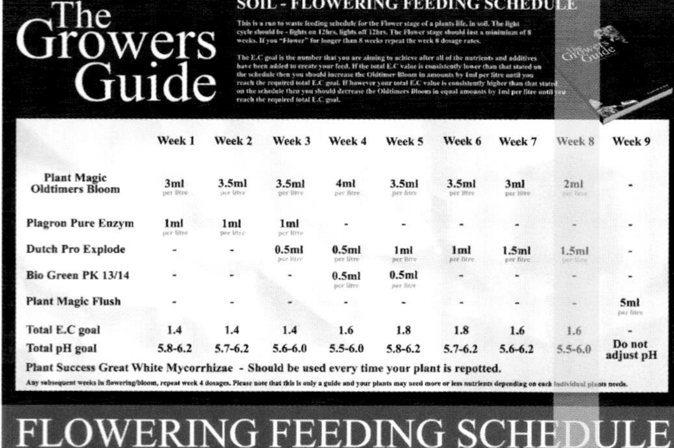

The Growers Guide

SOIL - FLOWERING FEEDING SCHEDULE

This is a run to waste feeding schedule for the Flower stage of a plants life, in soil. The light cycle should be - lights on 12hrs, lights off 12hrs. The Flower stage should last a minimium of 8 weeks. If you "Flower" for longer than 8 weeks repeat the week 8 dosage rates.

The E.C goal is the number that you are aiming to achieve after all of the nutrients and additives have been added to create your feed. If the total E.C value is consistently lower than that stated on the schedule then you should increase the Oldtimer Bloom in amounts by 1ml per litre until you reach the required total E.C goal. If however your total E.C value is consistently higher than that stated on the schedule then you should decrease the Oldtimers Bloom in equal amounts by 1ml per litre until you reach the required total E.C goal.

	Week 1	Week 2	Week 3	Week 4	Week 5	Week 6	Week 7	Week 8	Week 9
Plant Magic Oldtimers Bloom	3ml per litre	3.5ml per litre	3.5ml per litre	4ml per litre	3.5ml per litre	3.5ml per litre	3ml per litre	2ml per litre	-
Plagron Pure Enzym	1ml per litre	1ml per litre	1ml per litre	-	-	-	-	-	-
Dutch Pro Explode	-	-	0.5ml per litre	0.5ml per litre	1ml per litre	1ml per litre	1.5ml per litre	1.5ml per litre	-
Bio Green PK 13/14	-	-	-	0.5ml per litre	0.5ml per litre	-	-	-	-
Plant Magic Flush	-	-	-	-	-	-	-	-	5ml per litre
Total E.C goal	1.4	1.4	1.4	1.6	1.8	1.8	1.6	1.6	-
Total pH goal	5.8-6.2	5.7-6.2	5.6-6.0	5.5-6.0	5.8-6.2	5.7-6.2	5.6-6.2	5.5-6.0	Do not adjust pH

Plant Success Great White Mycorrhizae - Should be used every time your plant is repotted.

Any subsequent weeks in flowering/bloom, repeat week 4 dosages. Please note that this is only a guide and your plants may need more or less nutrients depending on each individual plants needs.

FLOWERING FEEDING SCHEDULE

welcome to the revolution.

This is where if you have followed my recommendation in week 7, the boost button on the dimmable ballast should really show you some results and you should really be able to see the difference by the end of this week. The extra 10% power that it produces is just what the plants need and is the perfect tool to give your fruits a final push. This "boost" feature is available on most models of digital, dimmable ballasts but not on magnetic ballasts so this is another advantage to bear in mind when you are deciding on what kind of ballast that you want to use. The fruits themselves at this point should be getting so heavy that they will begin to almost buckle the branch under the weight. As everything should be tied down by now it is of paramount importance that you are very cautious and do not knock or damage the plants as you will have to get underneath the canopy in order to feed them and this will obviously be quite hazardous now that so many plants are tied down. It is also probably now more important than ever to keep your grow room tidy and free from trip hazards as hopefully it will be incredibly cramped at this stage due to your plant's growth and there will be little space to move about and to trip and fall on your crop at this point would be a disaster.

At the end of week 8 your plants should be now ready to move on to the next stage. The Flushing stage. If you want to keep your plants in the Flowering stage for longer than the 8 weeks that we have, repeat week 8 feed/nutrient dosage rates.

Start of week 8

Coco Soil

End of week 8

Coco Soil

Flushing, Harvest and Curing

In this chapter we will look at everything that you need to know in order to Flush, Harvest and Cure your plant's fruits in the most effective way possible. It is very common for this stage to be carried out incorrectly through general impatience, rushing and the use of little or no technique. The result of rushing this stage will be detrimental to the crop and can mean a great yield is ruined and its full potential never reached. This really is make or break time.

By following the techniques in this chapter, you do not have to worry about your hard work going to waste. I will walk you through the method of flushing your plant properly by using a combination of flushing agents, water and a change of light schedule. We will also look at the 3 most commonly used techniques for Harvest and Curing from start to finish. This chapter should enable you to maximise on all your hard work and efforts so far, ensuring that you get the best taste and quality that your plant's fruits are capable of producing.

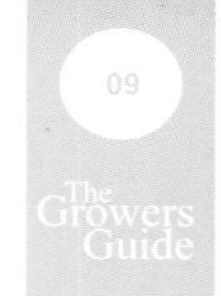

Flushing, Harvest and Curing

For flushing, the light cycle is - lights off 12hrs , light on 12hrs for 4 days – lights off for 24hrs for 3 days

For Harvest and Curing there is no light cycle, its just - lights off 24hrs.

The fruit of the plant is what we are really interested in.

The Harvesting and Curing stage of your plant's fruits is vital to understand and get right, which is often not the case. Done incorrectly, all the work, time and effort you have put in over the last few months will go to waste. Done right however, you will not only get the most weight out of what you have grown but also the best possible taste.

The equipment you will need for this stage is again minimal as we will be utilising some of the equipment that was used in the Flowering and Vegetative stages.

For the Harvest and Curing stage you will need the following equipment;

- **Flushing agent**
- **Trimming scissors**
- **Drying rack**

Flush agent – There are a lot of different flushes on the market but I would recommend using Plant Magic's Flush.

This is one of the only flushes that comes in both a hard water and a soft water version which is ideal for flushing your plants as fast as they possibly can be.

What does a flush do? At the end of your plants flowering cycle the plants will need to be flushed of all the extra nutrients which you have been using, this removes any unwanted chemical tastes and smells. This can be done by feeding the plants with water only for a period of time, using a flush however will half the time it takes and also help the plant to use up any stored nutrient elements that it has kept back.

The flush performs this action via the plant's vascular system. It is taken up by the plant through diluted water in the same way as you would normally feed the plant.

Flush in.

White outlined arrows represent the flushing agent full of nutrients leaving the plant.

Solid blue arrows represent the flushing agent entering vascular system the plants.

The flush is taken up via the root system.

As it passes up through the plant's vascular system it collects the nutrients which are left in the plant's system and in the fruits. As the flush is not something the plant needs it continues travelling and flushes/pulls the nutrients back down through the plant to the root mass as fast as it can.

As the flush has started to clean the plant of stored nutrients it will use any stored nutrients up at an accelerated rate, Thus ripening your plant's fruits to their full potential.

As the diluted flush is taken around the plant it picks up any nutrient elements present, drawing them back down the stem towards the root system. The name of the game is to draw as much of the nutrient elements away and out of the fruit as possible.

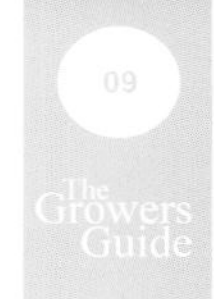

Trimming scissors – Some plant's fruit will need to be removed and prepared before the curing. For this we use special "Trimming Scissors". They are available in every hydroponic store. I recommend to use spring-loaded scissors. They are easy on your fingers, reduce hand cramp and are razor sharp.

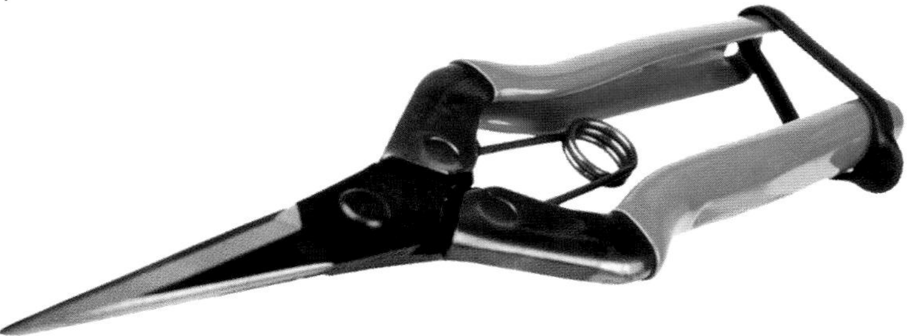

Drying Rack – If you are drying the fruit of your plant I would recommend the use of a drying rack. It's a great way to dry a lot of fruit in a relatively small amount of space. They come in all colours,shapes and sizes. They range in price but all in all they do the same thing. They come flat packed ready to use. you just need to hang them up. A few on the market have detachable sections, which can be very useful when space is at a premium or perhaps you are not in need of all the shelves. I wouldn't pay more than £20.00 for an XL drying rack.

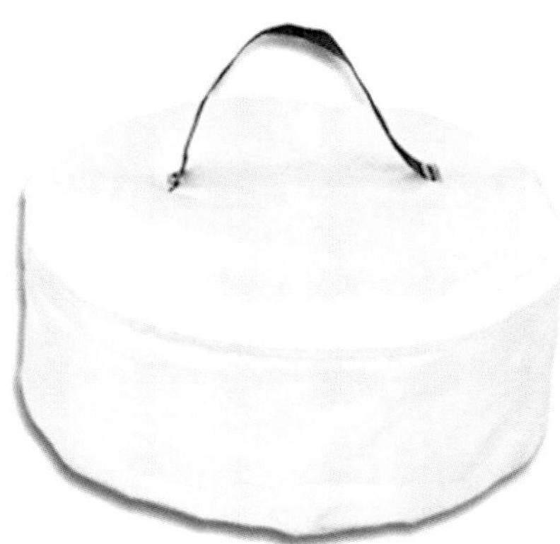

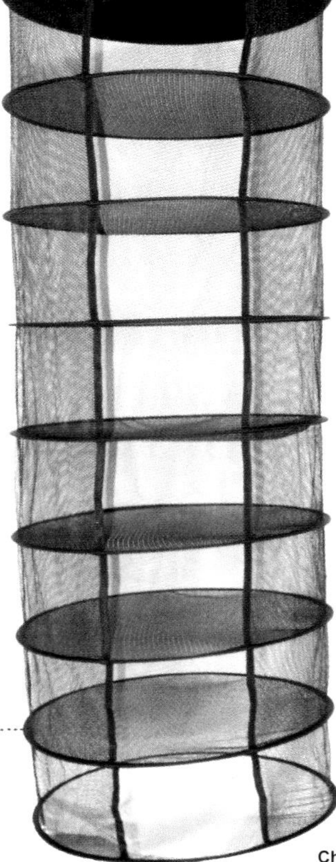

Top tip is to cut a piece of plastic the same size as the bottom shelf and insert it onto this shelf. this can then be used as a catchment tray for any small particles which may detach themselves from the fruit that you are drying.

I have broken the rest of the chapter up into 2 sections. 1.Flush and Harvest and 2.Curing. These chapters hold some of my best kept growing secrets. Using this information correctly will change your end product from good to the best it can be in flavour, smell, depth and weight.

Flush

Before your plants are harvested they need to be flushed. Here is the flush schedule we will be following.

Day 1 - Water with flush until run off.
Day 2 - Water with flush until run off.
Day 3 - Water only until run off.
Day 4 - Water only until run off.
Day 5 - Water only until run off..
Day 6 - Water only until run off.
Day 7 - Water only until run off.

As you can see we will be "flushing" for a week, there really is no need to flush any longer than this. Some people may say that you need to flush for two weeks.............. however, if they think that, then they are not doing it properly.

As you have done before throughout all of the feeds, you will need to leave the water you will be flushing with for 24hrs in order to let some of the lesser wanted chemicals in the tap water evaporate.

5ml per litre - 10ltr batches = 50ml of Plant Magic Flush.

The flush will need to be mixed with water at the right dosage. Once this is done you will need to feed your plants, to the point of run off. Run off – meaning until the liquid starts to come out of the bottom of the pot.

Each feed in "Flush" needs to see the plant be hand fed until the liquid starts to come out of the bottom of the pot.

In doing this you will clearly need to have a saucer or some sort of catchment tray for the run off to collect in.

Ideally the run off will then need to be removed from the saucer/ catchment tray.

As you can see on the schedule, the flush should only be used for the first two feeds/days, after that its WATER ONLY.

When you are in the stage of only using water, it's best to give the plants twice as much feed as they are used to taking. This will flush them faster but will mean that you will have a lot of run off.

Any run off will need to be removed from the grow room before you close the environment, by this I mean – close the grow room door. At this stage you need the humidity to be as low as possible, Ideally below 20%. The danger point is 40%, any higher than this and there is a very high chance that your fruit will rot or have serious mould or fungus issues. As previously stated the drier the better; which will be unachievable if you have not removed all of the run off from the grow room.

So here is a quick summary for the week.

Day 1 – Feed to run off with flush mix. Lights on 12hrs, lights off 12hrs.
Day 2 – Feed to run off with flush mix. Lights on 12hrs, lights off 12hrs.
Day 3 – Double feed to run off with just water. Lights on 12hrs, lights off 12hrs.
Day 4 – Double feed to run off with just water. Lights on 12hrs lights off 12hrs.
Day 5 – Double feed to run off with just water. Lights off 24hrs
Day 6 – Double feed to run off with just water. Lights off 24hrs
Day 7 – Double feed to run off with just water. Lights on 12hrs lights, off 12hrs.

Having 2 days of "lights off" before you harvest will accelerate and heighten the taste and potency of your fruit two fold.

Harvest and Curing

Harvesting your plants can be hard work and time consuming. Ideally it needs to be done in one sitting but it can take more than 12hrs to harvest the whole crop, taking you past the last flush time cycle (light cycle 12hrs on,12hrs off) If you do not manage to finish harvesting in one sitting then just stick to the 12hrs on, 12hrs off cycle and start again when the lights are on until the harvesting is completed. If you have managed to produce a crop of this size by using the set up in this book then....well done, you are on to good things!

As with most things preparation, patience and practice is key to success and never has that been more appropriate than here. Make sure that the area you are using is clean, tidy and well lit. When it comes to curing/drying your fruit you have to be patient, this is one stage that cannot be rushed.

Harvest and Curing go hand in hand and so I will spend the next chapter talking about them as a whole.

There are three main ways of Harvesting and Curing;

1. **Direct** - Harvest/cut the fruit directly off the plant as you go one by one, then dry/cure.

2. **Pay as you go** - Harvest/cut off a branch at a time and work on that until the fruit has run out, and so on, then dry/cure.

3. **Branching** - Cut off each branch individually and hang to dry/cure the fruit, then when its dry, harvest the fruit.

Direct

To start with you will need to hang the drying rack up ready for the trimmed fruit to cure on. As your grow room/tent will still be full of plants I suggest you hang the drying rack where you will be harvesting the plants. When all of the plants have been harvested

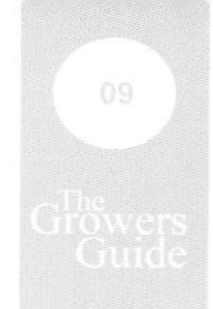

and removed from the grow room/tent then the drying rack can go back into the grow room for curing.

Cutting the fruit from the plant one by one can stress the plant quite a lot and will also create more airborne bacteria and smells than is necessary as you will be in constant contact with the whole of the plant, thus inadvertently knocking and agitating it.

If you do decide to use this method however, may I suggest that you start at the top of the plant with the largest fruits and work your way down to the smaller ones. Mentally separating the plant off into sections should help.

Large

Medium

Small

Cut here.

Branch.

As and when you start racking the harvested fruit it is best to keep each fruit roughly the same size per shelf. So, all the big bits on one shelf, all the medium bits on one shelf and so on.

When removing the fruit from the main branch it should be done at the point where the fruit's stem meets the branch or if your have super big fruit it should be as close as you can get to the main stem.

The next step is to remove any excess foliage. ie; leaves and stalks with the special trimming scissors. If the fruit you have grown is so big that the leaves and stalks disappear into the fruit then they should be cut right back to the fruit.

The fruit will then need to be placed on the drying rack as evenly spaced as possible ready for curing. The curing of the fruit will change from fruit to fruit depending on its size and the environment in which it is being dried.

When all of the plants have been harvested, remove what's left of the plants and the light from your grow room/tent and hang your full drying rack in the middle of the grow room/tent.

The temperature needs to be at a constant 21˚c.
The Humidity need to be as low as possible.

The extractor fan needs to be on constantly ie; 24hrs each day. The intake fan should be turned off.

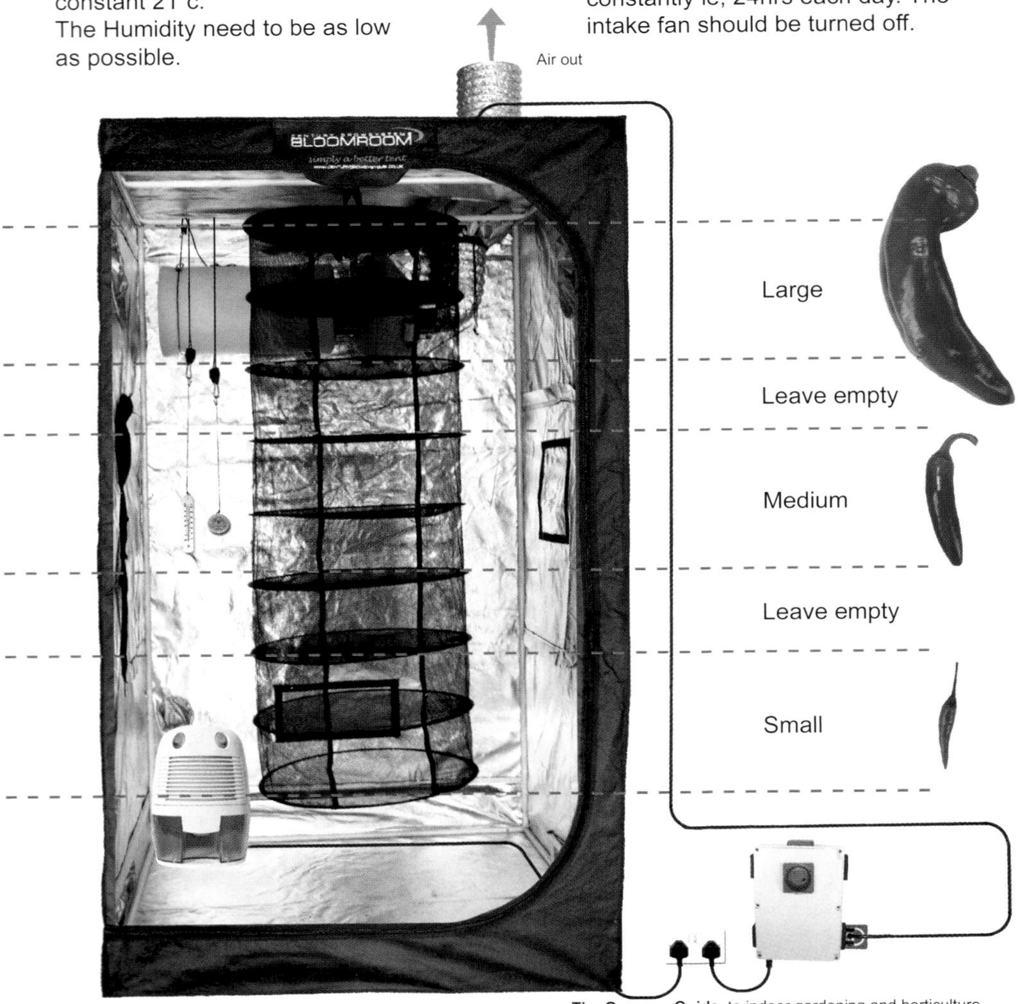

Air out

BLOOMROOM

simply a better tent

Large

Leave empty

Medium

Leave empty

Small

It's best to dry your fruit in the dark at 21°C. Any hotter than this and the fruits will dry too quickly and crisp up. The problem with this is two fold, the first is that you will be left with a crispy brittle end product. This is no good as when you touch it, move it or bag it, it will turn to a dusty powder. The second problem is that it will reduce the smell and the overall quality.

The humidity must be as low as possible ideally below 10%. Leaving your extraction on 24hrs will help with this, however, if you cannot get it low enough I would suggest using a dehumidifier. Just remember to empty the dehumidifier as and when required. If the humidity is too high your fruit will not dry and it may grow dangerous fungal spores and rot.

When the drying rack is in the grow room/tent, try and make sure that all fruit is evenly spaced as much as possible. This will help to dry your fruits evenly.

If done properly it should take between 7-14 days to completely dry your fruit this way. Each day your fruit is drying it will need to be turned in order for each piece to dry evenly. When turning try to be as delicate and as fast as possible, delicate so you don't damage the fruit and fast so that the drying fruit is exposed to the light for the least amount of time.

So in a nut shell, curing is;

- **Dry as possible**
- **Dark as possible**
- **Move/turn every day**
- **Good air flow out**
- **A constant 21°C and low humidity**

If you can give your fruits the full 14 days then this is all the better.

After all the fruit is completely dry it will need to be stored. This can either be done in air tight jars or sealable bags, whatever floats your boat. For the first few days it is good practice to open and air the jar and sealable bags at least once a day.

Pay as you go

I would recommend this way to harvest your plants. This is the way I harvest my plants. I have used this technique for years, it's easy, reliable, fairly mess free and most importantly successful.

I will run through the "pay as you go" system in its entirety, it's pretty similar to the "direct" method the only difference being that rather than taking each fruit individually off the plant you take a branch at a time. Doing this reduces the over all stress to the plant as it's only one cut per branch as opposed to several cuts per branch. It also reduces messing with the plant unnecessarily which will reduce the amount of airborne bacteria and smells by not inadvertently knocking and agitating it.

As with the previous method, you start with hanging the drying rack up ready for the trimmed fruit to cure on. As your grow room/tent will still be full of plants I suggest again that you hang the drying rack where you will be harvesting the plants. When all of the plants have been harvested and removed from the grow room/tent then the drying rack can go back into the grow room/tent for curing.

It's best when using this technique to go for the branches with the largest fruit on first. These will take the longest to dry so get them on the rack first.

The next step is to remove any excess foliage. ie; leaves and stalks with the special trimming scissors. If the fruit you have grown is so big that the leaves and stalks disappear into the fruit then they should be cut right back to the fruit.

Large

Medium

Small

As and when you start racking the harvested fruit it's best practice to keep each fruit roughly the same size per shelf. So all the big bits on one shelf, all the medium bits on one shelf and so on. This will help with the even drying of the fruit.

After the fruit has been trimmed it will need to be cut from the main branch. It should be done at the point where the fruit's stem meets the branch or if you have super big fruit then as close as you can to the main stem.

The fruit will then need to be placed on the drying rack as evenly spaced as possible ready for curing. The curing of the fruit will change from fruit to fruit depending on the size and the environment in which it is being dried.

When all of the plants have been harvested, remove what's left of the plants, the oscillating fan and the light from your grow room/tent and hang your full drying rack in the middle of the tent, Shown in the image below.

Humidity should be as low as possible.

Constant 21˚C.

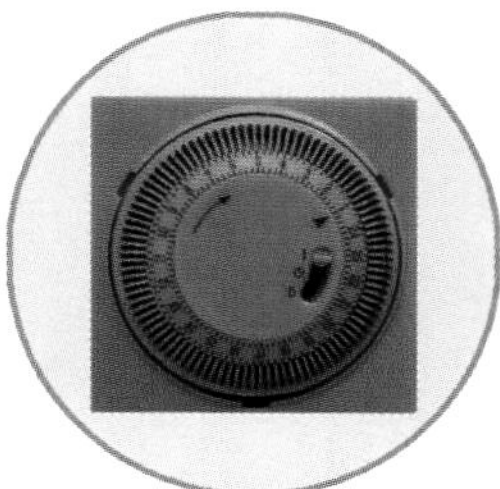

The Fan and filtering system needs to be on 24hrs a day. The timer on the contactor has 3 settings, off (o), timer (the image of the clock) and on continuously (I). The best way to do this is to either leave the timer on and put all the pins in the "on" position or to switch the timer to the constant "on" (I) setting like the above image.

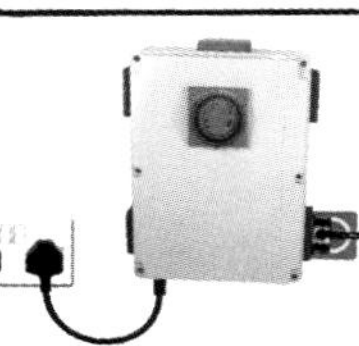

Its best to dry your fruit in the dark at 21°C. Any hotter than this and the fruits will dry too quickly and crisp up. The problem with this is two fold, the first is that you will be left with a crispy brittle end product. This is no good as when you touch it, move it or bag it, it will turn to a dusty powder. The second problem is that it will reduce the smell and the overall quality.

The humidity must be as low as possible ideally below 10%. Leaving your extraction on 24hrs will help with this however if you cannot get it low enough I would suggest using a dehumidifier. Just remember to empty the dehumidifier as and when required. If the humidity is too high your fruit will not dry and it may grow dangerous fungal spores and rot.

When the drying rack is in the grow room/tent, try and make sure that all fruit is evenly spaced as much as possible. This will help to dry your fruits evenly.

If done properly it should take between 7-14 days to completely dry your fruit this way. Each day your fruit is drying it will need to be turned in order for each piece to dry evenly. When turning try to be as delicate and as fast as possible, delicate so you don't damage the fruit and fast so that the drying fruit is exposed to the light for the least amount of time.

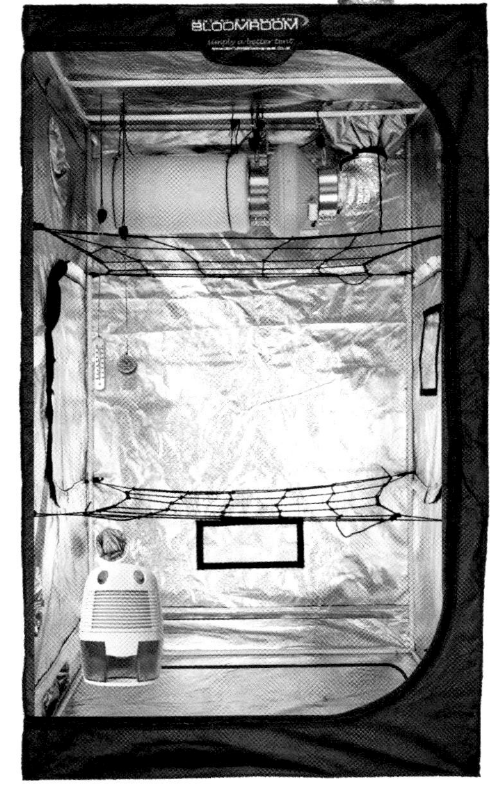

If you can give your fruits the full 14 days, the better.

Branching

This method is probably the most old school of all the techniques.

I will run through the "branching" system in its entirety but it's pretty much the same as the "pay as you go" method the only difference being that rather then cutting the fruit from the branch it is left and dried on the branch. You will also need somewhere for the fruit laden branches to hang. A washing line is cheap and perfect for this, you can either put some lines up in your grow room/tent when its empty or in a dark room.

You will not need the drying rack for this technique.

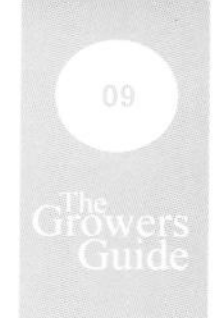

It's best when using this technique to go for the branches with the largest fruit on first. These will take the longest to dry, so it's best to trim them first so they have longer to dry.

Cut here, just before the branch and the stem's node.

All of the plants branches will be different. This one that I have removed first for example has a mix of large, medium and small fruits on it. I have chosen this one to give you an all round view of what to do in such a case.

The next step is to remove any excess foliage. ie; leaves and stalks with the special trimming scissors. if the fruit you have grown is so big that the leaves and stalks disappear into the fruit then they should be cut right back to the fruit.

Trimmed branch.

Then after the fruit has been trimmed it will need to be hung upside down to dry like so. It is important to make sure that the fruits are evenly spaced in order to help with consistent drying. Check them each day until they are completely dry through. When the fruits are completely dry they will need to be removed from the branches.

Humidity should be as low as possible.

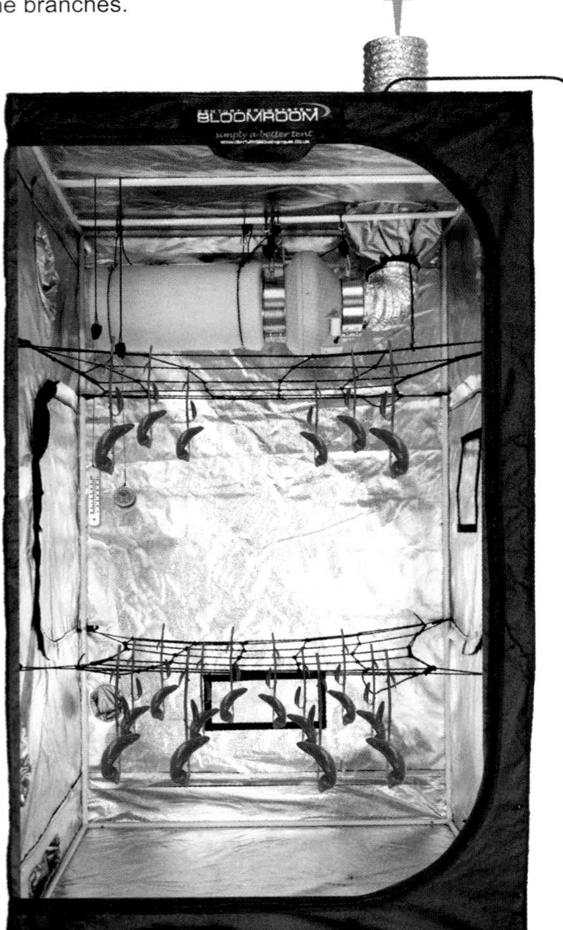

Constant 21°C.

Outake fan on 24hrs a day.

It's best to dry your fruit in the dark at 21°C. Any hotter than this and the fruits will dry too quickly and crisp up. The problem with this is two fold, the first is that you will be left with a crispy brittle end product. This is no good as when you touch it, move it or bag it; will turn to a dusty powder. The second problem is that it will reduce the smell and the overall quality.

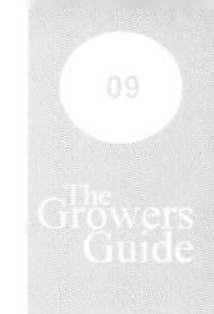

The humidity must be as low as possible ideally below 10%. Leaving your extraction on 24hrs will help with this however if you cannot get it low enough I would suggest using a dehumidifier. Just remember to empty the dehumidifier as and when required. If the humidity is too high your fruit will not dry and it may grow dangerous fungal spores and rot.

It should take between 7-14 days to completely dry your fruit this way if done properly.

If you can give your fruits the full 14 days, all the better.

After its all dry it will need to be stored. This can either be done in air tight jars or sealable bags. For the first few days they are in the jars or sealed bags it is good to air them at least once a day.

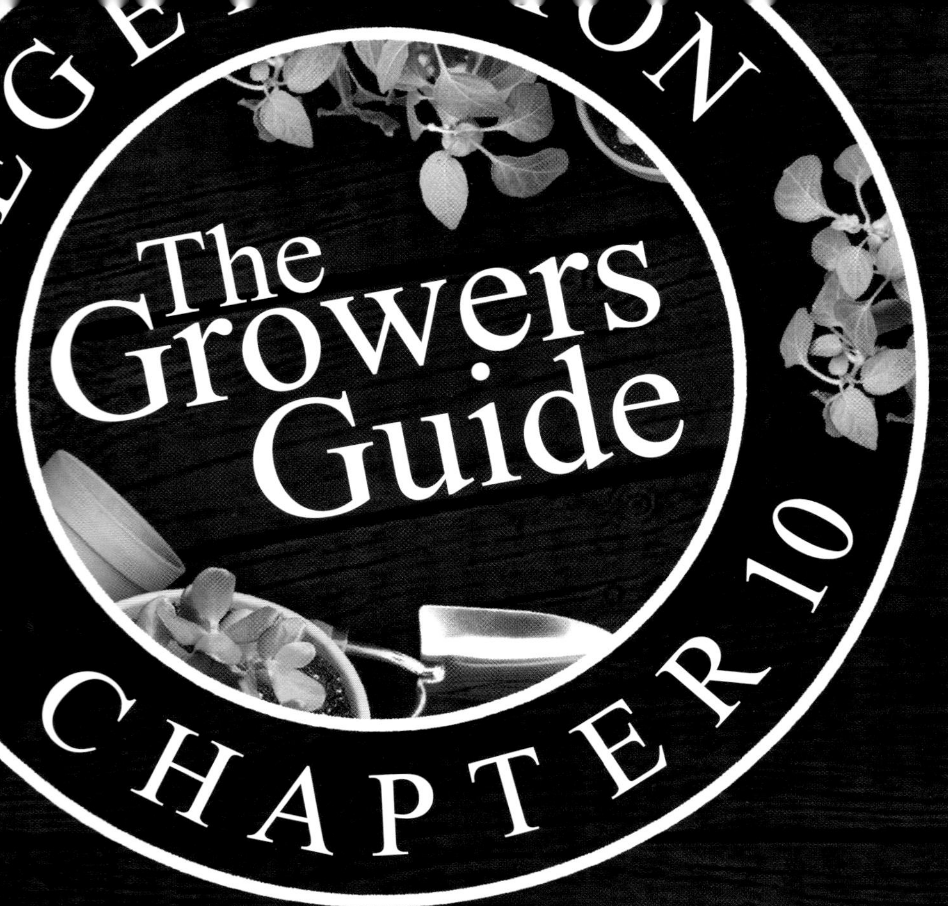

Pest control and prevention

Unfortunately, It is the inevitable truth that at some point you will have to deal with pests in your grow room. In this chapter we will look at the top 5 usual suspects that you are likely to find if you suffer from an infestation in an indoor growing environment. We will look at each insect individually summarising its lifecycle in order to get a better understanding of it. We will also look at what each pest does to the plant and what early warning signs you can look out for. It is true that prevention is the best cure so of course we shall cover how to avoid a pest attack in the first place and for the times that despite your best efforts things still spiral out of hand, how to manage and cure your grow rooms of an infestation.

Pests

Due to the nature of your fruit rich plants and their semi-closed environments, you will find that pests are highly attracted to them. Growing indoors does make your plants less susceptible to common garden insects but whilst saying that, when pests do find their way into your growing environment they will thrive if not treated.

The trick is to spot the early signs of pest infestation and treat them before the situation gets out of hand. One of the top ways of doing this is to make sure that you go through a "daily pest plant check list".

- **check that there are no flying insects in or around the growing environment.**
- **check the top side of the leaves for any patchy discolouration.**
- **check the top side of the leaves for any insects or larvae.**
- **check the underside of leaves for any insects, eggs or insect faeces.**

It is also good practice to remove a low level unimportant leaf once a week and go over it with a microscope. Looking for insects, their faeces, eggs and leaf damage. Pay close attention to the leaves creases and natural crevices.

9 times out of 10 pests will be brought into your growing environment via transfer.

Everybody at some point will have pests in their grow room. They are almost impossible to avoid unless you take steps such as avoiding hydroponic shops that have live plants growing in them, this is because pests can be transferred from the plants and so in this instance it is best to try and not brush your clothes on anything. Make sure that you wash your hands with an anti-bac after purchasing any hydroponic equipment, and clean everything that you buy thoroughly before letting it get anywhere close to your growing environment. Always wear disposable gloves when handling your plants and bear in mind that whilst it sounds a bit extreme, it is good practice to change into clean clothes before you enter your grow room in order to reduce any further risk of transfer. Unfortunately however even if you do go to these lengths the chances are that you will still get a pest infestation at some point.

Although your plants can technically get infested with most common garden insects and pests there is a usual suspect list. This is;

1. **Spider mites**
2. **Aphids**
3. **Thrips**
4. **Fungus gnats**
5. **White flies**

I will go through each pest individually and explain what they are, what they look like, how to spot them, what they do, the early warning signs and how to get rid of them/control them. I will also show you the best way to prevent them in the first place.

Spider mites

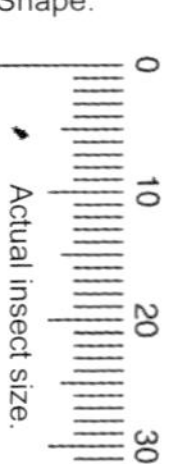

There are over 1,200 species of mite. They are normally found on the underside of leaves where they lay their eggs and spin a protective web. When their numbers start getting to an epidemic level they venture to every part of the plant, thus if you see spider mites on the top side of the leaves of your plant... the chances are that there are already hundreds if not thousands of them living on your plant. Unable to fly, the spider mite mainly relies on "transfer" as a means to travel on to new pastures.

Spider mites are very common. Adult spider mites are less than 1mm in size and are mainly red or white in colour. They breed at a rapid rate and lay their eggs on the underside of the leaf, in the crevices of the natural structure of the leaf. The eggs are initially transparent but seem a whitish colour to the eye/microscope. They sometimes spin a protective silk web over the eggs which is where they get the "spider" part of their name.

What do they do to the plant?

Spider mites bite holes in the top layer of the leaf in order to feed from its inside, these puncture holes in the leaf surface turn brown. They are visible to the naked eye but are not really noticeable (unless actively looked for) until they have started to dominate, at which point the leaf will start to turn yellowish in colour.

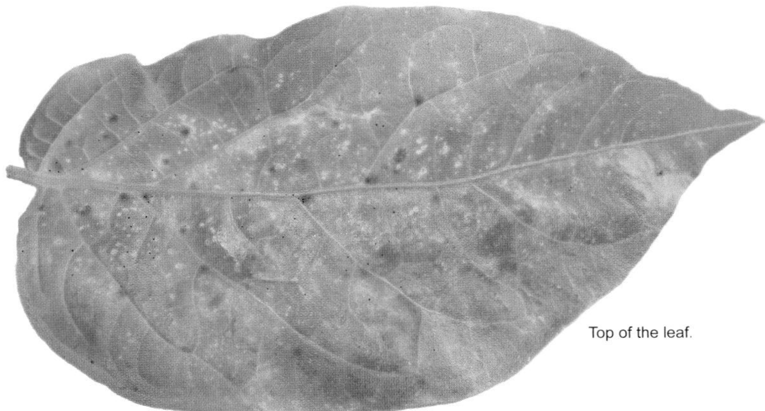
Top of the leaf.

Early warning signs of spider mites are tiny brown spots on the leaves of the plant.

Lifecycle – Spider mites thrive in hot and dry conditions and they can live anywhere between 2-4 weeks. Their eggs can hatch within 3 days and they can become sexually mature within 5-6 days. A female spider mite can lay up to 20 eggs per day, which is around 560 eggs in its lifetime. From that 560 eggs the offspring could produce 11,200 eggs a day!!!!!!! Which over a 4 week period could amount to 313,600 eggs all originating from 1 spider mite!!!!! So as you can see if not treated at the early

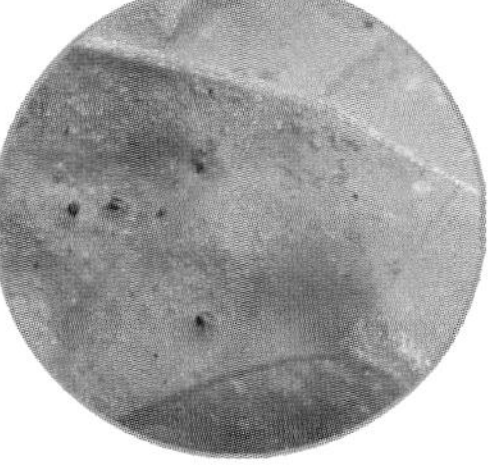

These are black spotted spider mites. The most common colour of spider mites are red or black.

stages the infestation can get out of hand very quickly. This rapid reproductive rate allows the spider mites to adapt very quickly to pesticides preventative measures.

Cure – There is no 100% effective cure for spider mites. Due to their rapid and aggressive breeding they can adapt very quickly to almost any chemical insecticides. There are two main types of insecticides out there in the market; sermetic and non-sermetic.

On a very basic level, sermetic means that when the insecticide is applied to the plant, the plant absorbs the chemical and then when the pests eat part of the plant they are poisoned. The issue with this is that by using a sermetic insecticide the poisonous chemical element from the insecticide will always be present within the plant and so also within the fruit which it produces. Non-sermetic means that the insecticide will kill the pests on contact. This is the type of insecticide that I would recommend.

Prevent – The best way to prevent pests in an indoor grow environment is to reduce the transfer rate, keep a clean environment and check your plants daily. Remember that the sooner you can spot a pest infection the higher the chances are that you will be able to eradicate it.

A good preventative measure would be to use a filtering sheet over the outtake of the ducting entrance and the intake entrance, commonly known as "bug barriers". These can be bought from most good hydroponic and gardening stores. If you can't get hold of a filtering sheet/cover you can always use a make shift cover with a pair of women tights stretched over the intake and outtake entrances. Black 50 denier tights are best to use, any thicker and they will reduce the air movement, any thinner and the spider mites will be able to easily pass through.

Another good idea is to feed your plant silicon. This will help your plants to form a strong cell structure system, in turn making the plant over all hardier to attack from pests and infections. Silicon may also help with an even uptake of nutrients.

You could also use an oil. Neem oil is the most commonly used oil in the hydroponics market, other oils such as sesame oil, horticultural oil, cinnamon oil and fish oil all do roughly the same thing. All oils come in different concentrations so for application it's best to follow the instructions on the bottle.

The basic principal with using oils is two fold, firstly it puts a protective layer between the plant and the pest. The younger of the pests will be unable to penetrate through the oil to get to the plant and thus starve. Secondly, it will coat the spider mite/pest in the oil on contact. This will slowly soften the pests shell and thus kill it. Covering a plant entirely in oil however can be almost impossible.

Oils should only be applied at lights out, when the grow lights have just switched off is best and during the Vegetative stage of the plants life (unless stated) differently on the bottle.

Control – Spider mites prefer a dry climate. A high level of humidity will slow them down.

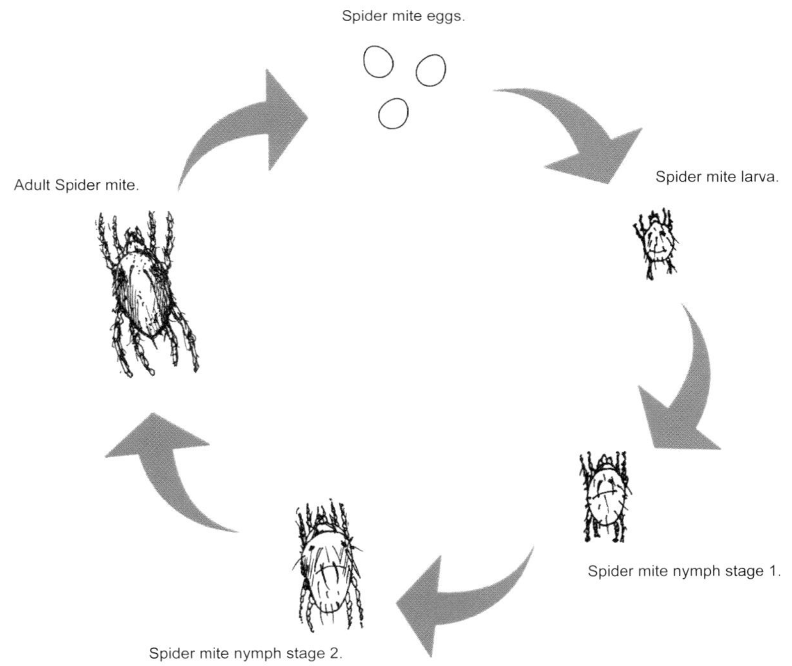

Aphids

Also known as plant lice, there are over 4,400 species of aphid. They can be found all over the plant and can vary in length from 1mm to 10mm. They have soft bodies and come in a variety of colours; mainly black, green, brown and almost a pinky colourless/transparent tone.

Some species of aphid have the capability to reproduce asexually. Geographically aphids can be found in every corner of the world, however, they do tend to prefer warmer climates. Their favourite mode of transport is either being carried by the wind or via transfer. However, if the crop/plants in which the aphids are feeding from become less favourable then they can produce offspring with wings in order to find new sources to feed from.

Shape.

0 10 20 30 40

Actual insect size.

Measurements are in millimeters.

What do they do to the plant?

Aphids are plant-sucking insects that feed by biting through the plants outer surface and sucking on the inner juices. Just like the spider mite does, they puncture holes in the leaves surface which eventually turn brown. Aphids are visible to the naked eye but are not really noticeable unless they are actively being looked for or until they have started to dominate the leaf. Unlike the spider mite some species of aphid will leave a silvery track line behind them where they have fed, at which point the leaf will start to turn yellowish in colour. A highly infested leaf is better removed than left to try and cure.

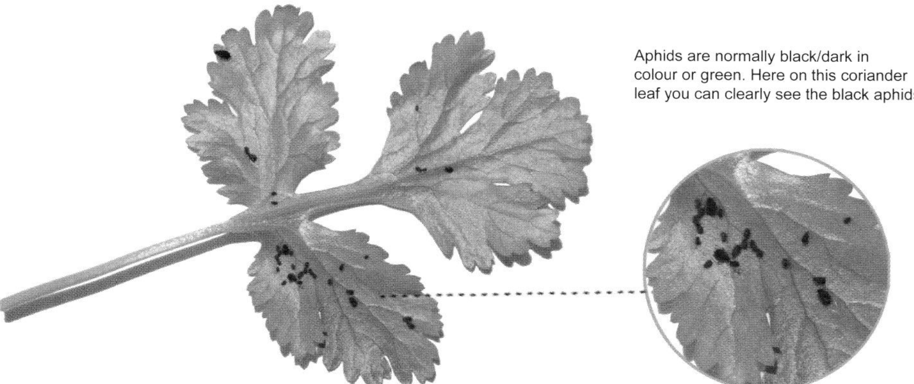

Aphids are normally black/dark in colour or green. Here on this coriander leaf you can clearly see the black aphids.

Unlike spider mites certain species of aphid can also feed from the roots in the same manner as above. This is much harder to spot as this happens below ground.

Aphids are well known for transferring diseases from one plant to another whilst feeding. The diseases which the aphid passes from plant to plant can and often do kill the plants that have been affected.

The early warning signs of aphids are tiny brown spots on the leaves and or silvery track lines on the top side of the leaf of the plant.

Lifecycle – Aphids prefer hot and dry conditions but can live pretty much anywhere. On average they live for 20 to 40 days. An adult can produce thousands of offspring and this rapid reproductive rate allows the aphids to adapt very quickly to pesticides preventative measures.

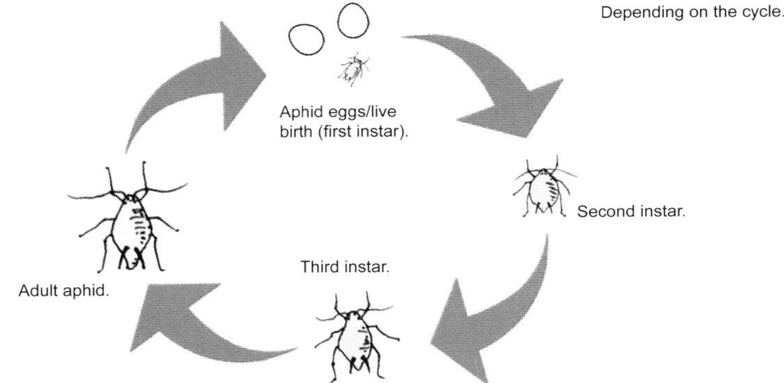

Cure – There is no 100% effective cure for aphids, they are among some of the most destructive pests known to cultivated plants.

I always believe that the best form of cure is prevention but if I had to I would use a non-systemic insecticide which can be brought at your local hydroponics store. I have used many different systemic insecticides over the years and all have been pretty good. I'm reluctant to give you a name as most of the good ones change their name on a regular basis. Don't ask me why.......... I really don't know. Ask your local hydroponics shop, I'm sure that they will be able to recommend a good one. It is possible however to stop aphids, as long as they are caught in the early stages.

Prevention – The best way to prevent pests in an indoor grow environment is the same every time.

Firstly, reduce the "transfer rate", keep a clean environment and check your plants daily. Remember that the sooner you can spot a pest infection then the higher the chances are that you will be able to eradicate it.

The second thing to do would be to use a filtering sheet over the outtake of the ducting entrance and the intake entrance. These can be brought from most good hydroponic and gardening stores. If you can't get hold of a filtering sheet/cover you can always use a makeshift cover out of a pair of women tights that you stretch over the intake and outtake entrance's. Black 50 denier tights are best to use, any thicker and they will reduce the air movement. Any thinner and the aphids will be able to easily pass through.

Thirdly, you should feed your plant silicon as this will help your plants to form a strong cell structure system, making the plant much hardier to attack from pests and infections. Silicon may also help to ensure an even uptake of nutrients.

Fourthly you can use an oil. Neem oil is the most commonly used oil in the hydroponics market however other oils such as sesame oil, horticultural oil, cinnamon oil and fish oil all work just as well and do roughly the same thing. All oils come in different concentrations, so for application it's best to follow the instructions on the bottle.

The basic principal when using oils is to put a protective layer between the plant and the pest. The younger of the pests will be unable penetrate through the oil to get to the plant and thus starve. The oil will also coat the pests which will soften them and make it very hard for them to move around the plant. Covering a plant entirely in oil however can be almost impossible.

Oils should generally only be applied at lights out. The best time to apply oil is when the grow lights have just switched off and during the Vegetative stage, unless stated differently on the bottle.

Another effective method of preventing aphids and gnats from destroying your plants is to try putting a thin layer of glass rocks over the top of the plants medium as seen in the images. Doing this reduces the chances of aphids or gnats getting to the roots of your plant.

For this I would recommend to use Growstone gnatnix.It is effective under both wet and dry conditions and also allows you to water your plants as normal directly through the top layer of gnatnix.

Thrips

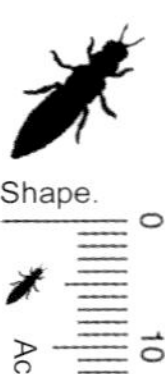

Thrips are some of the fastest growing pests in the world to date. They are very small slender insects which when winged can fly; though not that well (not all thrips have wings). The ones that don't have wings are good jumpers and have been know to jump if startled. Thrips are also known as

- **Thunder flies**
- **Corn lice**
- **Storm flies**

The presence of some thrip can be beneficial as they eat other pests, insects and plant harming fungus.Saying that however they have only ever had a negative effect on my crops over the years, damaging them and costing me a considerable amount of money.

They are normally 1mm long or less and they can grow to swarm numbers if not controlled quickly. They range in colour from a dark brown to a light translucent yellow. They carry diseases which can, and often are, passed from plant to plant. The diseases that they can carry range from mild (making your plant under perform) to severe (killing your plant in a matter of days).

What do they do to the plant?

Thrips are usually found on the top side of the leaf where they attack the leaf, scraping at the flesh until the leaf begins to release its sap which the thrips then feed on. Some thrips will inject the plant with a digestive liquid which makes the process of extracting the sap/cellular fluids easier. As the thrips do this they leave a distinctive silvery and sometimes bronze trail in their wake. As this dries, the scarred sections of the leaf which have been fed on will look almost scab like. Leaves can recover from a small amount of attack from thrips, however, once the leaf has been scarred its rate of photosynthesis will always be less than it was. Thrips can and do attack and feed on the stems of the plant also. They leave distinctive black specks/dots on the leaves and on the surface of the fruits, this is their excrement.

Lifecycle – An adult thrip in its life can lay 50 to 300 eggs. They lay their eggs in the plant's crevices and have been known to also insert their eggs under the surface of the leaves skin. Any eggs which fall off the plant and onto the soil/medium beneath the plant can also live and hatch within the soil/medium. This makes them very hard to get rid of once they have a foot hold on your plants.

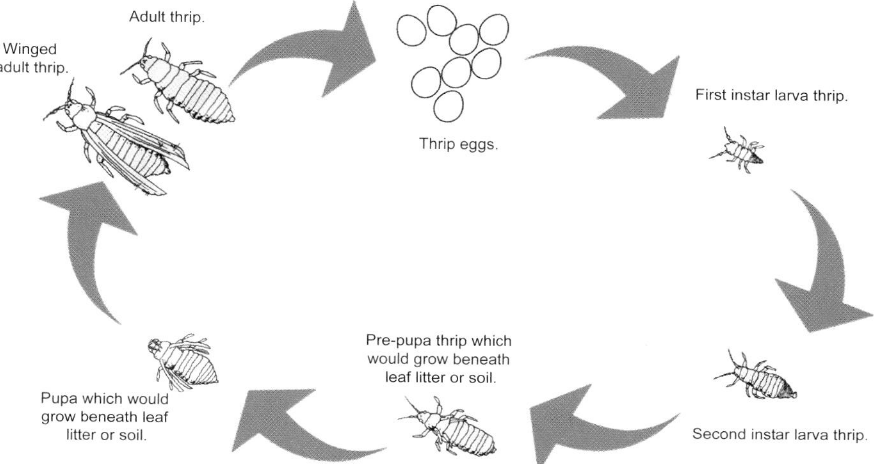

Cure – Thrips are attracted to the colours yellow and blue, so the use of insect sticky pads of these colours placed throughout your growing environment will have an immediate effect on their numbers. Not all thrips can fly so a smart move here would be to put the sticky pads at the base of the plant and to hang them resting on a leaf, making a bridge to the pad like in the image shown.

There is however no 100% effective cure for thrips. I always believe that the best form of cure is prevention.

Prevention – The first step is to reduce the "transfer rate". Keep a clean environment and check your plants daily. Remember that the sooner you can spot a pest infection the higher the chances are that you will be able to eradicate it. Thrip really do not like garlic, so keeping a few broken cloves of garlic within your grow room or at the entrance can help to deter them.

You can use a filtering sheet over the outtake of the ducting entrance and the intake entrance, to filter out the thrips.These can be bought from most good hydroponic and gardening stores.

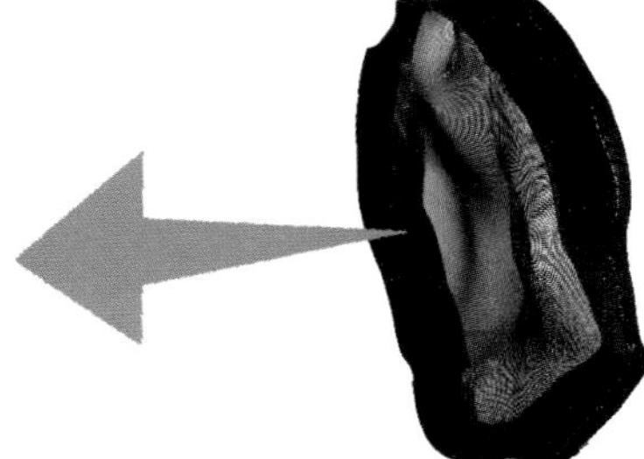

If you are going to use a filtering sheet then you will have to buy one which fits whatever size ducting intake you are using. In our case we are using 4" ducting, so thus we will need a 4" cover.

Another idea is to feed your plant silicon. This will help your plants to form a strong cell structure system, making the plant over all hardier to attack from pests and infections. Silicon may also help with an even uptake of nutrients.

Lastly but not least would be to use an oil. Neem oil is the most commonly used in the hydroponic market, However thrips in particular do not like strong oils such as capsaicin oil, garlic oil, cinnamon oil and coriander oil which all do roughly the same thing. All oils come in different concentrations so for application it's best to read the instructions on the bottle.

The basic principal with using oils is to put a protective layer between the plant and the pest. The younger of the pests will be unable to penetrate through the oil to get to the plant and thus starve. The oil will also coat the pests which will soften them and make it very hard for them to move around the plant. However covering a plant entirely in oil can be almost impossible.

Oils should only be applied at lights out, when the grow lights have just switched off and during the Vegetative stage of the plant's life, unless stated differently on the bottle.

Control – As they are so small and can live on the plant and also within the medium that the plant is growing in, it makes the situation very, very hard to control. Putting a barrier such as grow stones glass on the top of your medium will reduce the amount of eggs making it through to the medium as they fall from the main plant. If the eggs cannot make it to the medium they will die.

Fungus Gnats

Fugus gnats are very common indoors, they are dark, small flies with a short lifespan. They have four different states; egg, larvae, pupa and adult and they prefer moist warm areas. The adults are 3–4mm in size and black in colour. They are good fliers and can carry lots of diseases. The Larvae and pupa are an off-white, creamy colour with a black head. They only attack the root system of the plant and this is where they lay their eggs.

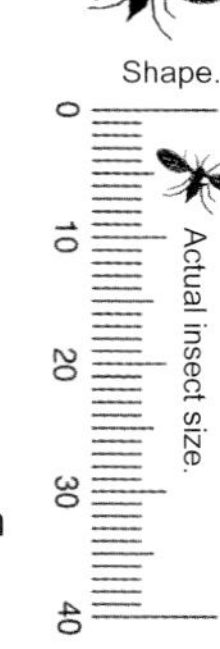

What do they do to your plant?

Fungus gnats lay their eggs not on the plant itself but in the medium that the plant is growing in. The larvae then eat the roots which in turn weakens and stresses the plant at the very beginning of the vascular system. They carry a wide range of diseases ranging from mild to severe which can kill the plant within a few days. They are particularly attracted to plants grown in an organic medium such as soil. When the larvae are active they can commonly be found1-3 inches below the top of the medium.

Lifecycle – Fungus gnats reproduce rapidly in an indoor environment. Each Female can lay hundreds, if not thousands of eggs in her lifetime. Their average lifespan is around 28 days and they commonly lay their eggs on the top of the medium, close to the main stem. The eggs take around 3-10 days to hatch. The larvae will then automatically head down to the roots and organic matter below the surface. They pupate under the surface and emerge as adults. The adult fungus gnat does not eat it only lives to reproduce. It can and still does spread disease at this stage too, via contact transfer. The most common of those diseases being Pythium.

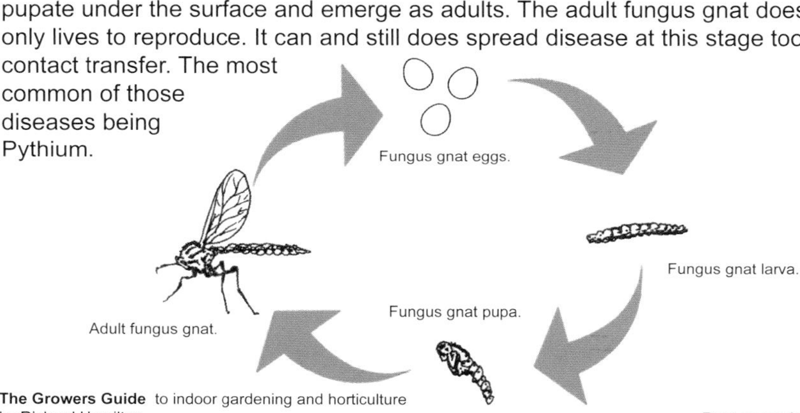

Cure – It is very hard to get rid of fungus gnats once they are below the soil. They prefer moist damp conditions so leaving your medium to dry out before re-watering will help to reduce the numbers. Also introducing a barrier on the top of the medium such as glass stones will have almost an immediate effect on the numbers. Insect sticky trap pads will reduce the numbers of flying gnats. You must try and remember, however, that the placement of a trap pad can be the difference between cure and control. Most people will hang an insect trap pad in their growing environment as a deterrent where there is space. To make this more effective it is better placed where the fungus gnat will be travelling or resting i.e. on the side of the plant pot or on the rim of the plant pot.

Prevention – Firstly as always the thing to do is to reduce the "transfer rate". Always keep a clean environment and check your plants daily. Remember that the sooner you can spot a pest infestation then the higher the chances are that you will be able to eradicate it.

Secondly would be to use a filtering sheet over the outtake of the ducting entrance and the intake entrance. These can be brought from most good hydroponic and gardening stores.

Thirdly, Putting a barrier such as grow stones or glass on the top of your medium will reduce the amount of eggs making it through to the medium as they are laid.

If the eggs cannot make it to the medium they will die. If any eggs do get through then the chance of them making it back out through the glass again is slim and this will reduce the numbers.

Using a standard closed sided plant pot will also help. Pots such as air pruning pots give a plethora of direct access points to the moist root rich medium to which the fungus gnats would be highly attracted to.

As you can see with so many access holes direct to the medium, if fungas gnats do infest your growing environment it will be almost impossible to cure if you were to use an air pruning style pot.

Control – If you do have an infestation of fungus gnats the best way to control them is to form a barrier between the medium and plant. If the adult fungus gnats can't lay their eggs directly onto the medium they will die before the larvae hatch. An upside down insect trap above the medium should catch any newly emerging adult fungus gnats.

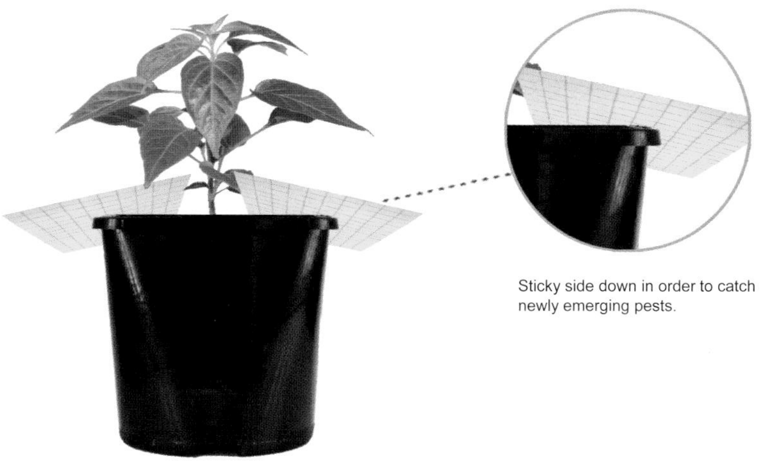

Sticky side down in order to catch newly emerging pests.

White Flies

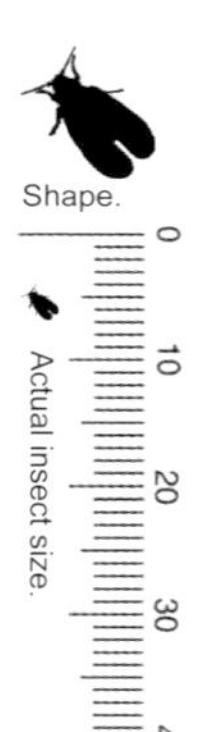

White flies are small moth shaped relatives of the aphid family. They are covered in a white powder which gives them their white appearance. They are common in both indoor and outdoor growing environments. Typically they are 1mm in size when adults. They have a staged lifecycle; Egg, larvae, instar, pupa and then finally, adult. They suck the sap and cellular fluid out of the leaves and stems of the plant.

Shape.

Measurements are in millimetres.

They are notorious for carrying and spreading disease. They can fly but not for too long, they are more comfortable walking around on the underside of the leaves.

What do they do to the plant?

Adult white flies will be found pretty much everywhere on the plant but they prefer the underside of the leaves. They feed on the sap and cellular fluid of the plant much like the aphid does. As they do this the leaf is left looking spotty where the white fly have been feeding from. As the leaf is attacked by the white flies it will appear droopy and lifeless. A quick way to check if you have white fly is to gently shake your plant, any adult white fly should almost instantly jump/fly off the plant for a few seconds before settling back down onto it.

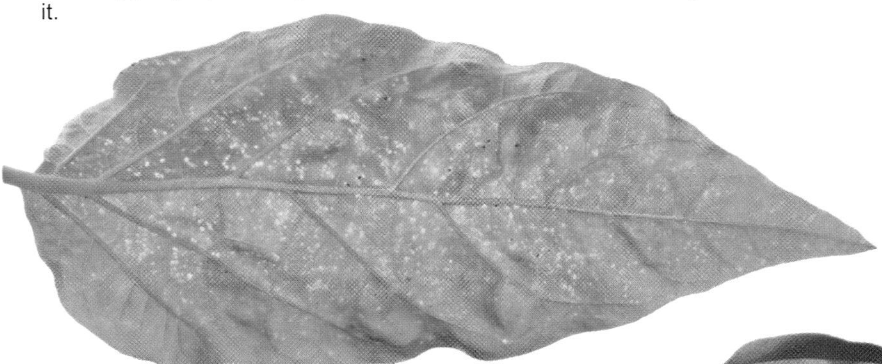

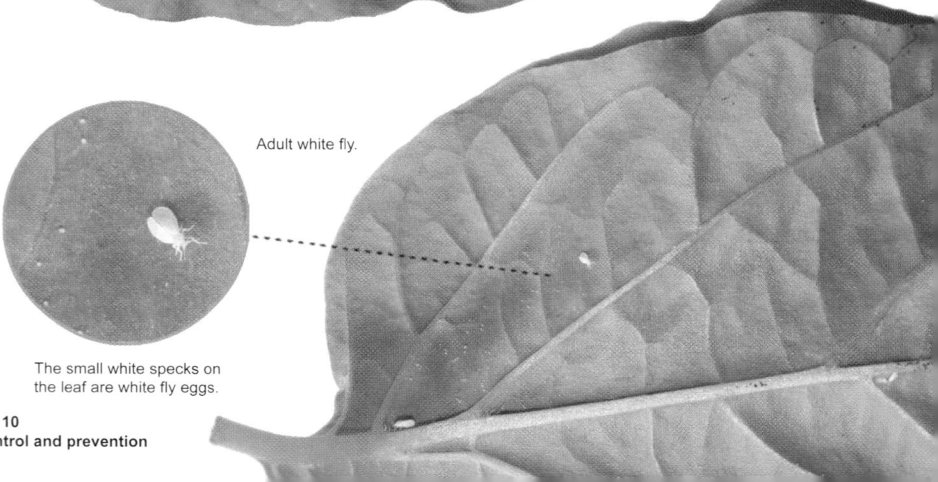

Adult white fly.

The small white specks on the leaf are white fly eggs.

Lifecycle – The life span of the white fly from start to finish is between 5 and 50 days. They lay their eggs on the underside of the leaves of the plant.

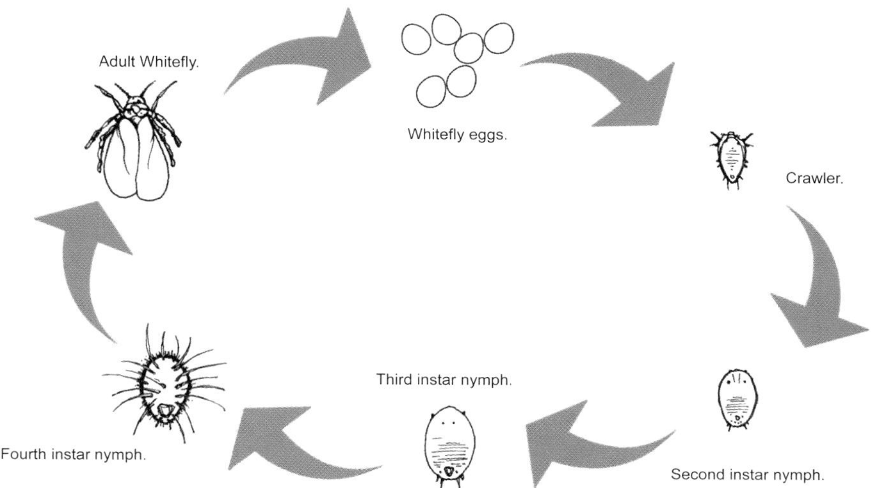

As you can see they have a staged lifecycle.

Cure – White flies are attracted to yellow, so the use of insect sticky pads of this colour placed throughout your growing environment will have an immediate effect. White flies as the name suggests can fly, so a smart move here would be to hang the sticky pads close to the plant. As stated before, the flies are unsettled easily, so by hanging the pads as close to possible to the leaves and gently shaking the plant the white flies should jump/fly off the plant and then before they have chance to settle back onto it they will be attracted to the sticky pads instead. This will have an effect on the numbers instantly, however it will only kill the adults. In order to prevent the larvae, pupa and instar from maturing into adults you will have to spray the underside of each leaf with neem or horticultural oil.

The basic principal with using oils is to put a protective layer between the plant and the pest. The younger of the pests will be unable penetrate through the oil to get to the plant and thus starve. The oil will also coat the pests which will soften them and make it very hard for them to move around the plant. Covering a plant entirely in oil however can be almost impossible.

Oils should only be applied at lights out, when the grow lights have just switched off and during the Vegetative stage of the plants life, unless stated differently on the bottle.

Prevention – As the white fly is from the same family as the aphid, the prevention of them would be pretty much the same. The first and most important thing to do is to take steps to reduce any risk of "transfer", keep a clean environment and check your plants daily. Remember that the sooner you can spot a pest infection the higher the chances are that you will be able to eradicate it.

The next step would be to use a filtering sheet over the outtake of the ducting entrance and the intake entrance. These can be brought from most good hydroponic and gardening stores. If you can't get hold of a filtering sheet/cover you can always use a make shift cover from a pair of women's tights stretched over the intake and outtake entrance's. Black 50 denier tights are best to use, any thicker and they will reduce the air movement, any thinner and the pests will be able to pass through easily.

Another good idea is to feed your plant silicon. This will help your plants form a strong cell structure system making the plant over all hardier to attack from pests and infections. Silicon may also help with an even uptake of nutrients.

Last, but not least you can use an oil, as stated earlier. Neem oil is the most commonly used oil in the hydroponics market however other oils such as sesame oil, horticultural oil, cinnamon oil and fish oil all do roughly the same thing. All oils come in different concentrations so for application it's best to read the instructions on the bottle.

Control – Insect sticky pads are always a good move with airborne pests, using them will give you a clear idea of the level of the pest problem that you are dealing with. A good way to control the numbers of white flies at the tipping point of infestation is to vacuum them straight from the air!! The best way to do this is to remove the plant from the growing environment, set up a vacuum and then shake the plant. White flies are easily dislodged and do not like being disturbed, so when the plant is shook they will either fall to the ground or try to fly, either way they can be easily vacuumed up. Clearly this isn't going to cure the problem but it will radically slow the reproduction of the white flies down.

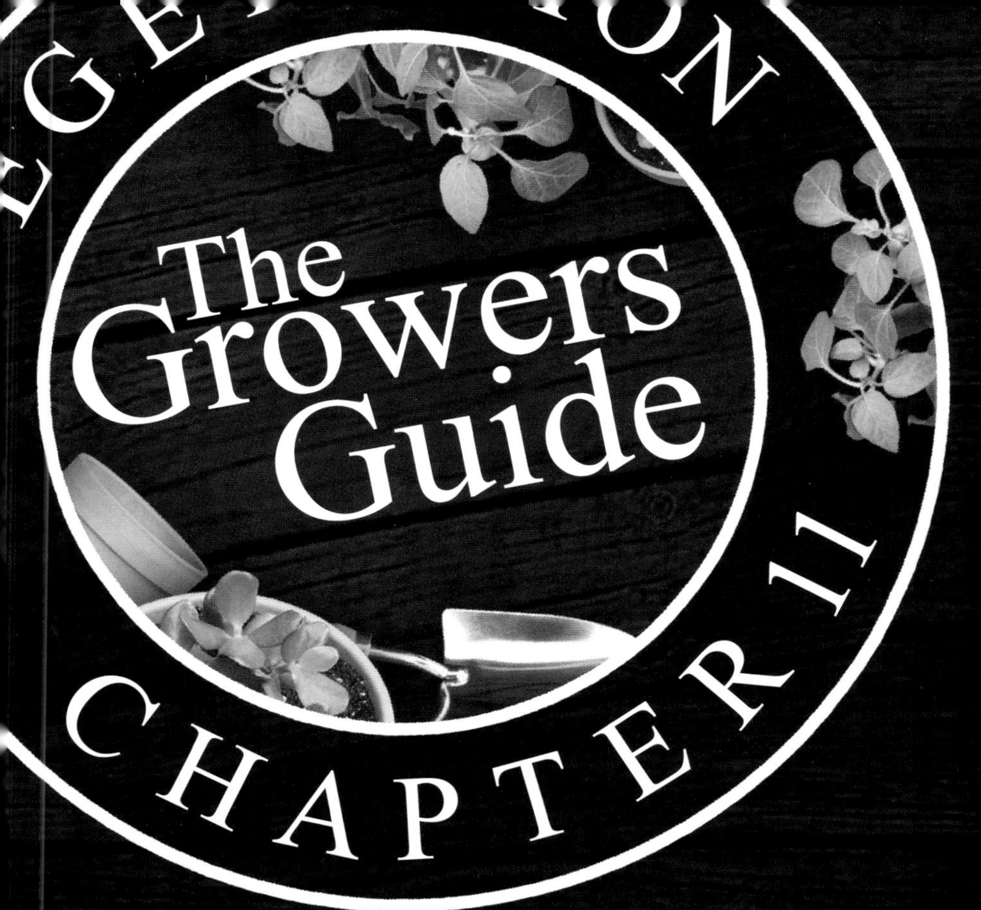

Feeding schedules and shopping lists

In this last part of the book you will find, for quick reference, all the shopping lists for all the items needed for each chapter in sequence. It also contains all the feeding schedules in a larger format.

The Growers Guide

COCO COIR - VEGETATION FEEDING SCHEDULE

This is a run to waste feeding schedule for the Vegetation stage of a plants life in coco coir. The light cycle should be - lights on 18hrs, lights off 6hrs. The Vegetation stage should last between 2 and 4 weeks. You may however wish to "Veg" for longer and if this is the case then just simply repeat the week 4 dosage rates.

The E.C goal is the number that you are aiming to achieve after all of the nutrients and additives have been added to create your feed. If the total E.C value is consistently lower than that stated on the schedule then you should increase the "A" and "B" in equal amounts by 1ml per litre until you reach the required total E.C goal. If however your total E.C value is consistently higher than that stated on the schedule then you should decrease the "A" and "B" in equal amounts by 1ml per litre until you reach the required total E.C goal.

For a full range of free Growers Guide downloadable feed schedules, visit us at www.TheGrowersGuide.co.uk

	Week 1	Week 2	Week 3	Week 4
Plagron cocos A	2ml per litre	2ml per litre	2.5ml per litre	2.5ml per litre
Plagron cocos B	2ml per litre	2ml per litre	2.5ml per litre	2.5ml per litre
Plagron Pure Enzym	-	1ml per litre	1ml per litre	1ml per litre
Dutchpro Take Root	1ml per litre	1ml per litre	1ml per litre	1ml per litre
Total E.C goal	1.2	1.4	1.4	1.6
Total pH goal	5.5-6.0	5.6-6.0	5.7-6.0	5.8-6.0

Plant Magic Evolution - Should be used every 5 days at lights off.

Plant Success Great White Mycorrhizae - Should be used every time your plant is repotted.

For any subsequent weeks in vegetation, repeat week 4 dosages. Please note that this is only a guide and your plants may need more or less nutrients depending on each individual plants needs.

VEGETATION FEEDING SCHEDULE

welcome to the revolution.

The Growers Guide

COCO COIR - FLOWERING FEEDING SCHEDULE

This is a run to waste feeding schedule for the Flower stage of a plants life, in coco coir. The light cycle should be - lights on 12hrs, lights off 12hrs. The Flower stage should last a minimium of 8 weeks. If you "Flower" for longer than 8 weeks repeat the week 8 dosage rates.

The E.C goal is the number that you are aiming to achieve after all of the nutrients and additives have been added to create your feed. If the total E.C value is consistently lower than that stated on the schedule then you should increase the "A" and "B" in equal amounts by 1ml per litre until you reach the required total E.C goal. If however your total E.C value is consistently higher than that stated on the schedule then you should decrease the "A" and "B" in equal amounts by 1ml per litre until you reach the required total E.C goal.

	Week 1	Week 2	Week 3	Week 4	Week 5	Week 6	Week 7	Week 8	Week 9
Plagron Coco A	3ml per litre	3ml per litre	3.5ml per litre	3ml per litre	3ml per litre	3.5ml per litre	3.5ml per litre	3.5ml per litre	-
Plagron Coco B	3ml per litre	3ml per litre	3.5ml per litre	3ml per litre	3ml per litre	3.5ml per litre	3.5ml per litre	3.5ml per litre	-
Plagron Pure Enzym	1ml per litre	1ml per litre	1ml per litre	-	-	-	-	-	-
Dutch Pro Explode	-	-	0.5ml per litre	0.5ml per litre	1ml per litre	1ml per litre	1.5ml per litre	1.5ml per litre	-
Bio Green PK 13/14	-	-	-	0.5ml per litre	0.5ml per litre	-	-	-	-
Plant Magic Flush	-	-	-	-	-	-	-	-	5ml per litre
Total E.C goal	1.2	1.4	1.6	1.6	1.6	1.6	1.8	1.8	-
Total pH goal	5.8-60	5.7-60	5.6-60	5.8-6.2	5.8-6.2	5.7-6.0	5.8-6.2	5.8-6.2	Do not adjust pH

Plant Success Great White Mycorrhizae - Should be used every time your plant is repotted.

Any subsequent weeks in flowering/bloom, repeat week 4 dosages. Please note that this is only a guide and your plants may need more or less nutrients depending on each individual plants needs.

FLOWERING FEEDING SCHEDULE

welcome to the revolution.

The Growers Guide

SOIL - VEGETATION FEEDING SCHEDULE

This is a run to waste feeding schedule for the Vegetation stage of a plants life in soil. The light cycle should be - lights on 18hrs, lights off 6hrs. The Vegetation stage should last between 2 and 4 weeks. You may however wish to "Veg" for longer and if this is the case then just simply repeat the week 4 dosage rates.

The E.C goal is the number that you are aiming to achieve after all of the nutrients and additives have been added to create your feed. If the total E.C value is consistently lower than that stated on the schedule then you should increase the Plant Magic Oldtimers Grow in amounts by 1ml per litre until you reach the required total E.C goal. If however your total E.C value is consistently higher than that stated on the schedule then you should decrease the Oldtimers Grow in amounts by 1ml per litre until you reach the required total E.C goal.

For a full range of free Growers Guide downloadable feed schedules, visit us at www.TheGrowersGuide.co.uk

	Week 1	Week 2	Week 3	Week 4
Plant Magic Oldtimers Grow	2ml per litre	2.5ml per litre	3ml per litre	4ml per litre
Plagron Pure Enzym	-	1ml per litre	1ml per litre	1ml per litre
Dutchpro Take Root	1ml per litre	1ml per litre	1ml per litre	1ml per litre
Total E.C goal	1.2	1.4	1.4	1.6
Total pH goal	5.8-6.0	5.8-6.0	5.8-6.2	5.8-6.2

Plant Magic Evolution - Should be used every 5 days at lights off.

Plant Success Great White Mycorrhizae - Should be used every time your plant is repotted.

For any subsequent weeks in vegetation, repeat week 4 dosages. Please note that this is only a guide and your plants may need more or less nutrients depending on each individual plants needs.

VEGETATION FEEDING SCHEDULE

welcome to the revolution.

The Growers Guide

SOIL - FLOWERING FEEDING SCHEDULE

This is a run to waste feeding schedule for the Flower stage of a plants life, in soil. The light cycle should be - lights on 12hrs, lights off 12hrs. The Flower stage should last a minimium of 8 weeks. If you "Flower" for longer than 8 weeks repeat the week 8 dosage rates.

The E.C goal is the number that you are aiming to achieve after all of the nutrients and additives have been added to create your feed. If the total E.C value is consistently lower than that stated on the schedule then you should increase the Oldtimer Bloom in amounts by 1ml per litre until you reach the required total E.C goal. If however your total E.C value is consistently higher than that stated on the schedule then you should decrease the Oldtimers Bloom in equal amounts by 1ml per litre until you reach the required total E.C goal.

	Week 1	Week 2	Week 3	Week 4	Week 5	Week 6	Week 7	Week 8	Week 9
Plant Magic Oldtimers Bloom	3ml per litre	3.5ml per litre	3.5ml per litre	4ml per litre	3.5ml per litre	3.5ml per litre	3ml per litre	2ml per litre	-
Plagron Pure Enzym	1ml per litre	1ml per litre	1ml per litre	-	-	-	-	-	-
Dutch Pro Explode	-	-	0.5ml per litre	0.5ml per litre	1ml per litre	1ml per litre	1.5ml per litre	1.5ml per litre	-
Bio Green PK 13/14	-	-	-	0.5ml per litre	0.5ml per litre	-	-	-	-
Plant Magic Flush	-	-	-	-	-	-	-	-	5ml per litre
Total E.C goal	1.4	1.4	1.4	1.6	1.8	1.8	1.6	1.6	-
Total pH goal	5.8-6.2	5.7-6.2	5.6-6.0	5.5-6.0	5.8-6.2	5.7-6.2	5.6-6.2	5.5-6.0	Do not adjust pH

Plant Success Great White Mycorrhizae - Should be used every time your plant is repotted.

Any subsequent weeks in flowering/bloom, repeat week 4 dosages. Please note that this is only a guide and your plants may need more or less nutrients depending on each individual plants needs.

FLOWERING FEEDING SCHEDULE

welcome to the revolution.

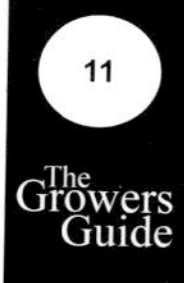

Cuttings and clones equipment shopping list

1. Scalpel - disposablel.
2. Cloning/rooting gel - Growth Technologies Clonex.
3. A clean cup to put the rooting gel in – disposable.
4. Medium (Something to transfer the clone into) i.e. rockwool etc.

Propagation equipment shopping list

1. Propagator - Heated if possible.
2. A light - 2ft strip light.
3. A spray bottle.
4. Temperature gauge.
5. Hygrometer.
6. Feed - FORMULA-XL.
7. Timer/contactor.
8. Pots – x4 3.5ltr black square to round.
9. Medium (Something to transfer the clone into) i.e. 3" rockwool etc.
10. Mycorrhizae - Plant Success Great White.
11. pH chemical test kit - GHE.
12. EC reader - HM Digital.
13. Mixing tub - Clean, water-tight 10ltr bucket.
14. Measuring Jug - 1ltr.
15. Measuring syringes - 10ml and 20ml.

Vegetation equipment shopping list

1. Light kit - 600w dimmable digital ballast, Dutch Hammertone shade, 600w dual spectrum or specific vegetation lamp.
2. Protective eyewear - Method Seven.
3. Contactor/time - 4 way.
4. Oscillating fan.
5. Grow Tent – 1.2m x 1.2m x 2m Bloomroom tent from Century Growsystems.
6. Ventilation Kit - RVK 6" fan, 10m 6" acoustic ducting, Dutch Touch 6" filter and x2 6" fast clamps.
7. Feed/nutrient range –

Coco

- Plagron cocos A – 1ltr.
- Plagron cocos B – 1ltr.
- Plagron pure enzym – 1ltr.
- Dutch pro Take Root – 1ltr.
- Plant Magic Evolution – 500ml ready to use in a spray bottle.
- Mycorrhizae - Plant Success Great White.

Soil

- Plant Magic Oldtimer Grow – 1ltr.
- Plagron pure enzym – 1ltr.

- Dutch pro Take Root – 1ltr.
- Plant Magic Evolution – 500ml ready to use in a spray bottle.
- Mycorrhizae - Plants Success Great White.

9. Medium - Coco coir – Nutrifield 50ltr bag, Soil - Dutch pro soil light mix 50ltr bag.
10. Equipment hangers - ractchet ropes.
11. Larger plant pots – x4 15ltr square to round black.
12. Saucers/catchment tray for pots - Garland.

Flowering equipment shopping list

1. A specific flowering lamp. If you are not using a dual spectrum lamp.
2. Larger plant pots – x4 30ltr round black pots.
3. Medium: - Coco coir – Nutrifield 50ltr bag, Soil - Dutch pro soil light mix 50ltr bag.
4. Intake fan kit - RVK 4" fan, 5m 4" acoustic ducting, x2 4" fast clamps
5. Dehumidifier – preferably with an adjustable digital humidity setting.
6. Flowering Feed/nutrient range –

Coco

- Plagron cocos A – 1ltr.
- Plagron cocos B – 1ltr.
- Plagron pure enzym – 1ltr.
- Dutch pro Explode – 1ltr.
- Bio Green PK 13/14.
- Mycorrhizae - Plant Success Great White.

Soil

- Plant Magic Oldtimer Bloom – 1ltr.
- Plagron pure enzym – 1ltr.
- Dutch pro Take Root – 1ltr.
- Dutch pro Explode – 1ltr.
- Bio Green PK 13/14 – 1ltr.
- Mycorrhizae - Plants Success Great White.

Flushing and harvest equipment shopping list

1. Flushing agent – Plant Magic flush – 1ltr.
2. Trimming scissors.
3. Drying rack – XL.

Note, that the above shopping lists are set out as if you were starting from the beginning of this book and working your way through it i.e. If an item is, for example, going to be used in multiple stages (like a temperature gauge) it would only be mentioned in the first shopping list that it is needed for, as it does not have to be re-bought and the same one can be used again throughout the different stages.

........................Notes..............................

..........................Notes..............................

Notes